Indian Eco Theology

Theory and Practice

Indian Eco Theology

Theory and Practice

Edited by
Namrata Kothari

MLBD
PUBLICATIONS

MOTILAL BANARSIDASS
PUBLICATIONS
4741/23, Ansari Road, Daryaganj, New Delhi - 110002 (India)
Email: mlbd@mlbd.com | sales@mlbd.com | exports@mlbd.com
Website: www.mlbd.com

Indian Eco Theology
by
Namrata Kothari

First Edition Published in July 2023

Published in India by Motilal Banarsidass Publications

ISBN : 978-93-91759-84-1 (HB)

Printed and bound in India

THE RAMAKRISHNA MISSION INSTITUTE OF CULTURE

(A Brandt Centre of Ramakrishna Mission,
P.O. Belur Math, Dist. Howrah, West Bengal-711202)

GOL PARK, KOLKATA - 700 029, WEST BENGAL, INDIA
Phone : 033-4030-1200, 2464-1303, 4030-1263
Fax: 033-2464-1307;
E-mail: rmicacc.goipark@gmail.com, golpark.rmic@rkmm.org;
Website : www.sriramakrishna.org

FOREWORD

The book entitled 'Indian Ecotheology : Theory and Practice' is a compilation of articles by experts in the field of Ecology and Theology. Religion and Environment are not two different concepts and our academicians have taken up the issue with all seriousness as it directly affects our life. We need to grow in spirituality in a serene atmosphere around us. Growing religiously also means creating consciously a conducive milieu in society. We can well remember the Hymn to Sweetness (Madhu) praying to the Almighty for sweet winds to blow, sweet rivers to flow, sweet mornings and nights to visit us everyday-break. Also, sweet be every God and Goddess towards us. In a word, the ancient Rishis used to invoke the celestial blessing for an extremely agreeable environment while living a Spiritual life. It shows that the concept of Ecotheology is not of modern minds. Even every faith in the world categorically put that this world belongs to the Almighty and Him alone. Hence we have no right to pollute it, ignore it. We shall have to make it better, at least, for our own sake.

Swami Suparnananda

(Swami Suparnananda)

हे प्रभो ! यह तेरापंथ

Arham 30-10-2021

For Dr. Namrata Kothari-

Your letter dated 21 oct. 2021 has been received by H.H. Acharya Shree Mahashraman ji. Acharya Shree has expressed his good wishes for your book "Santhara: A Jain ritual of fast unto death" and H.H. Acharya Shree has also expressed good wishes for book on Indain Eco-Theology being edited by you. It seems difficult to write a forward by H.H. Acharya Shree for book "Santhara: A Jain ritual of fast .... ." Whenever you get this message try to inform me.

Bhilwara, Rajasthan **Sadhvivarya Sambuddhyasha**

जैन श्वेताम्बर तेरापंथी महासभा

प्रधान कार्यालय–3,पोर्चुगीज चर्च स्ट्रीट, कोलकाता–700 001 दूरभाष : (033) 2235 7956 2234 3598 फैक्स : 2234 3666

शिविर कार्यालय संपर्क सूत्र – 07044448888 Email - office@terapanth.com

PREFACE AND ACKNOWLEDGEMENT

My interest in religion, particularly Jainism, has been rather varied. After my initial research on Jainism from a social political angle, I moved on to write about different themes of Jainism including human rights, peace, ahimsa, and death. I expressed many of my ideas about Jainism as a religion as well as the way of life in my book on "Jainism: An inquiry into its emergence, background and social political values in it". Shortly after that book was published, I engaged myself in teaching, researching and writing on various aspects of Jainism.

Suddenly one day I came across a book on sallekhana which was not read by me. I turned on its pages first, got curious, and soon riveted. Then I started my postdoctoral work on Sallekhana: A Jain ritual of fast unto death, a work which has not been done and thought by many. As I delved into it I was especially interested in the ideas related to Jain death with a sense of detachment, the relation between body and soul, conversant with the nature of life, and also in the manner in which these ideas are different from suicide and Euthanasia.

This book represents an expansion of those ideas, initial inquiries drawing on many other religious sources, situated within a continuous and comparative historical framework, in order to set large arguments. While I had, over the years, acquired experiences dealing with Jain Agamas and other secondary sources, editing this book gave me the opportunity to become acquainted with the concept of ecology embedded in the other religions like Hinduism,

Sikhism, Buddhism, as also in Jainism. This made editing this book a wonderful voyage of discovery.

My interest in comparative religion was accompanied by another realization of the need of the hour, that is how religion helps in the promotion, preservation and protection of ecology that look beyond a certain boundary. This wider spectrum makes it possible to place ecological thought with a comparative context, enabling us to recognise ecological connectivity of different religions of the world.

These ideas on religion and ecology require crossing not only spatial boundaries but also temporal ones. This book begins with explaining the conception of eco-theology and why it is so important for us today. The fact that ancient religious ideas and teachings continue to be invoked in modern India makes a new understanding of those ideas and teachings extremely relevant, indeed essential. Another reason for pondering on the connection between religion and ecology as present in different religious texts with the hope that it can perhaps help us to reflect on the escalating ecological violence in the world today.

I am indebted to those who have contributed a chapter in this book. Several people helped me in editing this book. My friends and teachers have been constant companions and sources of encouragement during highs and lows of editing this book, My husband and son, Vishal and Tej Veer, have been sensitive supporters throughout the process.

Finally, I would like to thank Motilal Banarsidass Publisher for the constant support, and cooperation, the entire team of Motilal Banarsidass publisher for their support, and efficiency, resulting to the publication of this book.

About the Contributors

Prof. Jayaraman Suresh is a Linguist with fifty years of research and teaching experience in various capacities and departments including UNESCO. After retirement he was attached with the Ramakrishna Mission Institute of Culture in the Centre for Indological Studies and Research. This is his last work before he departed his life.

Dr P S Bhatnagar, PhD is a scientist who has over two decades of experience in various issues concerned with the environment . He has written both in academic and popular media. He is widely travelled both within and outside India. His other interests include natural history films and museum related activities.

Swastik Banerjee, PhD Research Scholar, Dept. of Philosophy, Calcutta University trained in Trika Philosophy. He has completed his M.Phil in Philosophy from University of Madras and topped in M.A. He has qualified for the UGC-NET (Lecturership) Exam in 2018 July. He also assisted Dr. Julian Strube, University of Heidelberg for a Post Doctoral project on "Bengali Intellectuals in 19thand 20thCent." funded by the German Research Foundation (DFG). He published many national and international papers in books and journals.

Dr. Champak Bhattacharyya, an alumnus of the Presidency College, Calcutta completed his graduation and post-graduation in English Literature and Ph.D in History. He also completed graduation and post- graduation in Law.Presently working on the Management and Conservation of Indian Heritage.

Prof Kulwant Singh, Associate Professor (retd.) from the Postgraduate Department of English, Govt College, Chandigarh, with an M.A in English from Kurukshetra University and M. Phill Degree from Punjab University, Chandigarh on the novels of Australian novelist Patrick White, the 1973 Nobel Prize winner on literature, is presently Editor of the Quarterly Journal, "Abstracts of Sikh Studies", of Institute of Sikh Studies, Chandigarh. His two major publications of English translation in free English verse of two Sikh Classic texts are:

1. SriGurPanthParkash (1841) in two Volumes
2. Sri GurSobha (1711)

Another book written in collaboration with DrDharam Singh (retd), Former, Editor-in-Chief "Encyclopedia of Sikhism", Punjabi University, Patiala on ten Sikh classic texts is: *Know your Heritage* (2017), published by Institute of Sikh Studies.

He has participated in Seminars and Conferences and presented papers on Sikhism and Sikh related issues including two papers presented at UGC sponsored Seminar on "Multiculturalism in Literature: Re-inventing Identities" at Sri Guru Gobind Singh College, Chandigarh and Guru Gobind Singh International Sikh Conclave at Patna (Bihar) on September 22-24, 2016.

Dr. Ambalicka Sood Jacob has done her Masters of Art (Drawing & Painting), University Grants Commission (NET), PhD. 'Sculptures from Punjab with special reference to *Sanghol*'. She is serving as Associate Professor, Head, S.S.S., Department of Fine Arts/ In charge, Museum and Art Gallery, Punjabi University, Patiala, Punjab.

From 2015-2021 Joint Secretary, Office Bearers, Life Member, Indian Society For Buddhist Studies. 2015 Awarded with the 'Best Paper Presented Contribution in '*Waq- Shakti Ki Raksha,AaraadhnaEvamSavdharnaHetuSahityakSansatha*';'*Divj otWaq-ShodhaSanmaan*. Amrita Shergil Awardee; *MaaSaraswati Kala Manch; Jas Noor* Foundation'; at Museum and Art Gallery, Chandigarh.

Prof. Manjula Vibhasini Vithanapathirana, Professor in Educational Psychology at the Faculty of Education, University of Colombo, Sri Lanka is an interdisciplinary scientist. She graduated from University of Colombo with a Zoology Honours, completed postgraduate studies in Education with a Masters from Open University of Sri Lanka and PhD from Institute of Education (IOE) University College London (UCL) in the United Kingdom. She also secured a Post Graduate Diploma and a Master of Arts degree from Post Graduate Institute of Buddhist and Pali Studies of University of Kelaniya, Sri Lanka.

She has over 35 years of experience in teaching and research. She completed a tenure as the Dean of the Faculty of Education, University of Colombo from 2016-2019. She was elected as the General President of the Sri Lanka Association for the Advancement of Science (SLAAS) in 2016. She won a scholar award in the US government Institute for Secondary School Educators in 2011. She has extensively travelled for research to Japan, China, Vietnam, Thailand, Malaysia, South Africa, Eritrea, Nepal, Pakistan, England and Wales, Peru and Finland.

Prof. Vithanapathirana has delivered keynote addresses and speeches in around 40 conferences, international organizations and universities on different topics of varied range. She is a member of the editorial boards of more than 15 journals and an active article reviewer of more than 20 journals, mostly are international.

Her publications are on a range of topics on General Education, Teacher Education and Buddhist Psychology. One of her key articles is:

Critical Psychology in Sri Lanka: the Buddhist psychological perspective. *Annual Review of Critical Psychology*, 10: *Critical Psychology in a changing world; Building bridges and expanding the dialogue, 2013* (ISSN 1746-739X).

At present she is the National Coordinator of the teacher capacity building CONTESSA project for Sri Lanka, launched by University of Graz, Austria co-funded by EU in teacher education.

manjulav@edu.cmb.ac.lk or vibhasini@gmail.com

Prof. Suniti Kumar Pathak, MA in Pali & Buddhism, Calcutta University (Stood first, 1950); Disciplined in the Traditional methods in learning Pali, Sanskrit and the Purana(s) he passed Diploma examination with distinction marks in Chinese from Cheena-Bhavana, Visva-Bharati, 1956. He was awarded with the titles Suttavisarada (with a gold medal), Kavyatirtha, Puranaratna (with a gold medal); He was also awarded with Sino-Tibetan Research Scholarship by Calcutta University (1951-54) and deputed to Professor Dr. George N. Roerich, the Russian Tibetologist who was then at Kalimpong.

Christopher Key Chapple is Doshi Professor of Indic and Comparative Theology and founding Director of the Master of Arts in Yoga Studies at Loyola Marymount University in Los Angeles. A specialist in the religions of India, he has published more than twenty books, including the recent *Living Landscapes: Meditations on the Elements in Hindu, Buddhist, and Jain Yogas*(SUNY Press). He serves as advisor to multiple organizations including the Forum on Religion and Ecology (Yale), the Ahimsa Center (Pomona), the Dharma Academy of North America (Berkeley), the Jain Studies Centre (SOAS, London), the South Asian Studies Association, and International School for Jain Studies (New Delhi). He teaches online through the Center for Religion and Spirituality (LMU) and YogaGlo https://www.glo.com/preview/teachers/dr-chris-chapple.

Recent book: http://www.sunypress.edu/p-6860-living-landscapes.aspx

Master of Arts in Yoga Studies: https://bellarmine.lmu.edu/yoga/

Dr Jagat Ram Bhattacharyya, Professor, Department of Sanskrit, Pali and Prakrit, Bhasa-Bhavana, Visva-Bharati,

Santiniketan.He has completed his PhdfromUniversity of Calcutta, 1994,M.Phil, University of Calcutta, 1988,M.A. (Sanskrit, Specialization in Prakrit), University of Calcutta, 1986. He has teaching experience of more than 31 years. He has 44 articles published in journals and as single author published 4 books and 18 students have completed their PhD under his supervision. Other accomplishments are:-

- Honorary Language Consultant of Prakrit Anthology in Ancient Indian Literature project, Sahitya Academy, New Delhi, 1992.
- Editor of TulsīPrajñā, A Quarterly Peer Reviewed Research Journal of Jain VishvaBharati University, Ladnun.1998-2012.
- Teaching Prakrit in the Summer School of Prakrit Language and Literature organized by the BL Institute of Indology, Delhi, every year since 1993.
- Taught Prakrit to the Students of the Five Weeks' Prakrit Summer Course programme held at JVB centre, London in collaboration with the Institute of Jainology, London, 31st May – 3rd July, 2004.
- Taught Prakrit to the Students of the Four Weeks' Prakrit Summer Course programme held at JVB centre, London in collaboration with the Institute of Jainology, London, 14th July- 15th August, 2006.
- Registrar of the Jain VishvaBharati University from 22.11.99 – 19.07.2008.
- Associate Member – Centre of Jaina Studies, School of Oriental and African Studies (SOAS), University of London, UK.
- Visiting Professor 2014-2017 in the Department of Sanskrit and in the department of Buddhist Studies, University of Calcutta, Kolkata.
- Visiting Fellow, 2017 in the department of Sanskrit, Jadavpur University, Kolkata

Dr. Namrata Kothari, Post doctorate (The Ramkrishna Mission Institute of Culture, Kolkata), M.A(Double)(Poilitical Science and Jainology) and PhD (University of Calcutta, Kolkata). Currently, Assistant Professor, HOD, Political Science, South Calcutta Girls College, Kolkata. Contributed articles in 13 various journals and chapters in 12 books in different edited volumes. She has delivered lectures, participated and presented research papers in different conferences and seminars in India and abroad(Poland, Philippines, Brunei, China, Bangladesh, Suffolk University, Boston and American University of Paris, Paris). She also appeared in National TV channels CNN, India news, Republic Bharat, R.TV,Sahara TV as political analyst.

Books published:

1. Jainism: emergence and political values in it.
2. Raja Ram Mohan Roy: the first awaken soul of modern India.
3. Santhara: A Jain ritual of fast unto death.

Areas of interest are Jain religion and philosophy, comparative religion, Human Rights, ecology, religion and politics and Indian Constitution.

Contents

Introduction

"Protection of our natural spaces is a protection of home, for ourselves, for the wildlife and for future generations. Perhaps, in addition to the critical work for environmental justice, including protests, policy changes, restoration projects and the ongoing development of renewable energy, what is needed is the cultivation of ecology of belonging, of seeing oneself as part of the greater whole- not separate, superior, or even in charge of protecting- but emerged into the great web of being. This sense of belonging might be what saves us—mentally, physically and spiritually—especially when the challenges appear insurmountable."

—**Stephanie Corigliano**

Definition

Eco-theology, as defined here, is that reflection on different facets of theology as much as they take their bearings from cultural concerns about the environment and humanity's relationship with the natural world. It is, broadly speaking, a particular expression of contextual theology that emerges in the particular contemporary context of environmental awareness that has characterized the late twentieth century and early twenty-first centuries. Given the widespread secular engagement with environmental issues at global, national and local levels, such expressions of theology are highly significant. This development is not simply the concern of minority interest groups, but we reach out to include all those who are aware of global and local environmental problems.

In other words, it is hard to talk meaningfully about ecology in such a context, without also speaking about religion and theology as well. Ecology here means the broader context of ecological concerns, as well as that described by ecological science as such. In the loose sense, eco-theology is postmodern in that it takes context as its starting point and challenges the presupposition of much theology emerging in the so-called modern period. In the main, eco-theology turns against the tide of radical postmodern relativism for a confessional encounter reaction in that it accepts that environmental problems have a substantial and reasonable basis in reality.

At their best, postmodern critics show the limitations of scientific analysis and theological dogmas. Eco-theology can survive such criticism by also challenging the secular idea that the sciences are sufficient to solve environmental problems. Overall, eco-theology seeks to uncover the theoretical basis for a proper relationship between God, humanity and the cosmos. Humans are understood in Christian traditions to be created, but alienated from the natural world through their own tendency towards domination. Many approaches to eco-theology are those that seek to recover our sense of place on the earth, a reminder that the Earth is our common home, that the story of earth and that of humans are one. Theology is the study of religion. The word "theo" means God in Greek and logy means "the study of". Therefore, we expand it to mean the study of religion. It derived from the Greek word "theologia"—which means God and logic means utterance, sayings. Theology is defined as a collection of assembled religious beliefs, for the study of God and religion. According to Merriam Webster dictionary theology is the study of religious faith, practice and experience.

A new and urgent item on the agenda of all the religions of the world is the theological and ethical dimensions of ecological crisis. Highlighted by the United Nations "Earth summit" in Brazil, the issues covered in this volume raise unavoidable and fundamental questions of the lifestyle and different religions witnessed in the face of threats to the very survival of humankind and planet Earth.

Hindu, Christian, Sikh, Jain and Buddhist traditions have developed paradigms that have been and can be used in developing a viable religiously founded ecology. However, in life and thought of most religions today there is little awareness of such paradigms and even less action along the lines suggested by them. With great regularity Christian authority condemn and reject attempts to develop religiously relevant perceptions of nature and go beyond the folkloristic or metaphorical. Hindu traditions have been far too busy with political and other matters to pay much attention to the development of sound ecological theory from within the tradition.

Many fear that bringing religion into the environmental movement will threaten objectivity, scientific investigation, professionalism or democratic values. But none of these need to be displaced in order to include the spiritual dimension in environmental protection but it will rather help to create a self-consciously moral society which would put conservation and respect for God's creation first and delegate individualism, materialism and modern desire to dominate nature in a subordinate place. So no culture has remained immune to human irreverence towards nature. Then the question is how can we change the attitude of human beings towards nature?

Answering this, I believe that religion can evoke a kind of awareness in persons that is different from scientific or technological reasoning. Religion helps make human beings aware that there are limits to their control over the animate and inanimate world and that their arrogance and manipulative power over nature can be backfired. Religion instills the recognition that human life cannot be measured by material possessions and that the end of life goes beyond conspicuous consumption.

The entire lifestyle of human beings has been changed completely by the technological revolution and population explosion in the world. In earlier times, people were satisfied with minimal effort which they could derive from their narrow surroundings. But with technological growth people have started abusing the very surroundings which support their existence. Hence there is pollution.

Environmental awareness will help people to leave behind a world which is better than what it was in its lifetime. Would it be possible for men to satisfy their needs without exploiting the environment? The answer is "No". But even while exploiting the environment, people should feel that its fertility does not dwindle or degrade. In this context it appears worthwhile to examine how Indian religions have looked at the question of environmental awareness.

This book is very important in the present situation of post-pandemic period, because it makes the bond between human and nature most strong. At this juncture, the free model relation between the two for the established through the religious scriptures of different Indian religions.In other words, an in-depth analysis of the role of relation between religion/ God, nature and human beings and how this helps in the promotion, protection and preservation of the environment in today's modern technological developed world. In loose sense, eco-theology is postmodern in that it takes context as its starting point and challenges the presupposition of much theology emerging out of the modern period. Postmodern critics for the show the limitations of scientific analysis and theological dogmas. Eco-theology challenges the idea that the sciences are sufficient to solve ecological problems. Overall, eco-theology tries to unveil the theological basis for a proper relationship between God, humanity and the cosmos. In recent times, scientists have found that interacting with nature benefits humans in reducing many types of illness and lowering anxiety. For humans, close relation with nature connectedness leads to significant mental health benefits and manages our emotions. Many people are certainly realizing that there is no well-being without nature's well- being. Significantly, noticing nature through simple things like just listening to birds songs explain pro nature behavior. The message is clear -nature connectedness must run as a theme through our efforts to encourage people to do more for nature.

Noticing the good things in nature is vital and a clear tie with nature is crucial for sustainable and meaningful living. During the pandemic, more voices are talking about the need for a new relationship with nature which will be more firm through religion. Closer Bond with nature in different religions and religious scriptures embedded within our societies. We can create opportunities for everyday engagement with nature with the help of religious rituals. This can range from our models of health and well-being incorporating the benefits of nature, to our relationship with nature and religious values to be the part of education, urban design, employment and so on. We must control our use of nature now as humans, nature and religion is our real story. We need to protect that for our own narrative to continue. Otherwise, we face much larger catastrophes than the pandemic. I feel frightened when I think about climate change. I feel apprehensive for our children's future and I feel amazed that we are just carrying on headlessly, despite the mass extinctions, the ecological destruction, the science that is saving us that the virus emerged due to humans disturbing the natural world. All these should be enough to inspire us to change our ways. It's a very valuable endeavor because every bit of change matters now. Nature gives us joy- but we cannot afford to overlook the lessons it's teaching us. In our urban lives and our constant consumption, we have forgotten that we are very much a part of nature and this can be easily done for accomplishing true religion. Recalling that is essential now- both for our lives and for our souls.

Across the world, humanity is experiencing an unprecedented moment now. Facing a global pandemic, multiple nations have seen lockdowns, changed social interactions and challenging isolations. But in these testing times, nature and religion/ God is our constant friend. From our windows to the world, we have been comforted by nature›s presents all around us- like bird songs, trees, magical breeze, nights coverlet of stars etc. The covid-19 pandemic has been brought about by humanity disturbing nature›s ecological cycle. Similarly, climate change is being driven by humanity's exploitation of nature as a captive resource- our constant need to consume more and more is consuming the very planet we call our home. If we persist in damaging the environment in this way, then the pandemic may look small compared to the impacts of climate change. But we still have a chance. Indeed, nature has given us an epochal opportunity to transform ourselves and this can be achieved through religion.

Chapter 1

Religion, Society and Environment in the Context of Eco-Theology

Professor Jayaraman Suresh

"One of the first conditions of happiness is that the link between man and nature shall not be broken."

—Leo Tolstoy.

"Destroying our environment and our ecosystem is setting your own home on fire."

—Sir David Attenborough.

Earth is the planet of life. Life originated on this planet through organic evolution bringing plant life first followed by animal life, Animal life grew from primitive unicellular Amoeba to multicellular, bi-pedal human being over millions of years through evolution. The appearance of Man (Homo Sapiens) on the planet earth marked the beginning of history and initiated human activities. Primitive man was a "hunter gatherer" who led a nomadic life, roamed in the dense forest with sharp stone implements and sticks to hunt animals and to dig out roots and tubers for food and also to protect himself from attack by animals. He had no family and he roamed in the forest guided by his instinct. He lived with nature, thoroughly understood nature and led a sustained life with nature›s support. He was very much sensitive to nature and adopted his lifestyle as provided to him by nature. There was perfect harmony between primitive man and nature. He realized the importance of nature for his survival and began to respect nature.

With the passage of time and with the dawn of civilization primitive man grew to become a civilized man and was able to understand himself and his surroundings in a better way. He understood and realized his dependence on nature, environment and the living beings around him for his healthy life and survival. He also realized the importance of water, air, and fire for leading his life. He was able to enjoy the bounty of nature and found divinity in everything around him. He started worshiping the sun, moon, stars, mountain, rivers, rain, trees, fire etc., as he realized that they are his savior and source of his life. This firm belief in nature formed the basic culture of primitive society and led to the birth of "Animism" or primitive religion. The close and intimate encounter which the primitive man had with "Nature" and "Natural objects" made him realize the enormous power possessed by nature and he tried to encash them for his benefit and safe living. He ate whatever was available in nature and used selected plants, leafs, fruits, bark of trees etc. whenever he fell sick. Thus, his life was "Nature Centric" and very happy.

The human instinct in him kindled him to have a partner in life. He preferred to lead a settled life and became a cave dweller. This intimate life enabled him to understand the value of family life. He learnt the art of lightning fire and the method of doing agriculture. His lifestyle changed rapidly and he grew to become rational and developed rules for leading a systematic and organized life. This new life retained the total value for nature as the basis of the family life. When more and more families emerged they cleared the jungle to make space for their settlement. However, they desist from cutting trees and vowed to protect and preserve nature and worshiped nature as "Supreme Power."

The ever growing population *interalia* advancement of culture and lifestyle resulted in simple settlements grew to become villages which subsequently gave rise to towns and metropolis. This rapid and abrupt change necessitated destruction of the forest area to an incredibly large extent. This had chain reactions like more land for agriculture, communication, commerce etc. and completely altered the land pattern.

The Vedic seers realized the impending catastrophe and felt the need to impart the importance of nature for healthy living to the common man who are the actual practitioners and beneficiaries. They discussed various aspects in great details in a descriptive way in the Vedas, the principal source of knowledge for the common man. Temples became the centers for the propagation of this knowledge. The temples took initiative to develop Gardens on the campus called "Nandavanam" with flowering plants, trees, medicinal plants, fruit bearing trees and trees like Neem, Pipal, Banyan and a "Stala Vriksha" (a tree worshipped along with the presiding deity of the temple) which was temple specific. Besides every temple had huge tanks for providing pure water and the tanks served as the perennial source of water. The message conveyed through this was to emphasise on sanctity, purity and serenity. This was acceptable to all and practised in toto without questioning the need to maintain this.

At the same time there was a spurt in economic activities. This brought conspicuous changes in the human attitude to life. Wealth became the main yardstick for measuring progress and prosperity. The economic growth completely altered the common man's attitude to surroundings, his perception of the environment and the values attached to it changed, triggering concern among laymen. This was because these values formed the basis of their culture from the very beginning.

Religion and philosophy formed an integral part of man›s development from the earliest period. Religion, of whatever kind and in whatever place, had endeavored to establish dogmas and beliefs about events—real or mythical—with the object of enforcing certain precepts and canons of behavior. Most of these precepts and canons were such as to ensure the healthy continuance of the society which fostered them. If a particular society did not have a strong religious bias or philosophy with a moral and ethical base, it cannot guide the people in the conduct of their everyday life. I am giving a few examples to illustrate this.

In South India, women sprinkle water mixed with cow dung in the front yard of the house after brooming and put line drawings (Kolam) using rice powder. The scientific reason behind this practice is to make the area "pure". The cow dung mixture acts as a disinfectant and kills the germs and viruses. The line drawing made with rice powder acts as food for ants and other small insects.

Similarly a person affected by pox is asked to lie down on a bed made of tender neem leaf, also, turmeric paste is smeared on his body. This helps in the absorption of pox virus and helps in quick drying of the infection. Since this infection is contagious, application of turmeric with neem helps in restricting the spread among the other members of the family.

A very interesting belief is there in terms of curing leprosy. It is widely believed that if a leper takes a holy dip in the Nataraja Temple pond at Chidambaram in Tamil Nadu for one "mandalam" (48 days) he will be completely cured of the deadly disease. History goes thus: the famous Chola king Parantaka Chola was suffering from the deadly disease. He prayed to Lord Shiva and the lord answered his prayer. In his dream Shiva advised him to reach Chidambaram and take Holy dip in the pond for one mandalam (48 days) and also offer prayer to the Shiva Lingam lying under the "Punnai" tree. The king followed the divine order and was completely cured of the disease. The king built a huge temple for Shiva with the golden roof and developed the pond into a big tank for the benefit of the devotees. People suffering from the deadly disease (Leprosy) used to throng the temple to take the holy dip and were ultimately benefitted. This information is found in the inscription on the temple walls. People believe that this is a gift of god. A scientific probe done during 20th century showed that the temple tank contains a special kind of fish that is black in colour. It is deadly poisonous and not suitable for human consumption. The body of the fish contains a thick coat of an oily substance and this has medicinal properties. When the person with a leprosy wound gets into the pond, the fish comes and hits the wound. The oily secretion gets deposited on the wound. This continues for 48 days and the wound gets healed. A recent study conducted by the Marine biology department of Annamalai University and WHO confirm this. Despite these scientific explanations, people considered this as divine power and gave a deaf ear to scientific statements. Similarly people resort to such divine blessings and prayer for cure for diseases like pox, jaundice, hysteria, epilepsy, dementia etc. considering these diseases as divine curse. This shows that the people of India with their deep and firm religious sentiment and belief handle such situations.

During the 15th and 16th centuries, Christian dogma of supernaturalism described 'God' as the exclusive creator of man and the world. Clergy opposed scientific inquiry. However, struggling against all odds, including dogmatic religions, science and technology have enormously advanced to create a new world order. Science and Technology created the industrial revolution. Open and global economy has established a big market and met all the need of people for their living. A group of people, known as "Modernists", claim that faith in religion is meaningless in the modern socio-economic world. Modern science strikes at the roots of these beliefs. It has not said, "there is no supernatural force overseeing human destiny", nor stated "There is no life after death," but by its very silence it has produced a pervasive agnosticism.

Though conventional religions and philosophies continue to exist, they have lost their grip on "Modern man." The Time magazine article "God is dead" is symptomatic of the change. However, there are minds who cannot live without some faith and when old beliefs crumble people, out of dire need, turn to new ones, such as theosophy.

The advancements in Physics, Astronomy, and other

Sciences in the last three centuries, particularly in the 19th and 20th centuries attempted to provide logical and rational explanations of the phenomena occurring in the universe. The incredible advancements in technology created an impression that man has the power to control everything in the universe and bring everything under his purview. Scientists attempted to solve the mysteries of the universe and went to the extent of declaring that man can control nature since he can infer nature. This overconfidence resulted in arrogance and the feeling that man is above nature and that man can bring conspicuous changes in nature using his technology. Due to non-availability of rational, scientific and spiritual explanation towards religion, modern man has inadvertently developed an impression that religion is limited to dogmas and superstitions. While the evil of priestcraft reduced religions to blind faith and created fear of God in man, science and technology demonstrated the ability of man to understand nature and also use it. Consequently, modern man has raised the basic question "Is religion scientific?"

Explaining the role of religion with scientific basis, Swami Vivekananda says: when man finds that all the searches for happiness in matter is non-sense, then religion begins..........."

The ultimate goal of all mankind, the aim and end of all religions, is but one- re-union with God, or what amounts to the same, with the divinity which is every man›s true nature.

Emphasizing that religion is for realization, Swamiji asserts: "Religion is for realization: Not talk, not doctrine, nor theories, however beautiful they may be. It is being and becoming, and not hearing and acknowledging; it is the whole soul becoming changed into what it believes. That is religion. Thus,Swamiji strove to explain the meaning and the role of true religion to instill a spiritual orientation in modern man. Unfortunately his message went to deaf ears.

With the advent of new concepts in science and technology, life was given a new definition and direction. Everything was gauged in terms of economic growth and the age-old cultural values were side-lined as redundant. This led to the erosion of traditional cultural values and the loss of social norms. There was a sudden and abrupt change in the attitude and outlook of the people. In the name of modernization and development their voluptuous eyes fell on the natural wealth which was available in abundance providing a healthy environment for happy living. They could not resist the temptation of exploiting natural wealth for their own benefit and economic gains. They plundered and destroyed nature and natural wealth which brought chaos. The erroneous perception and application of science and technology caused irreparable damage to the environment resulting in atmospheric pollution, pollution of natural resources like water, soil etc. Destructive acts like use of atomic energy for non-constructive purposes, use of chemical and biological weapons, excessive use of outer space in the name of scientific and technological advancements, further damaged the environment. This resulted in the spread of several serious diseases, epidemic and incurable health problems. Despite several warnings, enacting stringent laws and putting restrictions, people continue to use plastics, cut trees, smuggle wood and animal skin, and poach wildlife for illegal wealth. This has resulted in serious environmental problem and bio-diversity imbalance.

Realizing the gravity of the situation scientists, environmentalists and nature conservationists initiated several programs to contain the grave situation. The objective was to establish a link between religion- science and nature in a harmonious way so that the modern man learns to live in harmony with nature.

In the late 19th and early 20th century several stalwarts like Vivekananda, Albert Einstein, Warner Heisenberg and others vehemently argued that religion is very much science. Swami Vivekananda asserted that "what we need today is western science coupled with Vedanta—The Spiritual knowledge. If this is systematically worked out, it will be for all times and all people."

Swami Ranganathananda declared that when relied on separately, science and religion can be counter-productive in the long run but when combined harmoniously can bring about an all round expression of human genius and total fulfillment.

Albert Einstein emphasized the harmony between science and religion for peaceful coexistence of people of various different religions, nations and cultures. He declared: "Science without religion is lame. Religion without science is blind."

On the invitation of Rabindranath Tagore, Warner Heisenberg visited India and during his stay in Bengal he visited Dakshineswar and Belur Math to listen to the ideas of Vedanta. Impressed by the Vedanta philosophy he was able to draw parallels between Vedanta and modern physics and based on that established the uncertainty principle.

Vivekananda explains the scientific analysis of religion as follows: "Religion deals with the truths of the metaphysical world just as the physical and natural sciences deal with the truths of the physical world. He concludes after much discussion that science of religion is based on the analysis of the human soul."

In a nutshell scientists were keen to bridge science—Religion and nature in a harmonious grid so that man learns to live in harmony with nature. They emphasized that if we start respecting "nature" and worship "nature" as god, giving due value, as did the earliest society,we can definitely live in absolute harmony, in a pure environment, good health and peace of mind.

However, modern society which is more towards materialism has completely neglected the traditional values and respect for nature and ignored the need for spiritual excellence. The life of a man has become more money centric and the man is ready to compromise on all fronts just for money without realizing that he is inviting trouble not only for himself but for the future generations as well. His greed to grab wealth by destroying nature really has made him blind. After carefully studying the situation theologians, social activists and NGOs have introduced new concepts, programs and projects to woo the attention of the modern man.

Although Hinduism had several concepts introduced indirectly to make the layman practice of environment related programmes, they lost their relevance in the mid twentieth century. To revive the tradition, a novel concept of "Ecotheology" was invented to make the programme successful.

Ecotheology is a form of constructive theory that focuses on the interrelation of religion and nature, particularly in the light of environmental concerns. Ecotheology generally starts from the premise that a relationship exists between human religions and spiritual world as also the degradation or restoration and preservation of nature. It explores the interaction between ecological values, such as sustainability and human domination of nature. The movement attracted the attention of many modern men and others alike resulting in numerous religious and environmental projects.

The burgeoning awareness of the environmental crisis has led to widespread religious reflections on the human relationship with the earth. Such reflections have strong precedents in most religious traditions in the realms of ethics and cosmology and can be seen as a corollary to the theology of nature.

It should be kept in mind that ecotheology explores not only the relationship between religion and nature in terms of degradation of nature, but also in terms of ecosystem management in general. Ecotheology not only seeks to identify prominent issues within the relationship between 'Nature' and 'Religion' but also to outline potential solutions. This is of particular importance because many supporters of ecotheology argue that science and education are not enough to inspire the change necessary in our current environmental crisis.

The relationship of theology to the modern ecological crisis became an aspect of great concern and an intense issue of debate in western academia in 1967, following the publication of the article, "The historical roots of our ecological crisis," by Prof. Lynn White, Jr., Professor of history at UCLA. Here Prof. White puts forward a theory that the Christian model of human domination over nature has led to environmental devastation, providing a voice for the ecological complaint.

In 1973, theologian Jack Rogers published an article in which he surveyed the published studies of approximately twelve theologians which had appeared since Prof. Whites' article. They reflect the search for an appropriate theological model which adequately assesses the biblical data regarding the relationship between God, humans and nature.

Although India had a pedigree of nature worship linking Human-Religion-Nature since the dawn of civilization, cultivated and developed over a period of time through the principles as expounded in the Vedas, its significance was lost during the late 20th and early 21st centuries. This was dealt at great length by the present author in the international seminar on the relevance of Vedas in the 21st century organized by the Yogakshema Trust, Chennai.

To revive the vital triangular link viz. Human-Religion-Nature, initiatives were taken by the heads of various religious myths to sensitize the modern man on his role in nature conservation for his own benefit and for the benefit of the future generation. In the 1970s Bangaru Adigalar, a school teacher turned religious head, established the Adiparashakti Trust and the famous temple at Melmaruvathur on the outskirts of Madras city. He organized "Vriksha Puja" on a grand scale and invited devotees to plant as many saplings as possible in and around the temple, a rocky barren land in the backdrop of a hillock. The devotees have to ensure the maintenance of the saplings. The saplings were mostly that of medicinal plants, fruit bearing trees and flowering trees. The objective was to make the barren area green and healthy. The program emerged not only successful but also acceptable to all communities. The temple authorities decided to convene annual conventions during which lacs of devotees would throng the temple carrying saplings from far and wide. In the three decades time the entire area has turned into a mini forest full of revenue generating trees catering to the needs of the pilgrims. This project attracted the attention of scholars and environmentalists all over the globe.

Taking the cue from this project the forest department in consultation with the authorities of various temples identified several plants for plantation around the temples. The temple authorities on their part identified each plant with one of the "the birth stars" and promoted that if the devotees plant sapling as required by his/her birth star he/she will get divine blessings. The temple authorities displayed the list of birth stars and the names of saplings (local names) for the benefit of the devotees. This initiative had a deep impact on human sentiment and mind and brought a positive result. This program transformed barren hills like Marudamalai, Palani hills, Thirumurthi hills and the temples on the Western Ghats into wonderful man made forest. The UNESCO has declared the Western Ghats as a treasure zone and an ecological hotspot.

Similar programs were also initiated in Sabarimala (Kerala) where devotees carry coconut saplings to plant on the hills during annual Maharajyoti pilgrimage. On the plains every major temple developed a sacred grove (Nandavanam) to keep the temple complex green and at the same time sacred.Besides every temple has a specific sacred tree (sthalavriksham) which is also worshipped along with the presiding deity.

In Sikkim, the forest laws are very stringent and cutting of trees is banned. Also, several lakes, ponds and water sources are declared sacred and fishing and all other tourism activities are prohibited—Lakes like Kichuburi, Aritar, Gurudangmar are declared sacred and believed to be created by Guru Padmasambhava. Mount Kanchenjunga is worshipped as mother goddess and mountaineering activities are totally forbidden.

TirupatiDevasthanam has initiated an ambitious project of developing the hill as a Sandalwood grove. Similarly forest areas are brought under surveillance and total protection. Some of the forests are declared as reserved forests and such forests are protected through joint forest management involving local tribes and foresters.

Traditional practices and lost beliefs are propagated through folk arts, folk songs, puppetry and organizing folk festivals. Rural population accepted them in the right perspective and adopted them easily. The urban population were reluctant and neglected them as primitive and unscientific and unhygienic. This has given rise to urban pollution and resulted in several health problems. Late 20th and 21st centuries saw several health, environmental and natural disasters because of our own negligence. Greed, unplanned development, mass destruction of forests, plundering of natural wealth, polluting the atmosphere, and unfortunately polluting air, water and land, excessive use of outer space in the name of technological advancement are some of the reasons for all the current problems. If a proper model is developed and promoted this current crisis can be mitigated.

Ecotheology should come out with a suitable scientific model linking man—religion and nature so that the future generation can live in peace with respect towards religion and nature.

Bibliography

1. Anton, J. Damilo.(1995). Diversity, Globalisation and the ways of Nature.Ottawa: IDRC.
2. Edwards, D.Miall. (1969). Philosophy of Religion. Kolkata, India: Progressive Publishers.
3. Gosling, L. David. (2011). Darwin, Science and the Indian tradition. The Cambridge Teape—Westcott lectures for 2009, commemorating Charles Darwin's Bi-centenary. Delhi, India: ISPCK.
4. Palsule, Sanjay Sharad.(2016). Swami Vivekananda, modern science and Human excellence, Chennai, India: RK Math.
5. Poddar, Arabinda (ed.,) (1970). Man,Science and Society. Shimla, India: Volume 9 IIAS.
6. Ray, Nihar Ranjan, (1965). Transactions of the IIAS.Shimla: Volume 1, IIAS.
7. Wulf, Andrea, (2015). The invention of Nature, Alexander Von humbold's New World. New York: Vintage Books.
8. Zimmer, Carl. (2002). Evolution—The triumph of an idea. London: William Heinemann.

Chapter 2

Eco-Theology: A Cosmopolitan View in Indian Context

Dr P S Bhatnagar

In a world where calamities and inexplicable adversities are parts of the conventional routines, the one who is lost in its slave morality, who cannot see the Sun and still chatters about shadows enthusiastically, may see the beauty and reach one's fulfillment, thanks to the relevant culture. When chaos is ready to burst into uncontrolled dreadful sequels, culture comes to bring light in the dark abysses, leaving every aspect of the world drowned into self-overcoming and satisfaction. Taking different existential forms, from the material and physical patterns produced by a society to a non material sacred culture such as ethics, language, beliefs and religions,the latter took an enormous edge of humanity's perspective nowadays. It differs from a group ethnic morality to another, to even a country's history to another. However, all religions aim to find the life balance, to give it a maximum of meaning and value through bright and dark days.

In fact, one of the most outstanding cultural areas that offers considerably a rich religious context is India. It is well known that the Indian milieu provides a cosmopolitan view of what is holy heritage, combining the sacred desires of original beauty and harmony. The first standpoint that Indian religions are framing is the beliefs on what we call the Eco-theology. Many philosophers and religious reverends admit in all ways that the eco-theology is the new theology. However, let us put ourselves in its theoretical aspect. What is eco-theology?

Mainly, Eco-theology is an interesting and special form of effective theology that focuses on the interrelationships and the interactions of religion and nature. The eco-theology helps to put humanity in a rational reality where the purpose of life keeps flowering with embracing the powers of environment and surroundings, decoding the best version of true beauty. The basic premise of eco-theology is that it is possible to be able to speak to nature, to appreciate the god's creations and to recognize the unlimited outcomes of the light of environmental concerns. The eco-theologians claim that praising god goes along with acknowledging nature as an interrelated system. It surely incorporates spirituality, understanding and action.

As Sigmund Freud said, during one of his most frustrating years, humanity is all driven by the pleasure principles. This psychoanalysis aspect inclines people towards easy physical and emotional rewards, and away from unpleasant things such as drudgery and discipline, leading them often unconsciously to dangerous reckless paths. On the contrary, people need to adjust to what Freud called the Reality principle, where all have to bow to this reality, shaped in better or worse kinds of adaptations, leaving the repression of the pleasure principle, and getting to understand more about the dynamics and the origins of our world. To the same extent, religion as a lifelong companion of humans should altogether focus on the reality-uplifting version. No one can deny that sustainability depends a huge amount on ecology. By ecology, we mean the science of living in a right devoted relation with the air, soil, water and life upon which we depend on. That is what reality propounds. Actually, ecology is the interdisciplinary study of primary reality, that which brought us into being, and which nourishes and sustains us and finally receives us when we die. This utter connection relates humanity with the primary reality that has only been trivial due to understanding what religion has to acquire.

Let us get back to India, where we cannot but admire the concrete extent of these notions. The country has a large historical culture, along with an abundant background of breathtaking landscapes and beautiful country views. Tourists never skip sightseeing the Himalayan Mountain Range, the Thar Desert, the Coastal Plains, nor the Indian Islands. The rocky terrains, the sprawling coastlines, the stunning deserts and the exotic islands- the true magnificence of India can be witnessed through its landscapes. It is, as simple as the word means, a treat for everyone that had the chance to visit. Thanks to these beautiful resources, people of India have always been devoted to raising the word sustainability into their cultural religion and education. Society preserves the ecology by all means, and religion has always been on its constant verge. What is better than a formal belief that puts all its people into harmony, reality comprehension and sustainability, knowing where they are, what they have and how to protect it? It surely is comforting, because a theology that does not embrace ecology as the very heart of it is certainly a theology that our great grandchildren will condemn us for. Indian society proclaims to live in a decent way that does not diminish or destroy the future generation but enhancing, enriching and preserving the health and well-being of the forests and fisheries.

In addition to that, we have to know that India has numerous religions inserted in the society. It is one of the richest countries that gave birth to many of the world's major religions. Hinduism, Buddhism, Jainism, Sikhism, Christianity, Islam, Judaism, Zoroastrianism and Baha 'I' Faith, are all religions that occupy different percentage of Indian population, and have been composed of innumerable sects and sub sects. These religions have been a nutritious chance to merge the religious beliefs one needs to the various ecological phenomenons one have to regard. Among these relevant religions, India converges into one major religion that carries a vast mass of its citizens: The Hinduism. With approximately 79.8% of the Indian population, and accounting 966 Million religious members, Hinduism recalls to be one of the largest religions in the history of India. The Rigveda, which is the oldest of the sacred books of Hinduism was written more than 3800 years ago, making then Hinduism one of, if not the oldest religion in the world. No wonder that the Hindu religion, as famous as it is in India, has been the most staggering icon of development of greater ecological awareness in the territory. Most of the Indian community practices Hinduism, although the Preamble of the Indian constitution implies that the State will not discriminate, patronize or meddle in the profession of any religion, which makes the constitution incredibly secular. It even shields individual religions or groups by adding religious rights as fundamental rights.

If we get a closer look at values of Hinduism, we will find that many of the gods mentioned in the hymns of Vedas, the ancient religious chants in India, are deeply related to the natural prodigies. How is that? Well, according to Hindus, religion is a way of life rather than structured following just instructions. It is normalized to admit that Hinduism is more of a culture and a code of behavior. Hindus believe that seeing the truth in things leads to eternal faith, and that every living being is sacred, owing to the fact that these beings are parts of God, and should be treated with respect and compassion. These statements are without the deviation to the nexus of ecology and reality's environment. By referring to sacred rivers, forests, mountains and even animals, Hindus grasp a superior care for the environment, all loving its innumerable features and beings consistently close to nature. For example, many villages that follow Hindu religion have sacred groves. These forest fragments deem to hold religious significance and are communally protected as sacred trees. In other certain villages, we can find holy lakes, surrounded by orchards to catch rainfall and protect the banks from erosion. Hinduism regards that the trees and plants possess divine healing properties, as also that every tree has a tree deity. Not only does the human aspect of ecological respect take an enormous part in the behavior of Hindus, but also there is the attempt to have morality in every day of their lives. There are two models; "devotional model" and the "renouncer model". Both of them can contribute in preserving the ecology of India. The renouncer model can help in reducing the over-exploitation of natural resources by limiting one's desire for more luxuries, and the devotional model can be of use to restore natural resources to their original beauty and harmony. A Jain householder is also expected to avoid injury to *trasa* beings (mobile) and is supposed to minimize injury to *sthavara* beings (immobile) while Buddhism has also emphasized on *Ahimsa* (non-violence), *Karuna* (Compassion) and *Metta* (loving kindness). '*Vasudhavkutumbakam*'; This Sanskrit phrase in Hindu texts means that "the world is like one family". How inspiring and warming that sounds!! When the balance between the resources and competences are met into one similar gap, it is very relevant to confess that crisis should no longer worry humanity and the present reality treasures assuredly the global environment conservation. That is exactly what Hinduism brings into one's spirit. The latter is lifted upon ethics that prioritizes the best interest of the Hindus, motivating them to act in the best form to sharpen their life expectations. These common ethics correspond to five *Yamas*, the scripture *Rig Veda* verses, of ancient Hindu religion. First, there is *Ahimsa*, as a non-violence principle. Secondly the *Satya*: the ethic of saying the truth and avoiding eternal falsehood, following the *Asteya*; referring to non-stealing and the *Brahmacharya* that mentions sexual abstinence and the control of all minds through self restraint and ascetic means and finally the *Aparigraha* or the non-possessiveness. These major five key beliefs are shared among Hindus core to lessen injuries to all human beings, and encourage peace and harmony, between men and nature.

Moreover, Hinduism points out that a human being gets to live many lives before its arrival on the earth, and a soul can be reincarnated into any form of life. For that reason, all living beings as parts of God, are essentially sacred because they are believed to have souls, and thus should be honored and cared for. The virtue of the defined simple and happy life that one can have is the inner peace that makes commodities and daily chores easy and uncomplicated, guiding the spirit through a lighter road. Hindus seek to reach the pleasant level when one finds delight in reality, and drowns into its resolution that the spiritual nature educates humanity by all manners. We start to limit our possessions, to reach the blissed state of mind, where only that matters is the rapturous morality and the energy brought from every pattern in our environment. All different consumptions and answers come from within, letting righteousness dominate our lives.

As it happens constantly, the Hindu community encourages in typical events to plant trees. They even consider such events as a religious duty that no one should miss. If we gather all these reasonable facts, we ought to mention that Hinduism is such an eco-friendly religion, multifaceted to traditional and ecological awareness in India.

Among other religions that has the right to get into the major thrones religions, and as the second largest religion in India, we had the chance to come across The Islam. No one can deny the weight of the polemic that this religion has worldwide. Regarding our eco-theology theme that we are discussing, Islam has been the solution to many environmental crisis the world is facing now-a-days. From climate change, pollution, biodiversity to deforestation, the Islamic virtues take detailed approaches to explain the failing process of human behavioral patterns. According to Islam, God created life through humans for a determined and specific purpose: to be trustworthy and an heir on the earth. The main key belief is to worship God in every level of human life. The Islamic community believes that every living being in the world, was, still, and will be under the control of one and only God. Plants, bacteria, insects, animals, trees, fishes, reptiles, humans and all kinds of living aspects are the creation of God, who entrusted its people to protect and guard them. Muslims are "the Khalifa", in other words, the preservers and protectors of the God's creations. Besides, does he not create flora and fauna? Certainly, God has praised the Muslim community with the privilege to live among fructuous and profitable natural creations providing each one of them the happiness to enjoy, the harmony it balanced and the benefits it generated. The only responsibility societies needs to sustain is to keep the viable respect and make a rational use of natural resources, while introducing evolving guidelines for continuously improving the environmental performance. That is again when religion and sacred beliefs meet ecology in its brightest tale. In fact, the central religious text of Islam, the revelation from God is The Quran. In one of its verses, (we call ayat, meaning signs and proofs of the divine), it is quoted as following: "He who produces gardens, both cultivated and wild, and palm trees and crops of diverse kinds and olives and pomegranates both similar and dissimilar. Eat of their fruits when they bear fruit and pay their dues on the day of their harvest, and do not be profligate. He does not love the profligate". In the same perspective, this human responsibility referring to ecology has taken the form of a predominant concept of Islamic religion: the *Tawheed*, or unity. The religious notion claims that God is one, and all his creatures live among common unity. All Muslims must therefore maintain the right cohesion and wholeness of the planet Earth, keeping humanity and nature in perfect order and polyphony. However, how Islam accomplishes this formality? So as to decipher the environmental requisition one is bound to attain, Allah encourages its people to avoid excess of natural resources leading to waste and desolation. Respecting the value of life, and entitling communities to fall in love with the beauty and pageantry of nature are some first steps to get the benediction of God. He does create everything in balance, and warns that misdemeanor of the balance shall surely have disastrous consequences. This holds true not just for the world around us, but also for our souls, for Islam, and as we previously mentioned, does not differentiate the world of man from the world of nature. On the top of that, Islam teaches as well that all people will be judged in the end by the only Allah, for how they have behaved, how they have discharged their responsibilities following the guidance of Islam.

All these principles have been a chance to show humans practical supervised paths for how to live, and preserve the well-being of the generations to come. We can find rituals to follow and to stick to, in the "Sharia". The word even means 'the way'.

It is more of a referring wide-ranging morals and broad ethical principles drawn from the Quran and the practices and sayings of Prophet Muhammad, known as "Hadith". From an early age, Muslim communities teach their kids different stories of Prophets at distinct time areas. As an example, Prophet Muhammad encouraged the planting of trees and the cultivation of agriculture. He also forbade the cutting of cedar trees in the desert since they provided shelter and shade to animals and continued to conserve water and all resources. Therefore, sustainable development is additionally in the Islamic attitude board, considered good deeds and acts of continuous charity.

Nevertheless, what has Sikhism to offer in community as an ecological religion? The monotheistic religion and philosophy first appeared in the North of India by 15th century, thanks to the founder Guru Nanak or 'Father Nanak'. Sikhism tradition takes a fundamental basis on ten Gurus—Guru Nanak, Guru Angad, Guru Amar Das, Guru Ram Das, Guru Arjan, Guru Har Gobind, Guru Har Rai, Guru Har Krishan, Guru Tegh Bahadur and Guru Gobind Singh: all of them believe that a single spirit inhabited them. Its members are known as the Sikhs, and the Sikh scripture is the Guru Granth Sahib. The latter is reviewed not only as the holy scripture of Sikhism, but also as the living Guru. Sikhism admits that achieving a blissful state and a righteous harmony with the earth and all God's creation is the optimum purpose of human beings. To put the world in the proof assay, Guru Har Rai, the seventh Sikh Guru had the firmness to carry on and to develop Kiratpur Sahib as a town of parks and gardens. Located on the banks of the tributary of the Sutlej, he planted flowers and fruit bearing trees all over the area. This created a beneficial and healthy environment, attracting beautiful birds and exquisite sciurid rodents to the town and turning it into an idyllic place to live in.

This Sikh scripture, or the Guru Granth Sahib insists in its hymns (Shabads), on the importance of life elements." Air is the Guru, Water is the Father, and Earth is the Great Mother of all". Owing to the fact that the earth is referred to as the mother, it plainly steers the first position with respect to all Sikhism society.

Great care needs to be taken all the way to ensure that no damage or defacement occurs to it while the Sikh is going about his or her daily life.

Further, we notice in the Guru Granth Sahib that water, earth and sky are God's home and temple. The sacred virtue means that life elements are sacred places, which need to be solemnly protected and taken with great consideration and valuable caution. For instance, the Sikh Gurus built many Gurdwaras, where Sikhs assemble and worship their God. The place offers food, shelter and companionship to those who need these. When building them, the Sikh Gurus made sure to surround its borders by sizable pools that supported aquatic life, especially fish. This was clearly a sign to live in harmony with nature rather than in conflict with it.

Guru Nanak in his philosophy states that humanity and nature are two different, but interrelated creations. The problems that the world had unfortunately faced all these centuries, from ecological to economic crises, were essentially caused by the inner conflict of humans. The current instability of the natural system of the earth is only a reflection of the instability and pain within humans. The increasing barrenness of the earth's terrain is a reflection of the emptiness within humans. That explains the correlation of consequences one part has to experience, depending on the other. Spirit and matter only appear erroneously as a polarity. They are otherwise; destined to live in unity and comprehensible integration, floating through all word's fields ever existed.

In the same philosophical extent, Jainism, the spiritual religion that exposes purity and enlightenment to acquire perfect understanding of reasons of life and knowledge of self and universe, has been well known for its extremely ecological and natural aspects. In India, Jainism, or the "Jain Dharma" is one of the oldest religions that involves avoidance of any form of violence, not only to human beings but also to all nature. The sacred religion emphasizes this non-violence and karma as the only true path that leads to inner peace and joy and then eternal liberation from rebirth. This common concern between Jainism and Mother Nature can be found in a mutual sensitivity toward living things. The Jain Dharma educates its people to respect and protect all living systems, thus that five main elements of nature; Prithvi (land, soil, stones), Jal (Water resources), Agni (Fire), Vayu (Air) and Aakash (Sky) are but living creatures and must be treated as living beings. The Jain community, or the Jainism keeps the empathy for all forms of life in their daily life. Most of them, if not all of them, are vegetarians. Their diet consists wholly of vegetables, fruits, grains, nuts and others, without any meat or fish. There is the Aparigraha premise in Jainism, which helps the society to acquire the habit of limiting the human acquisitions to non-material goods in the benefit to contribute to all society's commonwealth for the work on humanitarian charities and philanthropic causes. Once the material possession is limited, the factors of economic production become directly low and substantially affect the ecosystem. The demands of national economic growth and individual needs and desires are depleting the natural resources of the earth.

Constituting 2.3% of India's population, Christianity has been defined as another traditional religion that based its premises on the pursuit of graciousness and honorable happiness. The religion has left an indelible mark on the cultures, traditions and architecture of India. The country has the chance to uphold many beautifully embellished churches that adorn every city and town. Despite the material and artistic fractions, Christianity endorses cardinal morals that affect humanity and its surroundings. The Christian religion teaches, first, that God gave human beings a special responsibility within creation to cultivate the environment, guard it and use it wisely, as a form of stewardship. These values were enshrined in all the Christian testaments and presupposed by Jesus Christ, the son of God. According to Christianity, humans shall be grateful for everything, as long as all the materials given by God would satisfy their needs. "Everything that lives and moves about will be food for you. Just as I gave you the green plants, I now give you everything" (Genesis, 9; 3). "God took the man and put him in the Garden of Eden to work it and take care of it." (Genesis 2:15). These passages from the Bible, the sacred book that collects scriptures and religious texts, manifest in a very clear way, that Humans have the role of protecting all created things, not abusing or destroying them. Here is where it takes back to the interdependence of humanity and nature in another ecological realm. It is undeniable that Christianity respects the natural world, and offers guidance on different environmental issues. For the Christians, the guiding principles are to work, raise and stress the need for every individual and every nation to play their part, as well as to look after the environment in a variety of ways. The Roman Catholic Churches, as for example, organize reverent events along the year, to spread awareness of the ecological needs of future generations. They encourage their members to make changes in their lives, which enable them to live simply and minimize their exploitation of the Earth. Besides, India has a small percentage of Zoroastrians as well and Zoroastrians believe that everything including the natural environment has been created pure and should be treated with love and respect.

Men are now-a-days engaged in a new journey, a journey to search for ways and means to overcome ecological crisis. Natural catastrophes that rise at the other side of the planet, unexpectedly and easily find ways to expand and spread their feathers to reach every edge of each country, shaking out all homes and organizations to dread and terror. It is very important to emphasize and weigh the dangerousness of the natural situations we are living in today. Years passed by, and humanity realized that scientific solutions are not the ultimate answer to the problem. The sacred link to morality, culture attribution and religion affiliation are the palpable compounds to extend the life balance, and overcome its obstacles. India, having a cosmopolitan environment has taught us that appreciating nature shall be commonly first manners to apprehend. The multiracial religions and the many collections of cultural systems and beliefs have succeeded in playing an important role in influencing the world's daily and constant behaviors. No one can deny that the environmental crisis is caused by humanity's confrontation with nature. Having unflinching faith, men can take deep trust in the path God preserved for him in all circumstances. The peace within, and the extreme fulfillment and joy it brings, can but leave an exceptional trace into the nature sphere. Men become more aware of sustainability issues and take a good part to get the better of what nature ushers us. Thanks to all forms of religions, the natural world is seen as an embodiment of divinity, sacredness and even spiritual power. Moreover, what is better than a blessed and grateful world? Men can still have credence in what tomorrow will hide. The unity of men and nature is after all, an organic presence. The environment, although outside them, had within them not only its image, but also its material energy and information channels and processes. When the external principles disappear, men themselves disappear from life. That is said if we lose nature's image, we definitely lose our life, and if we live closer to nature, adopted and accompanied by a sacred religion, its eternal laws will protect us.

Notes and Bibliography

1. Hinduism: Coward H. (2003) Hindu Views of Nature and the Environment. In: Selin H. (Eds) Nature across Cultures. Science Across Cultures: The History of Non-Western Science, vol 4.Springer, Dordrecht. https://doi.org/10.1007/978-94-017-0149-5_21

2. Nelson, Lance. Purifying the Earthly Body of God: Religion and Ecology in Hindu India. Albany: SUNY Press, 1998.

3. Chapple, Christopher Key. "Hinduism, Jainism, and Ecology" in Earth Ethics, vol. 10, no.1, fall 1998.

4. Donald K. Swearer, The Harvard Theological Review, Vol. 99, No. 2 (Apr. 2006), pp. 123-137 (15 pages), published By: Cambridge University Press

5. Prime Ranchor. Hinduism and Ecology.New York, Caael Publishers Ltd. 1999.

6. Basics of Jainism: https://medium.com/bliss-of-wisdom/5-fundamentals-of-jainism-d61e82304b29, https://www.soas.ac.uk/blogs/study/jainism/

7. Beyond the pleasure principle and other writings by Sigmund Freud, Translated by John Reddick

8. **Quran References:**

   "He is Allah, Absolute oneness, Allah, the Everlasting Sustainer of all. He has not given birth and was not born. And no one is comparable to Him" (Surat al-Ikhlas: 1-4)

   "What is in the heavens and the earth belongs to Allah: He encompasses everything" (An-Nisâ, 4:126)

   "He who produces gardens, both cultivated and wild, and palm trees and crops of diverse kinds and olives and pomegranates both similar and dissimilar. Eat of their fruits when they bear fruit and pay their dues on the day of their harvest, and do not be profligate. He does not love the profligate" (Surat Al an'âm, 6:141)

9. **Guru Granth Sahib References:**

   "Air is the Guru, Water is the Father, and Earth is the Great Mother of all", Guru Granth Sahib, page 8

10. The dominion granted to man by the Creator is not an absolute power, nor can one speak of a freedom to 'use and misuse', or to dispose of things as one pleases.Evangelium Vitae, Section 42 (1995)

11. The Christian View of Nature, by the reverend David Stacey, M.A Eastbourne, The expository Times, Published September, 1956

12. **Christian Bible References:**

    "Everything that lives and moves about will be food for you. Just as I gave you the green plants, I now give you everything" (Genesis, 9; 3).

"God took the man and put him in the Garden of Eden to work it and take care of it." (Genesis 2:15).

13. **Jainism Reference:**

    Jainism, Dharma and Environmental Ethics by Pankaj Jain.` https://academiccommons.columbia.edu/doi/10.7916/D8Q531B9/download

14. **Zoroastrian Reference:**

    https://www.bbc.co.uk/religion/religions/zoroastrian/beliefs/god.shtml#:~:text=Zoroastrians%20 believe%20that%20 everything%20he,'the%20first%20ecological%20religion'.

Chapter 3

"Experiencing *Sarvaṃsarvātmakaṃ*": Tāntric Journey to Non-Dual Eco-Theology, with Special Reference to Trika Philosophy of Kashmir

Swastik Banerjee

Introduction

Sakalabhuvanodayasthitilayamayalīlāvinodyuktaḥ/
Antarlinavimarśaḥ pātu maheśaḥ prakāśamātratanuḥ//[1]

India has been a land of seers and spiritual thinkers. Here the world, the individual and the God, here the very discussion of theology or philosophy has a purpose. It is therefore called *darśaṇa*[2], a way of seeing life. It is also a way of living life. Life in harmony with the *other.* This *other* is not just the other person but the entirety of existence. For many *advaita* philosophy

1 The invocation of *Kāmakalāvilāśa* pays homage to the Supreme Being, from which all the existence springs out, sustains and dissolves. In whom is *svatantryaśakti vimarśa* resting, and because of that *prakāśa* all else shines. This summarises the idea of the Supreme to be discussed hence forth.

2 An etymological derivation can clarify their differences. The word darshana comes from the root dṛś (seeing) and the suffix *lyuṭ* is added. The word Philosophy comes from the words *philos* and *sophia,* which literally translates to love for knowledge.

became popular, and a central way of understanding spirituality. Even now, if we meet spiritual teachers, several of them choose to follow the doctrine of non-dualism. This theory of non-dualism suggests that there is no second, or whatever exists is one with that which is *the Reality/Highest Truth*[3]. We can more simply say that, if we say God is the ultimate reality then the world and the individual are not separate from God. If we believe something other exists outside, then it would incur contradiction. Since everything is ultimately in *That*, it seeks to promote of holistic approach. The world, the individual and God are one and the same. Even for a dualist the idea that the man is made in the image of God to have dominion over the nature[4], is unacceptable. Instead for them the world and the individual *belong* to God[5], man only serves God and treats the world to respect and care. Thus a holistic Eco-theological tendency came into being. Here we find the concept of *ṛṇas*[6], which develops from the doctrine of cosmic harmony. Therefore, what is taken has to be given back. We take knowledge of the ṛṣis, essentials of living from the *bhutas*, our body from our parents and ancestors, privileges of nature from *Devas*, and social needs from other humans. Thus *ṛṣis, bhuta, pitṛ, deva* and *manuṣya ṛṇa*s have been mentioned in the śāstras to revoke the debts respectively. These are done by performance of duties towards them by teaching, giving back to the nature, birth of children, performing rites and social service respectively. Even the four āśramas, or stages of life, reflect the same ideals.

---

3 In *Taitteriy*a Up. 2.1.1 after śikṣāvalli, it opens with the statement as Brahman is *satyam*, i.e. the *Truth*. Knowing which one moves in the great sky, i.e become liberated.

4 If we read Genesis 1:26 we find, the statement of God sating, "Let us make man in our image, after our likeness. And let them have dominion over the fish of the sea and over the birds of the heavens and over the livestock and over all the earth and over every creeping thing that creeps on the earth.".

5 Whereas in Indian religion we find that in Bhagvad Gita 10.20 "*aham ātmā guḍākeśha sarva-bhūtāśhaya-sthitaḥ", i.e.* the God says he is present in all living beings. Thus for the dualists, who serve God, has to respect the creation.

6 For better clarification see the concept of *Ṛta* (cosmic order), and *ṛṇa* in Vedic ethics.

One cultivates the inner nature and acquires knowledge in the first āśrama, *brahmacārya*, then moves on to become a householder as *grihasta*, and fulfills duties towards the family and society. After this, he is supposed to go for vanaprasta-retire to a hermitage and finally, by practice of renunciation should take up *sannyāś*. The very cultivation comes to the point where one knows this worldly pleasures are momentary. Thus in Vedic tradition the cultivation of *vairāgya* through *nitya-anitya-viveka*[7] is emphasised by the schools.

Tāntric Nonduality

The *tāntric* systems have a rather unique way of seeing the world. Neither do they believe that this worldly existence is suffering, nor do they see the sensual pleasures to be bondage. Instead they state that, all these are the creative expression of the Supreme God Consciousness. This Supreme God Consciousness, has been called by several names- *Anuttara, Kaula, Pramaśiva,* Ādyāśakti, *Parabrahman,* and so on.

Whatever name we may use, it is an indication of the non-dual reality, *Caitanya.* This *Caitanya* is the Self, ātmān. This *Caitanya* is inseparably associated with the power of absolute freedom, *svatantryaśakti.*[8] *Svatantryaśakti,* out of her own free will reveals this multiplicity[9] (of 118 *bhuvanas* and seven *pramātās*) on her own screen of awareness. For *Tāntrics* (or more accurately *Kaulas*[10]), everything is sacred. They do not see distinction of any objective awareness, and experiences *Caitanya* as the reality in all. This is their highest state of realisation. Since the world is identical, they need not give up the world and senses to attend *moksha.*

---

7 This is a core requirement for the study of *Vedānta* falls under one of the *sādhancatuṣṭayas*.

8 See *Śiva Sūtra's Vimarśinī* by *Kṣemrāja* commentary on the first aphorism "*tasya bhāvaḥ caitanyaṃ...svātantryam ucyate.*"

9 See *Pratyabhijñāhṛayam* by *Kṣemrāja's* commentary on the sūtras 1-4.

10 The world *Kaula* is technical, it means the union of *Kula* (the differentiated totality), and *Akula* (the undifferentiated totality). The Kaulas are those who reside in the state of *annuttara.*

But for them the senses which are seen as *mātrikāśaktis*[11] help in evolution of the *sādhāka* to attain the state of *Bhairava*. It is this journey of *Vāmamārga*[12], that is in reverse of the creation where one understands the true identity of oneness—*ekatmabhabna,* that is at play in this multiplicity.

The Seeker's Journey

This journey starts with the rise of self inquiry, *who am I?* We seek to find an identity that defines me. The answer is not simple, like reading a book and realizing that, "Oh! I am *Brahman"*. But it involves a journey, a journey which takes place by trying to figure out my place in this world. And this brings us to the question of, *what is my purpose of life?* Or *does life have a purpose? What gives life its meaning?* The world, my being there , figure out a purpose, all make us wonder *if there's a God(dess).* This very inquiry is considered to be rare, and therefore the Upanishads call this the path of śreyas[13]. This knowledge of *Self* has been considered as the key to liberation.

However, there has been no single answer for this throughout the history. Some choose to take the path of atheism[14], while some resort to agnosticism. Then there are others who develop some form of theism. Even in a theism, there is no absolute answer. We find views of—pantheism[15], polytheism[16],

11 In several Trika texts, like the *Sambitcakrastava* of Abhinavagupta, we find the *aṣṭamātṛkās,* mentioned as presiding *śaktis* over the instruments of knowledge.

12 One of the several definitions of *Vāmamārga* comes from the name of Goddess *Vāmeśvarī*, or the form of mother who is beautiful since She is revealing the world, she is *Vāmā* because she is also the gateway in reverse of creation.

13 In Kathopanisad 2.2 Yama speaks of the path of self enquiry as *śreyas*.

14 In india we find Lokāyatas who are sceptics, even now we have atheists. Philosophers like Karl Marx and his followers have taken this course. Even if we see thinkers like Daniel Dennet they would reduce all these to simple neurological impulses.

15 Spinoza's pantheism was heretic at the same time a popular view.

16 Several pagan cultures like Helenic, and Egyptian is believed to be polytheistic.

monotheism[17], and so on. In India we have found non-dualism, and *Trika Tantra* follows a version[18] of this. It stands in contrast to the most popular view of *Advaita Vedānta*. The *Advaita Vedānta* school states *Brahman* is the sole reality[19], this world of our experience is just a mere superimposition of *Brahman*, therefore not real. The individual self is not different from the *Brahman*[20]. Trika agrees with Vedānta regarding *jiva*, but disagrees regarding the world and calls it real.

Now here comes the challenge- there should not be two for non dual. For Advaita Vedānta, *Brahman* is non-dual and cannot be spoken of or having something that qualifies or has activity. It is just bare consciousness since involving anything would simply hinder the quality of non-duality. Trika on the other hand develops a perfect Eco-theological view, where the individual realising the truth, does not reject the world but becomes a sustainable member of the society. This can be realised by understanding two processes-(1) the way of revealing the multiplicity (2) experiencing the oneness.

Visvamunmīlayati: Revelaing Multiplicity:[21]

In *Pratyabhijñāhṛayam* the first two sūtras state—*citiḥ svatantrā viśvasiddhihetuḥ & svecchayā svabhittau visvamunmīlayati"*. The *Caitanya* out of its own free will unfolds the multiplicity in her

17 The Abrahamic religions like Islam and Christianity are monotheistic, however in India, if we see the Brahma Samāj, they have proposed a form of monotheism as well.

18 The non-dualist schools are having their own views. There are those like Śaṅkara, who see the jagat as mithyā. The Vaiṣṇavas see it as real but Viṣṇu as the Godhead. Trika is a Śaivite school, which is not entirely Vedic, and thus has their own ways.

19 For the Vedantins a thing to be 'real' must be *abādhita* and *anadhigata,* that is it must not be sublated and not be a subject of another cognition.

20 The philosophy of Advaita Vedanta is often summarised in the popular half sloka- *"Brahma satyam jagan mithyā jivo brahmaiva nāparaḥ"*.

21 In this section I have combined the concepts of *pramātā, kalās* and *tattva* from different texts, and co-related them to explain the process of world revelation.

own screen. This *Caitanya* is *prakāśa-vimarśamaya*, the union of Śiva and Śakti. They are inseparable from each other, just as there is no difference between fire and its power to shine or burn, so is the case of Śiva-Śakti. The word *prakāśa* comes from the root '*kāś*' which means to shine upon, it is prefixed with "*pra*" as in the sense of *prakṛṣṭha* and '*ac*' suffix is added to give the sense '*prakāśate*'. The word *vimarśa* comes from the root '*mṛṣ*, (to analyse/reflect), with '*vi*' prefix, and '*ghañ*' suffix, to bring forth the sense of '*vicāra*'. These two words simultaneously are used following the grammar rule of *prakriyā daśā,* where a single concept for the sake of linguistic and conceptual clarity is broken into two. Thus though two words are in use, one must remember the indication is '*not-two*'. This may also be understood using the *svarūpalakṣana* of *Brahman*, '*Satcitānanda*'. In that manner, Śiva is *sat,* or mere existence, while Śakti is the nature of Śiva. The two *citśakti* and ānandaśakti are in union with Śiva'. *Vimarśa* is *pūrṇāhamtā,* a pure I-sense which floats in the *Caitanya*. Consciousness cannot be devoid of activity, and thus it is intentional, therefore this pure 'I' is what floats in the awareness. It is where the entirety of the possibilities and impossibilities rest. This word AHAṂ consists of three segments. First the letter 'A indicating Śiva, and the letter 'H indicating Śakti, the Consciousness Śiva reflects on the mirror of Śakti, and in the mirror it experiences down to the H, which indicates the Śakti's womb. The Ṃ indicates the concentrated oneness of experience as *bindu*. These /A/ /H/ /**Ṃ** together forms the *pūrṇāham.* The aspect also deals with the united state of *Yāmala,* where the letter *visargaḥ* indicated by '*aḥ*'is called the *sitak*āra, a primordial orgasmic urge to create, which is in union with the *bindu, aṃ,* the joining of the two, which is termed as *saṅghaṭṭa*[22], known as *aham.* The *bindu* here is experiencing the reflection of itself as *visargaḥ*[23]. This experience causes a churning, which is in the form of supreme bliss, termed as ānandaśakti. This ānandaśakti is the experience of *svatantrya.*

---

22 Literally means a meeting with friction.

23 If one keeps a mirror infront of *bindu,* or point it reflects and both appears as the *visargah* ":".

As and when the very first urge rises, the Śiva tattva[24] appears, it start to split that which was one to two, one rests while the other takes motion and triggers the process giving birth to *iccāśakti*, this is when the Śakti tattva gets prominence, At this state Śiva pramātā[25] resides in the all pervasive Śāntātitakalā[26]. These three form the first triangle.

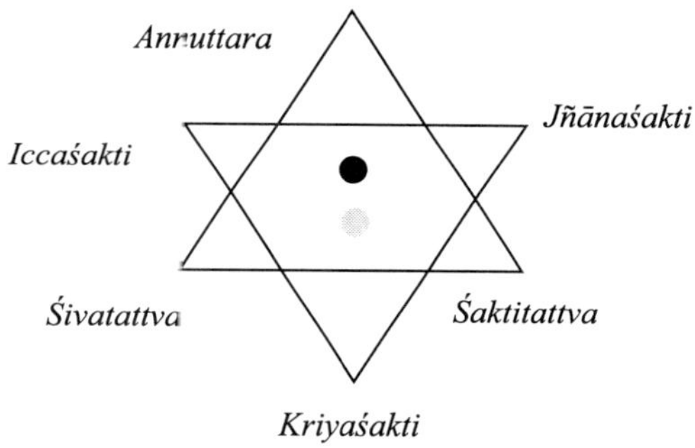

The upward triangle indicates dissolved whole, while The downward is the womb of creation, The *bindu* becomes *visargaḥ* being reflected in the mirror of *Śakti*.

With the start of descent, and the formation of the downward triangle, the Śāntakalā comprising of 18 *bhuvanas*[27] and three *tattvas* [ii]comes. The split which happens within the *annuttara* gives birth to the first embryo of *idam*. This *idam* or objectivity has not become clear yet, and as a mere intention to create, like the urge to speak, it is where *iccaśakti* becomes prominent. This in the level of speech is called *paśyanti vāk*, as it cannot quite be explained but merely seen. This holds a double intentionality, one where all the speech that is springing out towards duality is tied

24 Tattva may be understood as the abode or level where *Caitanya* appears in a certain manner.

25 *Pramātā* is the cognitive agent at a particular state, they show how the other is experienced at a level.

26 The name *Śāntātita* implies that it is transcending the *Śānta kalā, or all pervasive.*

27 A single *bhuvana* contains the entire cosmos or universe with physical laws etc.

as a knot of thread, and other rising from the *Parāvāk.* The being starts to experience the objectivity as *aham-eva-idam,* and is thus called the *Mantramaheśvara pramātā.* This state of revelation is where the *annuttara* is revealed as the *Sadāśivatattva.*

As the experience of the objectivity becomes more prominent, the cognitive agent starts to see the *idam* as one whole, and within the *aham.* Thus in the form *idameva aham* the experience happens, and the being comes to be known as *Mantreśvara pramātā.* This state is equated to *madhyamā vāk*, which resides in the mind with clear picture of the word and the object meant. This is the level where *jñānaśakti* becomes prominent and the Supreme reveals as the Īśvara tattva and we look upon Īśvara as God/Goddess residing here.

After the Īśvara tattva, the *mantra pramātās* appear, these are the forces like minor gods and goddess, the deities and so forth. Their experience has a distinct *aham* and *idam.* The *kriyāśakti* is prominent over here, and so is the *Vak* ,that from this point is known as *Vaikhari.* This level is called the śuddhavidyā , and the last of the śāktānda.

Just below the state of śuddhavidyā we have a layer of beings, who are called *vijñānakala pramātās,* , in the gateway of being liberated , getting a taste of *aham.* They reside just above the *māyā.*

The *māyā* as the *parāparaśakti*, tends to make *idam* overpower *aham,* and binds the *svatantra* through the five *kañcukas*. They together form the *māyānda*, where the cognitive agent becomes devoid of awareness and thus is called as *sūnya pramātā*. These five *kañcukas* cover the true nature of the Self. Therefore forgetting the *svatantrya* nature, the vision becomes limited,what is essentially *pūrṇa* starts to appear as *apūrṇa.* These five *kañcukas- Kalā, Vidyā, Rāga, Kāla and Niyati* respectively limit the Consciousness in aspects of efficiency, knowledge, desire, time and causality and space. From this point, due to concealing *aham,* only the *idam* aspect remains. But since just objectivity cannot exist, therefore the *idam* splits to create an objective subject *'idam-aham'*, which we know as the jiva or *puruṣa* This is the *vidyākalā* consisting of the 28 *bhuvanas*. Beyond this comes the *pratiṣthakalā* which consists of 56 *bhuvanas* extending till the *tattva* of *apah* (fluid/ water). The first *tattva* of this is *prakṛti,* which is the *idam idam.* Here the *prakṛtyānda* appears, and extends till the subtle senses. The experiential object first manifests as *idam idam,* which takes the form of *prakṛti,* which is *triguṇātmikā,* that is consisting of the three *guṇas* (strands of rope), *sattva rajas and tamas.* It is by the power of these three strands that the *prakṛti* binds the *puruṣa* into experiencing the world. This makes the *puruṣa* glance upon *prakṛti* only to see that as *vikṛti.* In the state of deep sleep, or when one falls unconscious, there is a state of dissolution of awareness, which is a bit oblivious than the void awareness in *sūnyapramātā.* This state is pralayakala pramātā. It forms its own screen, to experience the object. In that screen the three psychic apparatus of *antaḥkarana,* appears as follows,

(1) *Buddhiḥ:* The ascertaining intellect, which is of two kinds:
   (a) External: the one that identifies objects as jar, etc.
   (b) Internal: which processes the memory impressions.

(2) *Ahamkāra:* The *buddhiḥ* identifies the subject of experience, and forms the limited ego. This gives us the cognition of 'I am so and so'.

(3) *Manas:* This is a product which rises out of *ahamkāra,* which helps in building up concepts, it is usually termed as decisive.

They create the embodied cognitive agent, the *sakala pramātā.* Hence sequentially the five *karmendriyas*, and the five *jñānendriyas* appear,from which the five subtle elements comprising of the senses come. This forms the subtle body, *puryasṭaka*. This subtle body moves from one physical body to another. After this the gross level of creation known as *prithīvyānda* comes, which consists of the *pañcamahābhuta*s- ākāsa, tejas, vāyu, apah and prithīvi. The process of revelation comes to halt at prithivi, which is called the *nivrittikalā.* Here there are 16 *bhuvanas*, and at the lowest level resides *Kālagnirudra. Prithīvi tattva* deals with our universe, the physical realm.

This entire process describes how the *anuttara* reveals in each level of being. Here the Supreme never loses the nature, but can manifest as both in the immanent world as the tattva, and the transcendent absolute *Caitanya,* this very aspect of immutability makes consciousness absolutely free and non-dual.

"Bhūyaḥ syāt pratimīlanam": Recognition of Oneness

The prior section dealt with understanding the Trika's approach towards the non-duality manifesting as the world. This section deals with the individual realising this truth. The path of *Vāma*[28] is the path reverse of *sṛṣṭi*. These are known as *adhvans* (path). The word has a dual meaning, in one sense it means the path that one must discard, and in the other it means the one the sādhāka should take. The path to discard is the way towards objectivity, and the path to be taken is introspective one, that looks inwards. This is where the role of the master comes. The Siva is said to constantly carry out the five acts, even when manifesting as the limited being. These are- *tirodhāna* (concealing the real nature)*, sṛṣṭi, sthiti, laya* and *anugraha* (revealing the real nature). However, due to the presence of *mala*s we are unable to experience these acts, and grasp the real nature. These *malas* or ignorance reside in our *buddhi* (intellect) and *pauruṣa.* Though with intellectual analysis one may overcome the ignorance residing in our intellect it is with śaktipāta, or grace, a sudden urge of *samavesa* rises.[29]

---

28 See note 10. There are four primary powers: (i) *Ambikā,*identical with the Great Consciousness, the whole. (ii) *Vāmā*, the power which flows to create, the act is compared with vomiting the world into existence. (iii) *Raudrī,* the fearsome one which makes the individual directed towards objectivity. (iv) *Jyeṣṭhā*, which pulls and throws the mind towards Higher awareness. The idea is that the later two are powers which are existing as offspring of *Vāmā*, so since She is the stream at play, the reverse stream shall show *Ambikā.*

29 See *Tantrāloka* 1.36-44, section dealing with the nature of knowledge and *dīkṣā.*

This awakening is also known as *dīkṣā.* It is through *dīkṣā* that the *pauruṣājñāna* is removed. The act of śaktipāta is constantly happening, however the intensity differs. The intensity has been categorised as, *tibra, madhya, manda.* Those who experience *tibra* śaktipāta, they have direct experience without human intervention. The *madhya* category has an urge, and requires human *Guru*,whereas the *nimna* category ranges from those who seek only to escape the worldly pain, till the level of those absorbed in materialist slumber.

Since most of the people are absorbed in the world of objective duality, this vision of identity does not come so easily. This requires practice of withdrawing from the object through phenomenological reflection. With the yogic practice, it starts to get more subtle. Subtler the experience, more does this objective world dilute and the consciousness shines forth. Each state of being, which resides in a *tattva* or *kalā*, has its own way of perceiving the reality. With evolution of the consciousness it gets closer and closer to the state of *annutara.*

The idea is to look within, since the objective vision has been a central factor of bondage. This process of looking back at the source, and experiencing the non-duality has been taught in the system as upāyas. The act itself is called *pratyabhijñā.* Since we are trying to remember our true nature, the act is like looking into a mirror and trying to see self. The problem is that the mirror has dirt in it, causing hindrance to vision. The way to clean the mirror of awareness is given in the texts called *upāyas.*

There are those who being devoid of any *upāya* is directly able to experience the reality. This is called *Anopāya*. Ānadamoyee Mā is one such personality who automatically manifested such characters. However, for others three upāyas have been stated. First is the Śambhavopā*ya,* it is where the yogi simply shifts the focus and have the experience. Then comes *Saktop*ā*ya,* where through one pointed focus, or through the use of intellect one cuts through the veil of duality. And for those who are in a scattered mental state, the practice of Ānavopā*ya* is discussed. This comes from the word *anu,* which means small. Here several small factors are used together to bring forth gradually the experience. Each of the upāyas leading to its own *samavesas*, exclusive in nature, is used simultaneously by the yogin to constantly maintain the state of *Bhairava Consciousness.* The way has been summed up in *Vijñāna Bhairava*[30] as,

> *Mānasaṃ cetnāśaktirātmā ceti catuṣṭyaṃ/*
> *Yadā priye parikṣīraṇaṃ tadā tadbhairavaṃ vapuḥ//*

With constant practice of maintenance of awareness the yogi becomes capable of experiencing the non-duality. As the individual starts to remember the true nature, so does the entities which at each layer binding the individual, dissolves into the greater Bhairava. It is like becoming the CEO of a company, through gradual promotion from a clerical stuff, as one gets to higher posts the number of people above becomes lesser, and one obtains more and more power and influence to exercise. Only in this case, the individual has an expansion of awareness, and the śaktis become absorbed in that awareness to be a part of it. The object which appeared outside due to bodily identification, now floats in an unified holistic awareness. Thus it is said in the *Spanda Kārikā* regarding such an individual,

> *Iti vā yasya saṃvitti krītvenākhilaṃ jagat/*
> *Sa paśyansatataṃ yukto jīvanmukto n saṃśayaḥ//*[31]

Conclusion : The way Non-Duality

> *Īśā vāsyamidaṃ sarvaṃ yat kiṅca jagatyāṃ jāgat/*
> *Tena tyaktena bhunjñithā mā gṛdhaḥ kasya svidhanaṃ //*[32]

---

30 Trans: When the *manas, buddhi, prāṇāśakti* and the limited ego dissolves then, Beloved (Goddess) the state of Bhairava appears. (*Vijñāna Bhairava 138*).

31 Trans: For such an individual, who is united with the divine. S/he views the entire world as the of the Self identical with Śiva, and becomes liberated while alive. (*Spanda Kārikā, 2.5*)

32 That *Īśa* resides here, everywhere, covering the entirety of existence and beyond. One who realises that verily rejoices in renunciation, as for whose sake is this wealth. (*Īśa Upaniṣad,1*)

Now, after all this discussion the question comes up—How does this idea of non-dualism help? We are all familiar with the Īśā *Upaniṣad*. It is said that one who has realised this non-duality, s/he does not hate the other[33]. The first mantra of the *Upaniṣad* if read in the line of *Trika* would be clearly understood as speaking of that *Caitanya* which is omnipresent in the entirety of our experience, that is the immanent, and also beyond, the transcendent. It is those who have become absorbed in that realisation, can truly act out the statement, *tena tyāktena bhuñjitā.* That is the person can, through sacrifice enjoy the world. How is this seemingly contradictory act possible? Here the individual has transcended so much beyond the restricted identity, that s/he identifies the object of experience as it is in the Consciousness. The very act of experience becomes an aesthetic act of *rasanā*. Where the emotions like *rasas* in a *sahṛdaya* spectator arise and again, then submerge in that great stream of Consiousness, which is that eternal *Spanda*[34] principle. And to explain such an ecstasy *Kṣemrāja* uses the statement[35], '*yattatvaṃ yasya viśvaṃ sphuritamayamiyadyanmayaṃ viśvametat",* which we can read in reference to the first half of the mantra; this immediately follows "*svācchandyānandavṛndochaladamṛtamayānuttaraspandatattvaṃ"* to explain the drunken state of the *yogin* absorbed in the *annuttaraspandatattva,* which is overflowing in his/her awareness. Being *pūrṇa* the experience of other is not reallyseparate from the subjective being. The other is engulfed within the self, and only the *pūrṇāhamta* remains. That yoginis said to be ever awake, *viraḥ*[36] Forsuchan awakened soulitissaid,

> *Prakāśamāneparamāthabhānau naśyatyavidyātimire-samaste/*
> *Tadābudhā nirmaladṛṣṭ'pikiṃcannapaśyatibhavaprapañcaṃ//*[37]

---

33 Ibid, 6 "…tato na vijugupsate"

34 Synonymous with Supreme reality, lit. Divine Pulsation.

35 See invocation of Śivasūtravimarśinī.

36 See vimarśinī.commentary on Śivasūtra 1.11 triteyabhoktāviresaḥ.

37 Tr: The shine of the Sun of supreme knowledge banishes all the darkenss of ignorance, and then when the awakened soul sees with their pure eyes, they see not the differentiated multiplicity(but the Self shines forth), *Kṣemrāja's* invocation in *Stavacintamaṇi* of *Bhāṭṭānārāyaṇa.*

This realisation of non-duality may be a key to a more sustainable way of approaching the world.When the person sees the other not as something separate but as the same as what one experiences as the individual being, then the question ofharming or exploitingwillnot rise. Thebeautyin theworldwill beenjoyed asameans of creative expression of the same. The views of another, will be seen as a wayof expression of the same great consciousness. This supreme understanding of Trikapaves the way of diversity, that can manifest in oneness. This is just paving the way for an uniqueEco-theology, where we do not forsake the world, nor exploit the world, but try toreach to a deeper holistic identification and develop a sustainable vision towards the other.

Bibliography

1. Bhattacharya,Sukhamāyā.*AbhinavaguptapraṇītaTantrāloka.* Kolkata:TheAsiaticSociety,2015.

2. Dasgupta,Surendranath.*A History of Indian Philosophy, Vol.1-5.* Delhi:MLDB, 1975.

3. Dyczkowski, Mark S.G. *The Aphorisms of Śiva-Śivasūtrawiththe Bhāskara's commentary, the Vārtika,* NewYork: SUNY Press,1992.

4. Dyczkowski, Mark S.G.. *The Stanzason Vibration.*New York: SUNY Press, 1992.

5. Gutroo, Neelkantha. *ŚrīŚrīParātrīśikā.* Delhi: Motilal Banarasidass, 1985.

6. Pandey, K.C. *Bhāskarī: Vol.I-III.* Lucknow: Superintendent, Printing and stationary, 1954.

7. "Marjanovic, Boris. *Stavacintamaṇi of Bhaṭṭa Nārāyāṇa with the Commentary of Kṣemrāja,* Varanasi: Indica, 2011.

8. Pandey,K.C.*Abhinavagupta: an Historical and Philosophical Study.* Benaras: Chowkhamba Sanskrit Series Office, 1935.

9. Rastogi, Navjivan. *Abhinavguptakā Tantrāgamīya Darśan:Itihāsa-Saṁskṛtti-SaundaryaaurTattva-cintan.* Sagar: University Publications,2012.

10. Rastogi, Navjivan. *Introduction to the Tantrāloka:A studyin Structure.* Delhi:Motilal Banarasidass, 1987.

11. Rastogi, Navjivan. *Kāśmīr* Śivādvayavādakīmūlavadhāraṇae. Delhi: Munshiram Manoharlal Pub. Pvt. Ltd., 2002.

12. Laxman Joo, Swami. *Kashmir Saivism: Secret Supreme.* Srinagar: Ishwar Ashramtrust,1988.

13. Laxman Joo, Swami. Śiva *Sūtrasthe supreme awakening.* NewDelhi: Munshiram Manoharlal Publications, 2007.

14. Mahadevan,T.M.P. *Invitation to Indian Philosophy.* New Delhi: Arnold-Heinemann Publishers,1974

15. Mahadevan, T.M.P.*The Philosophy of Advaita.* Chennai: Ganesh & Co., 1957

16. Sen Sharma, Debabrata. *Aspects of Tantra Yoga.* Varanasi: Indica Books, 2007.

17. Sen Sharma, Debabrata. *The philosophy of sādhanā: with special reference to the Trika Philosophy of Kashmir.* NewYork: SUNY Press, 1990.

18. Sen Sharma, Debabrata. *Kāśmir* Śaivadarshan. Kolkata: RMIC, 2016.

19. Sen Sharma, Debabrata. *Ṣaṭtriṁśsattattva Sandoha.* Kurukhsetra: B.N. Chakravarty University Press, 1977.

20. Singh, Jaideva. *Parātrīśikā Vivaraṇa: The secret of Tantric My sticism.* Delhi: Motilal Banrasidass, 1998.

21. Singh, Jaideva. *Pratyabhijñāhṛdayamthesecret of Self-Recognition.* New Delhi: Motilal Banarasidass Publishers Pvt. Ltd., 1979.

22. Singh, Jaideva. Śiva *Sūtrastheyoga of supreme identity.*New Delhi: Motilal Banarasidass Publishers Pvt. Ltd., 1979.

23. Singh, Jaideva. *Spanda Kārikāsthedivine creative pulsation.* New Delhi: Motilal Banarasidass Publishers Pvt. Ltd., 1979.

24. Singh, Jaideva. *Vijñānabhairavaor Divine Consciousness.* New Delhi: Motilal Banarasidass Publishers Pvt. Ltd., 1979.

25. Swami, Gambirananda.*Upaniṣada Granthābalī.* Kolkata: Udbodhan Karyalaya, 1962.

26. Torella, Raffaele. *The* Īśvarapratyabhijñākārikā *of Utpaladeva with the author's Vṛtti: Critical edition and annotated translation.* Rome: Serie Orientale Roma, 1994.

Chapter 4

ECOTHEOLOGY AND FOLK RELIGION: DELTAS OF SUNDARBAN

Dr. Champak Bhattacharyya
Dr. Namrata Kothari

Nature refers to the world around us, as well as to our deepest sense of self. Yet, how nature is defined and understood today popularly is rooted in mechanistic and materialistic assumptions about reality. Hinduism as a religion is considered a complicated one in the sense that it is an indigenous as well as global religion.

The interaction and interdependence between the natural environment which will include water, soil and forest on the one hand and religion which includes the entire web of life of human beings, that is, social, political, economic, and cultural milieu is commonly known as eco-theology. It is this aspect of ecotheology that suddenly becomes alive in a fragile, dynamic and ecological setting of the region of Sundarban, in the time of great ecological crisis.

Even if we look back in the annals of history we will find that the seals of IndusValley Civilization, the vedic texts, the ancient texts, epics, agamas, the slokas of Upanishad,ThePuranas and Smriti all demonstrated a concern for nature and its promotion, protection and preservation. This is very much reflected in the rituals, worship of Gods and Goddesses and rites performed by the tribal people which show great reverence for nature and use its resources for survival not out of greed which is a punishable offense for them.

Therefore, this chapter will focus on the environment and livelihood of the forest dwellers with special reference to their rites and rituals in the Sundarban delta of West Bengal. This will bring forth the unique bond between nature, human and divinity and their interdependence. Before discussing the livelihood and rites and rituals of forest dwellers of the deltas of Sundarban it is important to know the geographical location of this region which helps us to understand the occupation and belief of the people residing in that region.

The word 'Sundarban' is a Bengali name meaning 'beautiful forest'. It may have derived from God Sundri or Sundari, the local name of the mangrove species Heritiera. Alternatively, it has been proposed that the name is a corruption of Samudraban, Shomudro Bon ("sea forest") or Chandra Bandhe, the name of a tribe.

Sundarban is situated in the Brahmaputra Delta falling in India and Bangladesh. The larger part is situated in Bangladesh(60%) and the smaller portion lies in India(40%). It forms the western part of the largest delta in the world, and confluence of three rivers Ganges, Brahmaputra and Meghna in the Bay of Bengal.It is the largest mangrove forest and also a UNESCO World Heritage site.

The Sundarban is intersected by a network of tidal waterways, mudflats and small Islands of salt-tolerant mangrove forest. The interconnected network of waterways makes almost every corner of the forest accessible by boat. It is a home of diverse species of animals and plants. It is an abode of salty water estuarine crocodiles, Royal Bengal Tiger, deer, gangeticdolphins,red crabs, prawns, snakes etc. The fertile soils of the delta have been subject to intensive use for centuries, and the ecoregion has been mostly converted to intensive agriculture, with few entries of forest remaining. The remaining forests, taken together with the Sundarbans mangroves are an important habitat for the endangered tiger.

The mangrove dominated Ganga Delta—the Sundarban is a complex ecosystem comprising one of the three largest single tracks of mangrove forest of the world covering 20,400 square kilometers. Mangrove forests are not home to a great variety of plants. They have a canopy and undergrowth is mostly seedlings of the mangrove trees. It is salt tolerant and is adapted to life in harsh coastal conditions. They contain a complex salt filtration system and complex root system to cope up with salt water immersion and wave action. They are adapted to the low oxygen conditions of water logged mud. Mangrove swamps protect coastal areas from erosion, storm surge and tsunamis. Its root system is efficient at dissipating wave energy and slows down tidal water. It is also an important source of blue carbon and it provides measurable economic protection to coastal communities from tropical storm impacted communities globally. It also acts as an ultrafiltration mechanism to exclude sodium salt from the rest of the plant. It holds soil from erosion, its wood is used for furniture making. Its wood is resistant to rot and insects, making it extremely valuable. Many coastal and Indigenous communities rely on this wood for construction material as well as for fuel. Thus it supports a wealth of life from flora to fauna to people.

Its leaves are also used as animal fodder. The researchers have found that the world's largest mangrove system; which has been degraded because of unbridled human activities in the past, is showing signs of stabilization and it is gradually becoming resilient to climate change. Thus the mangrove forest acts as a buffer against frequently occurring cyclones, helping to protect local settlement including the two most popular sites of the world Kolkata and Dhaka, against their effects. Mangroves are diverse and highly productive ecological communities which provide important ecosystem functions. Located at the land-sea interface, they protect coastal areas against natural hazards such as cyclones and tsunamis, they retain terrestrial sediment and recycle nutrients, thus supporting clear offshore water, which is in turn favors the photosynthetic activity of phytoplankton as well as growth and robustness of coral reefs, seagrass beds and reef fish communities; this serves as an important habitat, nursery and refuge, providing food for countless organisms including humans. These ecosystems are also vital carbon sinks, either storing carbon temporarily with organic peat soils,or dissolving carbon in ocean sediments at greater depth, offsetting climate active greenhouse gasses for longer periods. Because of the collective ecosystem services, mangroves are of great economic value. However, owing to both anthropogenic and climate factors, mangroves the world over are threatened, and, with current global annual loss rates of 1%-2%, no such forest may be left by the end of the 21st century, if the current trend continues.

In this context, the role of folk religion and beliefs and rituals followed by the people of Sundarbans played a very important role to strike a balance in the environment for its promotion, preservation and protection by following the precepts of religion.

The Sundarban stands supreme in the habitat map of the world because very few areas are there in the world with such diversity in flora and fauna that live in a complex environment. The forest dwellers on the one hand have to fight with the environment for their very survival and at the same time they are dependent on the environment for their livelihood. They considered the forest as sacred because forest is their only source of income, as a result of people living in this region developed a peculiar habit and have tremendous faith in certain myths, legends etc.

The inhabitants of the Sundarban region are in general forest workers. They are dependent on forest and water for their livelihood. As they are dependent on the environment, there is a strong bond of unity, collectivity among the people. As a result communal harmony is preserved in the Sundarban. Basically the forest workers of the Sundarban are highly religious minded. They have tremendous faith in their famous forest deity goddess Banabibi. They also worship other folk deities like Barakhan Gazi, DahshinRai, Manasa, Sitala and many other Gods and Goddesses. The forest workers of the Sundarban can be divided into following categories:

(i) honey collectors, (ii) fisherman, (iii) prawn seed collectors, (iv) crab- seed collectors.

Collecting is the most dangerous occupation among them. Before entering the forest they always offer prayers to the goddess Bonbibi. They believe that they work under the protection of Banabibi. They consider Royal Bengal tigers as their "brothers' 'and so to harm or disturb their "brothers" will extremely be detrimental to the relationship between humans and the forest. Another occupation is prawn seed collection, this is also a very risky occupation and female centric in nature. Women who pull prawn seed nets along the river banks are at huge risks of attack by crocodiles, sharks even tigers as well. The forest workers of the Sundarban subscribe to a characteristic folk religion, syneretic culture, keeping track with the mainstream of religion practice in India. The worship of the forest workers of the Sundarban is different from Pie gazis. The religious worship of these forest workers are not completely based on The Puranas or the holy scriptures. Through RaiMangalaKavya BanabibiJahurnama and similar oral and written literary traditions there have been developed in Sundarban through Hindu and Muslim cultural contact and fusion a wonderful mingled folk cultural tradition that affords a rare example of unity amidst diversity.

In the largest continuous mangrove forest of the world, humans reside amidst the thriving population of crocodiles, snakes, sharks and man-eating Royal Bengal Tigers. Many of them depend on the forest for their livelihood as fisherman, track collector and gatherer of the thick and strong honey that grows in the comb on the hetal,gorgon, and sundari mangrove trees.

In one of the most ecological fragile regions of the world, strict code is laced to the belief in Bonbibi. The islanders believe that one must enter the kingdom without carrying any weapons. They often explain that Bonabibi had left them the injunctions that they were to enter the forest only with pure heart, pure mind and empty hands. The islanders claim that they have to identify completely with Dukhe, whose deep faith in Bonbibi saved him.

In a landscape such as this, Bonbibi becomes a focal point for faith and absolute devotion. The residents of Sundarban, who depend on the forest for their daily survival by fetching wood, honey, wax, fish, and crabs are the primary worshippers of Bonbibi. The word 'ban' in Bengali means 'forest', while 'bibi' originates from the Persian word denoting lady or wife; the word 'Bonbibi' thus literally means the 'lady of the forest'. Bonbibi is an Islamic deity, almost an oxymoron according to our present normative understanding, and is believed to have traveled on Allah's orders from Medina to Sundarban to protect the distressed residents as well as the animals of the forest. Bonbibi is one of the syncretist cults of Bengal, as both Hindus and Muslims of the region pray to this deity.

The lore of Bonbibi, like any other oral literature, has changed forms and contours, still exists in a flexible state in the present society and appears to transform further. The myth of Bonbibi-r Palagaan is built on an intricate system of myths which trace their origin to important socio-political changes in the history of Bengal—the rise of Islam around the 13th century followed by the liberal spirit of Sufism in rural lower Bengal in the 15th century and thereafter developing Hindu-Muslim syncretism in the medieval period.

The jungle (forest) with its looming presence is an unavoidable part in the lives of the people of the region. Sundarban is comparable to the sea as depicted in J.M. Synge's play, Riders to the Sea. It is like a maze that the residents cannot resist, and thus they constantly get caught in it. As the islanders have to depend on the forest for their survival—they often encounter danger and deaths in various forms. Losing lives become a regular phenomenon. The dynamic of perpetual war at the same time dependence translates into worship of nature and the intertwining of fear and faith makes them praying some super power of nature, embodied in the form of the cult goddess Bonbibi, considering as the guardian of the forest. An integral part of the puja, the performance, can be seen as a way to mitigate the wrath of natural forces. Bonbibi-r Palagaan thus exhibits the struggle for survival.

Certain sacred rituals are also practised during the performance, such as the body of the actors are to be kept clean, actors are barred from eating non-vegetarian food, women actors do not take part while menstruating etc. Such rituals are faithfully followed so as to maintain the sanctity of worship.

Sanjit is a regular member of the audience of Bon Bibir *Pala Gaan*, whose story can be found in a 19th-century text called Bon Bibi Johuranama (The Chronicles of Bon Bibi's Glory). "It is difficult to confirm whether the performative text of the *palagaan* precedes the printed journals or vice versa," writes Mousumi Mandal, Assistant Professor, Presidency University, in Bonbibi-r Pala Gaan: Tradition, History and Performance, on Sahapedia. The language of the Johuranama is *Musalmani Bangla*, written in the Bengali script, but with the book opening to the right, in the Arabic style. "Her worshippers do not think of her in terms of 'Muslim' or 'Hindu' but as a 'forest super-power' who extends her protection over individuals of all communities equally," writes Jalais. "When people read Bon Bibijohuranama, they punctuate the verses with a chorus of 'Allah Allah Bol (Say the name of Allah)'," adds Mehebub Sahana, a research associate in the School of Environment, Education and Development, University of Manchester, the UK.

Ma Bonbibi originally emerged as a "super power" to protect the fishing community, honey-gatherers, wood-cutters and others,entered the jungle from tiger attacks. A 19th century booklet, Bonbibi Johuranama, tells her story in Bengali, probably authored by a Muslim – written from left to right, but back to front to emulate the Arabic script.

The composition of Bonbibi-r *Palagaan* goes beyond the narrative mentioned in Johuranama and draws its material from local myths. The narrative of the story can be partitioned into three sections:

- Janmakhanda or Bonbibi's birth in the tidal land
- Narayani-r Jang or battle with Narayani
- DukheyJatra or the travails of Dukhey

Following are the outlines of these three sections of the plot.

Janmakhanda

Fakir Ibrahim and his wife Phulbibi used to live in Medina. They were childless and decided to pray to Rasul for a son. Rasul informed them that no child would be born to Phulbibi, but if Ibrahim were to be married again, he would have twin children. Phulbibi consented to Ibrahim's second marriage, on condition that he would grant her a karaar (promise), which she could demand as and when necessary. Without suspecting her wicked intentions, Ibrahim readily agreed to it and married Gulal, the daughter of Fakir Shah Jalil of Mecca.

Meanwhile, Allah commanded Bonbibi and Shah Jangali, who had then been residing in *beheste* (heaven), to take birth on earth from the womb of Gulal to accomplish a divine mission. They were sent to Atharo Bhati-r desh (land of 18 low tides, i.e., the Sundarban) to protect the land from the 'Hindu' deity, the half-Bramhin sage, half-tiger Dakshin Rai. When Gulal's nine months of pregnancy was over, Phulbibi reminded Ibrahim of his promise and demanded that Gulal be exiled to the forest. Ibrahim, trapped by his own vow, pledged to deceive Gulal though with a disconsolate heart. Ibrahim led Gulal into the forest and left her there when she fell asleep. When she woke up, Gulal looked for her husband, but could not find him. She cried her heart out only to realize that her husband had left her in the desolate and dangerous forest all alone. Eventually, Gulal gave birth to twin children—Bonbibi and Shah Jangali—in the forest; and these children were none other than the messengers of Allah.

Without any access to food in the forest, Gulal became tired and hungry. She left her daughter and took her son with her. Allah sent a deer who breast-fed little Bonbibi and took care of her. Shah Jangali, on the other hand, was growing up under his mother's care and protection. After seven years, Ibrahim, overcome by guilt, returned to the forest in search of Gulal. Ibrahim found Gulal and Shah Jangali in the forest and offered to take them back home. Immediately, Bonbibi reminded Shah Jangali of their divine purpose and why they were born in the forest. Shah Jangali and his sister set out together to seek their final orders from the rasul in Medina. After receiving khilafat (heirship) from the rasul they headed back to Hindustan. After crossing the Ganga, they reached the east of India and finally arrived at Baadaban.

Narayani-r Jang

Bonbibi and Shah Jangali commenced their pursuit with *azan* in Baadaban. *Azan* became a call of warning to the earlier residents of the forest. The land was the realm of Dakshin Rai and his mother Narayani. They were the Hindu god and goddess ruling over the region. Narayani first fought against Bonbibi, claiming that only a woman should fight with a woman. In the fight, Narayani was vanquished and accepted Bonbibi's supremacy by offering her entire ascendancy to Bonbibi. But Bonbibi declared that she had no intention of disheartening her. She called Narayani her '*soi*' (friend) and proposed to form a union to rule the land together.

DukheyJatra

In another locale in Barijhati village, there lived a poor shepherd called Dukhey with his widow mother Bibijaan. They eked out their livelihood by working in other households. Dhana, a honey collector and a trader, approached Dukhey and offered him work. He tempted Dukhey by offering to teach him the trade and also promised to get him married. Owing to their extreme poverty, Dukhey readily agreed to work for him. Dukhey's mother was unhappy about this decision for she thought that since the forest was dangerous place Dukhey would unnecessarily be at risk. But seeing that Dukhey was so steadfast in his decision to go to the forest and collect honey, she just informed him about the power of Bonbibi and instructed him to seek her help if he ever were in danger in the forest.

Dukhey and Dhana, along with other sailors, set sail towards the forest. After crossing Barunhati, Santoshpur, Kanaikathi, and

Herobhanga, and the rivers Raimangal and Matla, they finally reached the jungle (forest). Astonishingly enough, they could not find a single drop of honey in the forest since the bee hives were completely empty. The Hindu god, DakshinRai, played the trick since they had entered the forest without offering worship. DakshinRai told Dhana that he would find honey in the forest only if he would sacrifice Dukhey to him. If Dhana chose to disobey him, all the sailors and he himself would be killed by Dakshin Rai's adherents, i.e., the tigers in the forest and the crocodiles in water. Dhana was instructed to go to Kendokhali where they would get ample amount of honey to fill seven boats. In return, Dhana had to leave Dukhey as revenue. Dhana was thus left with no choice.

Dukhey heard the entire conversation between Rai and Dhana. Frightened, Dukhey remembered what his mother had told him. He started praying to Bonbibi, and she appeared immediately before him. After listening to Dukhey, Bonbibi consoled him saying that she would be able to protect him only after he is abandoned in Kendokhali by Dhana. When they reached Kendokhali, all were amazed to see the amount of honey that was available there. Finally, as Rai had instructed him, Dhana convinced the other sailors and left Dukhey on the shore. Dukhey was sent to the forest to fetch wood for fuel and was finally duped. Seeing the boats sail away from the shore, Dukhey kept crying and requested them in vain not to leave him.

Dakshin Rai lurked in the forest in disguise of a tiger. Bonbibi appeared in the forest to rescue Dukhey. Shah Jangali and Dakshin Rai engaged in battle, and finally, Rai was defeated by Jangali. DakshinRai fled and reached Barha Khan Gaji's abode. Shah Jangali chased him, and on reaching Gaji's home, reprimanded him: being a Muslim fakir, how could he give refuge to a beast like DakshinRai? The three of them finally decided to go to Bonbibi for final judgment. Gaji explained to Bonbibi that she should forgive DakshinRai since he was like her son. Surprised, Bonbibi asked him, 'KemoneDakshinaRai beta mor hoy?' ('How can DakshinRai be my son?'). Gaji cleverly illustrated that Bonbibi had once called

Narayani her '*soi*' (friend) so, Bonbibi should treat Narayani's son as her own. Unable to refute the argument, Bonbibi accepted DakshinRai as her son and pardoned him. DakshinRai promised to give Dukhey honey and wax and Barha Khan Gaji assured him of seven vessels of wealth. Bonbibi rescued Dukhey and sent him back to his village. Meanwhile, Bibijaan, the mother of Dukhey, became blind and grief-stricken at the loss of her son. Bonbibi cured Bibijaan and brought back her son. Bibijaan and Dukhey were mesmerized by the miracles of Bonbibi. They pledged to go around begging in the village to collect money in the name of Bonbibi and distributed kheer-khairaat (rice pudding) amongst the people and told everyone about the miracles of Bonbibi.

With the wealth that Barha Khan Gaji had promised, Dukhey became prosperous and powerful. Dukhey's status rose and he became a Chaudhury[15] in the village, at the mercy of Bonbibi. Dukhey wanted to punish Dhana for betraying him, but Bonbibi pointed out to him that it was because of Dhana that Dukhey could meet Bonbibi and sought her refuge. So he should pardon Dhana and marry his daughter, Champa. Abiding by Bonbibi's command, Dukhey married Champa. The tale ends with their marriage ceremony.

No forest worker enters the jungle without being accompanied by a bauli or tiger-charmer, or having received instructions from them. They claim to have powers given by Bonbibi to protect others from tigers. The charms that the bauli use are in Arabic, reflecting their derivation from Sufi saints who contributed to the reclamation of land from the mangrove forest, the control of tigers and the spread of Islam in this area in the 16th century. (Although baulis can be Hindus too, those I met were all Muslims.)

Many find Islam as a magical technique to control evil spirits and demons in Sundarban. The baulis generally are humble and peaceful. They have a profound emotional impact on the forest workers. Often, however, the tiger-charmers are mocked by forest officials, who insist that they feed upon the innocence of the locals and have none of the powers they claim to possess.

Given the fear of tigers among most of us outside Sundarban, it is interactions with outsiders that the people living in these jungle areas regard as violent. To them, the forest serves to unite and equalize people..This is why the majority of the Bonbibi shrines, especially those in the island blocks, have no doors, and are located along common areas such as pathways and river banks. They are accessible to all. People also create temporary shacks, made of branches and twigs, and sometimes decorated with flowers, within the forest, where they invoke her blessings before entering the realm of the tiger.

It is the belief of the local people that everything that happens there is according to Bonbibi's will, and nothing can be done behind her. There is a story of a group of woodcutters died out of snake bites about 10 or 12 years ago. Locals believed that they just contaminated the forest and not respected the ethos of the region. Therefore Bonbibi punished them.

Bonbibi's egalitarianism is symbolized and enforced by the repeated re-enacting of her stories by people from multiple *jatis* (various caste, race, or religion.)

Another common thread that binds forest dwellers is the belief that escalating greed has prompted many to enter the jungle and ruin its tranquility. Collectors of prawn seed, a new breed of forest worker, are often blamed when things go wrong. All forest workers agree, however, that the increasing strife among themselves as well as the regular intrusion of noisy tourists cause the tigers feeling insecure and disturbed. As a result, tiger attacks are on the rise. The tales of Bonbibi passed on from generation to generation are embedded in this land's folklore. Hindu and Muslim mythologies have blended here to ward off the shared perils of life. Religious differences melded into a way of life can only be experienced in Sundarban.

Thatched shrines bearing the goddess mounted on Raja Dakshinrai, accompanied by her brother Shah Jangali, are common sights along the riverbed. It is from these shrines that chants of "Ma Bonbibi Allah, Allah" effortlessly mingle with those of "Baba DakshinraiHariHari" as the honey collectors and fishermen pay obeisance before venturing into tiger territory.

The islanders of the Sundarban believe that the forests are meant only for those who are poor and who have no intention of taking more than what they need to survive. Life here is for only 'pure hearts' and 'empty hands'. The 'agreement' between humans and other inhabitants permits both to depend on the forest, and yet to respect the requirements of all. The 'purity of the heart' means that they should enter the forest without greed or violent disposition. The 'empty hands' mean they will enter the forest without firearms.

Bonbibi is a personification of the forest itself and the overriding faith among the villagers is the reaffirmation of their commitment to forest and tiger conservation. The Bonbibijatra (enactments of the folk tales of the valor of the goddess, performed by local artists) has become an art form synonymous with the Sundarban. These performances are melodramatic, yet the underlying message is clear: "If the forest exists, then the tiger lives and only then can we flourish."

The faith towards the goddess Bonbibi. unites the villagers of Sundarban against all dangers. Hindus as well as Muslims, all the people of Sundarban bow towards this goddess before they make entry into the jungles. When animals attack, they do not differentiate between Hindus and Muslims. That is why people of both the communities worship Bonbibi here. She is called the patron goddess of the Sundarban. She teaches them that when your need is fulfilled in the forest, then you return. Do not be tempted to possess too much.

The story of Bonbibi is mentioned in Amitav Ghosh's The Hungry Tide, and also referred to in his The Great Derangement: Climate Change and the Unthinkable. Even today, many members of Scheduled Tribes with the surname Singh are found in the Abads. Man is the greatest predator in the Sundarban. Often on the river banks, we find small makeshift huts or brick structures with a red cloth flying over it. These are Banbibir Than or Temple.

Banbibi or Bandevi is the guardian of the forest. According to the folklore, when the first human settlers could not cope with the Tiger God DakshinRai, and his army of wild animals and demons of the forest, they prayed to Bon Devi or Bon Durga or Bonbibi. Bonbibi defeated DakshinRai and established her supremacy over the forest and protected her followers. Bonbibi decked in red sari and crown, rides on a tiger and is revered by both Hindus and Muslims. No fisherman or Honey collector known as Mouli will go to the deep Jungle to catch fish or collect honey without offering prayer to Bonbibi. Bon bibi Puja is an annual function in the Sundarban. The Banabibi festival is celebrated once a year in January or February and RamRudrapur's fair is one of the oldest and biggest ones.

However, the worship ofBonbibi is receding now as modernity intrudes into the jungle. In Bakkhali, a small tourist resort at the border of Sundarban forest, the Bonbibi mandir is located on the beach. It is, however, sparsely visited now even as more orthodox Hindu festivals such as DurgaPujo are celebrated fully. Muslims do not worship idols like Hindus, but in Sunderban, one can see the rare sight of Muslims offering 'bhog', a predominantly Hindu custom, to Bonbibi. It is an equally beautiful and rare situation where the god's name is suffixed with 'bibi'—a revered, sacred name among Muslims—and is worshipped by Hindus of the region as well.

This devotional story of Bonbibi finds place in Banbibir Keramati (magical deeds ofBonbibi) also as in BanbibirJahuranama (glory to Bonbibi).Thus through the worship of Bonbibi it is clearly exemplified that the interdependence and need of man and environment can be achieved through religion for the preservation, protection and promotion of the environment. It is the only way through which we can ignite the minds of human beings the importance of the environment for our very survival on planet Earth .Religion truly helps us to achieve that purpose.

References

1. Das, Girindranath. 1998. BanglarPirSahityar Katha. Kolkata: Subarnarekha.
2. Das, Shasankasekhar. 2004. Banabibi. West Bengal: Loksanskriti O AdibasiSanskriti Kendra.
3. Eaton, Richard M. 1994. The Rise of Islam and the Bengal Frontier: 1204-1760. New Delhi: Oxford University Press.
4. Ghosh, Aditya, Susanne Schmidt, Thomas Fickert and Marcus Nüsser. 2015. ‹The Indian Sundarban Mangrove Forests: History, Utilization, Conservation Strategies and Local Perception'. In Diversity 7:149–69. Online at doi: 10.3390/d7020149. (viewed on December 3, 2016).
5. Haq, Muhammad Enamul. 1975. A History of Sufi-ism in Bengal. Dacca: Asiatic Society in Bangladesh.
6. Khater, Morhum Munsi Mohammad 1881. Bana Bibi Johura Nama. Kolkata: Gaochiya Library,Mechuabajar.
7. Mandal, Mousumi. 2011. 'Banabibi-r Pala Gaan of the Sundarbans: An Interpretative Analysis'. Unpublished M.Phil.Thesis.Centre of English Studies, Jawaharlal Nehru University.
8. Mandal, Sujit Kumar, ed. 2010. Banabibir Pala. Kolkata: Gangchil.
9. Mukhopadhyay, Amites. 2009. 'Cyclone Aila and the Sundarbans: An Enquiry into the Disaster and Politics of Aid and Relief'. In CRG Annual Winter Course on Forced Migration. Kolkata: Mahanirban Calcutta Research Group. Online at http://www.mcrg.ac.in/pp26.pdf (viewed on November 21, 2016).
10. Rahim, Abdul. 1986. BanabibiJohuraNama: KonyarPunthi. Kolkata: Osmania Library.
11. Grove H. Richard, Vinita Damodaran, Satpal Sangwan

(edited)—Environmental History of South and Southeast Asia, 'Nature and the Orient',Oxford University Press 2000; pg 3,4

12. Grove H. Richard- 'Green Imperialism, Colonial Expansion,Tropical Island Edens and the Origins of Environmentalism,1600-1860', pg 1; also see Glacken .C.J 'Traces on the RhodianShore:Nature and Culture in western thought from ancient times to the end of the 18th c', Berkeley, Calif. 1967 .
13. Guha Ramachandra—Environmentalism : A Global History, Longmans Publications 2000; pg 25.
14. Wikipedia 'Social Ecology', http://en.wikipedia.org/wiki/Social_Ecology
15. Clark John (art) 'A Social Ecology' (Anarchy Archives) http://library.nothingness.org/articles/anar/en/display/303
16. John Clark art 'A Social Ecology' (Anarchy Archives A History of the Social Ecology of Sundarbans: The Colonial Period Page 45
17. http://library.nothingness.org/articles/ anar/en/display/303 global environmentalism and its recent trends see 'Environmental History, Recent Dialogues'- (ed) by MahuaSarkar, Gyan publishers 2007)

Chapter 5

*Balhari Kudrat Wasiya**
SIKH THEOLOGY ROOTED IN ECO-THEOLOGY

Kulwant Singh

What differentiates Sikhism from some of the major oriental and Semitic religions is that it reposes its faith on the single impersonal cosmic power which permeates the entire cosmos in all its environmental and ecological segments. It is a kind of energy, a kind of kinetic impulse that energizes and enervates all the animate and inanimate objects. Unlike Hinduism which personifies natural phenomena of procreation, nurture, and annihilation and worships these phenomena as gods and deities, Sikhism worships and eulogizes the only one primal energy which expands, flourishes and contracts at its own will in an inscrutable manner. Instead of worshipping and invoking a hierarchy of subordinate gods and goddesses and seeking their blessings, Sikhism acknowledges the universal sovereignty and supremacy of a single most, unitary cosmic power with some of its broadly identifiable attributes such as its being the sole creator, whose writ runs large till and beyond eternity, with its dispassionate disposition towards its creation, with no fear and favor and inbuilt universal compassion and benevolence towards every created being. It is this declaration of

* Hail! The creator resides in the Creation.

unshakeable and firm faith in the existence and eternal presence of this unitary cosmic power with which the thirteen lettered preamble, visualized and written by Guru Nanak and added to the body of the text of the sacred Sikh scripture Sri Guru Granth Sahib in Gurmukhi script of Punjabi language deals. It encapsulates the fundamental theology of Sikhism which is deeply rooted and has its genesis in the inextricable integration of nature and its creator which, in a branch of modern scholarship engaged in the study of environmental and humanities ecology, is formally known as eco-theology. The preamble runs as follows:

ੴਸਤਿਨਾਮੁਕਰਤਾਪੁਰਖੁਨਿਰਭਉਨਿਰਵੈਰੁਅਕਾਲਮੂਰਤਿਅਜੂਨੀਸੈਭੰਗੁਰਪ੍ਰਸਾਦਿ॥

Ikoankaar Sathnaam Karathaa Purakh Nirabho Niravair Akaal Moorath Ajoonee Saibhan Gurprasaadh||.

> *He is the Sole Supreme Being; of eternal manifestation;*
> *Creator, Immanent Reality; Without Fear;*
> *Without Rancour; Timeless Form; Unincarnated;*
> *Self-Existent, Realized by grace of the holy Preceptor.*[1]

Guru Nanak's use of the mathematical numeral 1 before the open ended letter (ੳ) pronounced together as *Ek Onkar* reflects the unity of the creator and creation besides the sole sovereignty of the Divine creator. The remaining twelve epithets following this first dual numeral-letter ੴ in the preamble facilitate the reader to identify the true nature of the Divine Cosmic power. It lends primacy to the fundamental principle of Sikh theology which consists of the monotheistic identity of the Divine cosmic power and its absolute sovereign sway over all kinds of created species across earthly continents, nether and celestial regions. It also obliterates the existence of a host of multiple deities, gods and goddesses and the human need to placate them for securing personal favors. It projects an impersonal kind of cosmic power whose appeal is universal and attitude is indiscriminately compassionate and benevolent. It is immune and impervious to all attempts at personal appeasement and invocations to the detriment of others. No doubt, the daily congregational Sikh prayer in the

Sikh shrines (Gurdwaras) all across the globe concludes with an appeal for the welfare of all.

(*Sarbat Da Bhalla*). Further, the second and third word (*sat nam*) together denote the enduring nature of the cosmic power as compared to the temporariness of created objects and species. The Fourth and fifth epithets taken together (*Karta Purakh*) embody the creative power and exclusiveness of the sole cosmic creator. The next sixth and seventh epithets (*Nirbhau, Nirvair*) taken together are symbolic of the indiscriminate, dispassionate nature of the cosmic power towards its created species as it energizes and nurtures them without any fear and favor. The eighth and ninth signifiers (*Akal Moorat*) together signify the eternal existence of the cosmic power beyond dimensions of time, space and physical forms. The tenth and eleventh signifiers (*Ajooni Saibhang*) stand for its formless, self-existent and transcendental existence free from the cycle of birth and death. The last concluding combination of two words (*Gur Parsad*), signifies the benevolent nature of the Divine Cosmic power which corroborates its already existing quality of indiscriminate dispensation without any sense of fear or favor, rancor or malice towards anyone. It also implies the concept of grace of both the Divine power as well as of the spiritual mentor (Guru) who leads a religious devotee across the spiritual voyage. Thus, the preamble, in its totality, sums up the core of Sikh theology which derives its vision from Guru Nanak's realization and enlightenment about the universal, eternal existence of the single most monotheistic cosmic power and human need to abide by its cosmic laws. The entire gamut of Sikh theology, stems from its unshakeable faith in the sovereignty of the Divine cosmic power and man's need to understand the working of the Cosmic laws and his need to fine-tune the human impulses to synchronize with the cosmic laws. Guru Nanak terms the cosmic laws of nature as *Hukam* (Divine will expressed in the sense of a commandment) in the concluding line of the very first verse of *Japuji* and believes that human beings are mandated to abide by the Divine will if they are desirous of their own emancipation:

Through obedience to His Ordinance and Will,
Saith Nanak: This blessing too is pre-ordained.[2]

Sikh devotees are inspired by the Sacred Gurbani verses to streamline themselves and their egoistic impulses by repeated references to the spontaneous operation of cosmic law of Gravity and other forces which govern the movement of planets and other celestial bodies in space and their almost error-free compliance of these cosmic laws since eons of time. Besides *Hukam* (Divine Will), Sikh theology terms this speechless command as *Bhoy*/Awe of the Divine cosmic power which controls and governs this vast universe consisting of an infinite number of planets, satellites, stars, galaxies etc. In another representative verse from his collection of verses known as *Asa Di Var*, Guru Nanak, observing the location of the planets and other celestial bodies in the space and their precisely regulated movement as if these bodies were in awe of their regulatory force, lays down the first principle of Sikh theology which consists of abiding by the Divine Will termed as *Hukam* or *Bhoy* or *Bhau*. This verse runs as follows:

In fear of the Lord moves the air in a hundred gusts,
In fear of the Lord flow millions of streams.
In fear of the Lord does fire perform its labour,
In fear of the Lord is the earth placed under its burden.
In fear of the Lord do clouds roam about bearing burden of water on the head.
In fear of the Lord Dharamraja at His Portal dispenses justice,
In fear of the Lord Move sun and moon,
Roaming Millions of miles without end,
In fear of the Lord stand Sidhas, enlightened ones, gods and yogis,
In fear of the Lord are spread the skies;
In fear of the Lord stand the mighty heroes,
In fear of the Lord arrive and depart swarms of beings,
Over the head of all has been recorded the writ of fear,
Saith Nanak: The formless Eternal solely is from fear exempt.[3]

It catalogs the five elements water, air, fire, earth and sky as also celestial bodies like sun, moon and myriads of stars and galaxies along with all the mythological gods and deities which stay, move and behave in tandem at the dictates of the single most fearless controlling Divine Power. All these bodies have been strictly following the encrypted script since their creation. In another complementary verse in the same collection, Guru Nanak refers to all pervasive environment or nature called *Kudrat* created by the creator which has a bearing on the behavioral activities of all the elements constituting nature or environment or ecology. Its impact is visible in whatever we see,perceive, hear, eat, drink as much as in the primal elements of nature, over, above, and beneath the earth. What is unmistakably evident in these two verses is that the creator and the creation are integrated at the deepest level and it is the sovereign writ of the Divine Creator that determines the behavior of all its components from the biggest heavenly bodies to the smallest organisms. The Sikh Gurus, while composing their sacred Gurbani verses, have been mainly inspired by their observation of the cosmic laws of nature which govern this universe and emanates from the fountainhead of all pervasive cosmic Divine Power. It is this spontaneous, non-stop compliance of the Divine Will by the Cosmic bodies and the acknowledgement of the unquestioned authority of the sovereign cosmic power which becomes a source of inspiration for the Sikh Gurus while laying down the core values and principles of Sikh theology through their inspirational verses. Sikh theology consistently lays emphasis on the cultivation of human virtues of curbing of one's personal egoistic impulses, and abiding by the Divine Will, self-control, contentment and streamlining of One's physical mental and spiritual faculties, love and service of humanity irrespective of fellow human beings' caste, creed, color as also universal brotherhood of man and fatherhood of monotheistic Divine power. These are all derivational corollaries of the cosmic laws which constitute the Eco-theology.

Since Eco-theology is the study of the relationship between God, the ultimate Cosmic power and cosmos, Sikh Gurus' keen observation and study of this relationship led them to design and build the rudimentary infrastructure of Sikh theology and its major rituals and practices based on the pattern of eco theology. Before elaborating the conceptual spirit of Sikh values and their application in some of the major Sikh rituals and practices, we shall look into some other insights of Sikh Gurus into Nature, its creation and even its pre-creation state. As recorded in his masterpiece creation *Japuji*, Guru Nanak, in his deepest intuitive, mystical peep, provided a glimpse into the origin of the universe which at one end rejects the Hindu mythological view of earth resting on the horns of the proverbial bull and on the other looks forward to the modern 20th century scientific discovery of "Big Bang" theory of earth's creation acknowledged by modern scientists in 1950s which was originally put forth in 1931 by Georges Lemaitre.[4]

It theorized that the universe originated from a single primordial atom and its explosion resulted in the ever expanding universe and galaxies. Thus, what was discovered by the scientists in the 20th century about the creation of the universe through empirical experimentation and scientific tools was revealed by Guru Nanak five hundred years earlier through his meditative, intuitive realization of the cosmos and its creation from the Divine Cosmic power in its primordial State. He summed up this whole creation saga in two lines in Gurmukhi script in *Japuji*. He stated:

> *All the endless expansion of creation arose out of one Note,*
> *Giving rise to millions of streams.*[5]

This insight into cosmology led him not only to reject the bull horn mythological belief but also gave a moral slant to the human existence on this planet. Stating another law of Sikh theology, Guru Nanak emphatically declared that human life would endure on this planet earth as long as it would comply with the cosmic laws with the observance and practices of the three moral values - Dharma, compassion and self-restraint. It is the network of these three values which sustain life on this earth.

Guru Nanak emphatically declared:

Bull of Dharma offspring of compassion,

And contentment have established a network to hold the creation together.[6]

It may not be wrong to infer that as there is an increasing erosion of these values among the humanity at large and human societies in general in modern times due to excessive human greed for grabbing material things and exploitation of nature, there is a concomitant degradation of environment resulting from excessive pollution, global warming and other damaging ecological effects. Thus, we find almost every tenet of Sikh theology emanating from the formulations of eco-theology.

Guru Nanak's meditative, intuitive and mystical enquiry did not stop at the point of creation of earth or cosmos but went deeper even into its pre-creation state. He stated that the Supreme Divine Cosmic power created the universe out of nothing or from a state of complete vacuum according to his own Divine Will. In other words, the Supreme Divine was in a State of primordial trance and a state of complete stillness prevailed before it created the universe. He stated:

For millions upon millions, countless years was spread darkness,

When existed neither earth nor heaven, but only the limitless Divine Ordinance,

Then existed neither day or night, nor sun or moon;

The Creator into unbroken trance was absorbed.[7]

The veracity of this mystical revelation has also been confirmed by the scientific enquiries of modern astrophysicists like Stephen Hawking. In his path breaking work "A Brief History of Time" (*A Brief History of Time: From the Big Bang to Black Holes.*) Stephen Hawking observes that there was nothing before Big Bang and Gravity created the universe.[8] This fact has been further corroborated by the findings of scientist Francis Collins.[9] From this primordial state of the Divine Cosmic power, Guru Nanak and his successor Sikh Gurus, who composed Gurbani verses included in the sacred Sikh scripture, drew another analogy from the pre-creation stage of cosmos for describing the corresponding stages of their spiritual voyage. A Sikh devotee or spiritual seeker of truth, during his meditational journey starts with the verbal recitation of the sacred name of the Divine Power (*Satinam*) and then goes deeper and deeper into the Divine mystery to reach a state of complete stillness and silence where all human as well as material desires cease to exist and a stage of perfect bliss and peace prevails. It is a feeling of peace that passeth understanding. This state is called the fourth stage *Chautha Pad or TuriyaPad* in Gurbani parlance. It is identical to the primordial state of the Divine before the creation of the universe.

Another dimension of Sikh theology is its spiritual and moral aspect of human life on this earth. Beginning his spiritual quest with his keen observation of the infrastructural set up of environment consisting of elements of nature such as air, water, fire, earth, sky and nature's cycle of seasons through the circle of alternating days and nights, Guru Nanak considered the planet earth as the focal point of human activities, his *Karam Bhoomi* which he called *Dharamsal*.

It is on this earth that human beings and other species conduct their business of life and get evaluated by the Divine power for their further evolution. Thus, earth is not only a field for human physical activity but also a testing ground for covering the probation period for their further emancipation and evolution on the basis of the moral actions. Those who qualify and become worthy of Divine grace are stamped to be eligible for being endowed with spiritual enlightenment. They have been branded as *Panch Parwan* (Chosen ones). This verse runs as follows:

He created Night and Day, seasons and occasions;
So also Air, water, Fire and the nether Regions;
Amidst these has He fixed the earth, the place for Righteous Action.
In it are numerous kinds of creatures and their ways –
Of names many and illimitable.

All creatures on their actions are judged

In God's court, just and true.

At His Court are seated in celestial beauty the saints, Elect of God,

Who through His glance of grace are marked with His approval.

At the Court alone may be known the false from the true:

Only in the world to come may God's true judgement be revealed.[10]

It is because of this evaluating nature of earth besides its being a field for human existence and physical activity that Sikh theology upholds the earth and its constituent elements as sacred and worthy of worship and preservation. It is not to be defiled, damaged and polluted since it not only creates life but also sustains life. It is our pater-familias to which we owe our origin. Earlier in the verse *Asa Di Var*, Guru Nanak referred to water as the source of all life. It states.

The first of living thing is water, whereby is each object sustained.[11]

Earth, water and air being sacred, Sikh theology holds these in great reverence as because not only the whole mankind and human life in this world physically exists due to these basic elements of nature, but also because of the kind of life lived on this earth only determines the next state of human soul after its bodily death. Those who live in continuous remembrance of God's sacred name and meditate upon that in their present life on this earth not only get emancipated themselves, but become instrumental in liberating others as well. Thus human existence in order to realize its full potential is inextricably integrated with nature. Guru Nanak beautifully summed up this close knit human-nature relationship in the concluding *sloka* of his masterpiece verse *Japuji* as follows:

Air is the vital force; water the Progenitor;

The vast Earth the mother of all;

Day and Night are nurses, fondling all creation in their lap.

Of all, the righteous Judge weighs merit and demerit himself.

Approval or rejection by God comes from each one's actions.

Those who, meditating on God have earned merit through hard endeavour-

Saith Nanak – Their faces are radiant with the Divine Light

Many shall find release through them.[12]

This *sloka* in Sikhism is as sacred as *Gaytri Mantra* in Hinduism. It is recited daily at the end of almost every Sikh congregational service and ceremony because it highlights the man-nature relationship and its enduring nature.

The most comprehensive vision about nature, cosmic power and its monotheistic identity as well as its eco-diversity, that may fall into the ambit of eco-theology, occur in Guru Nanak's *Arti* verse in *Raga Dhanasri* in the sacred Sikh scripture Sri Guru Granth Sahib on page 663. It is believed that Guru Nanak was inspired to compose and recite this unique invocational verse to the universal cosmic Divine power by watching the Hindu ritual of evening *Arti* being performed by the Hindu priests at Shree Jagannath temple at Puri (Orissa- India). Contrary to the recitation of invocatory chants in praise of a lesser and imaginary deity/ god, Guru Nanak visualized the ultimate Divine power in the largest possible dimension with its absolute sway over the entire universe and the entire nature in all its ecological diversities engaged in a joint choral singing of its magnificence and rare beatitude. Before quoting this verse in full, it would be beneficial to provide a gist and sequence of its movement. Following the procedural and cataloged inventory of items used in the customary *Aarti* being performed in Shree Jagannath Temple, Guru Nanak conceived of sky or the entire environmental space as the salver in which the sun and the moon placed as lighted lamps in the midst of millions of twinkling sparkling stars placed as precious gems and stones (rubies) being rocked to and fro by the cool breeze scented with the fragrance of vegetational blossoming flowers coming from the Himalayas in an eternal rhythmic musical orchestra, played in praise of the

Divine Cosmic power. This verse then goes on to pay a tribute to the immanent and transcendental attributes of the supreme Divine as all the visible forms of nature are manifestations of the invisible cosmic energy. This spontaneous, rhythmic participation of nature in this song and dance sequence is a rare tribute to the monotheistic Divine light which illuminates the whole universe. The verse concludes with a human prayer for the human soul to be endowed with grace and glimpse of the Divine to the praying devotee who is as desperate as the rainbird (*sarang*) for the first drop (*swanti boond*) of the rain from the skies. The whole verse runs as follows:

> *Placed on the salver of heaven are the lamps sun and moon,*
> *With bright pearls of the constellations –*
> *Thy offering;*
> *Fragrant mountain breezes Thy incense, the wind Thy fan;*
> *The entire blossoming vegetation thy Flower-offerings,*
> *Wonderful is this arati, of the entire creation to thee,*
> *Thou annuller of transmigration;*
> *The unstruck harmony; Orchestrates Thy worship.*
> *Thousand Thy eyes, Thy shapes,*
> *Thousand Thy Lotus feet; of thousand waves Thy wafted fragrance,*
> *Yet invisible, Wonderfully captivating Thy essence.*
> *Thy light in all creation – Thou who art Light!*
> *Thy effulgence illuminating the visible universe!*
> *The Master's Word alone makes manifest the light!*
> *Whatever action pleases Him, is the highest prayer!*
> *My Heart yearns for touch of Thy lotus feet fragrant,*
> *In thirst ever unquenchable;*
> *Bestow on the Chatrik (Sarang) Nanak the water of Thy bounty:*
> *In thy name grant him abode!.*[13]

This verse attracted Gurudev Rabindra Nath Tagore and he admired the cosmic vision of Guru Nanak.[14]

II

Besides this spatial link between Eco and Sikh Theology, Sikhism has also formulated most of its philosophical, spiritual and moral tenets on the basis of Sikh Guru's observation and choice of natural phenomena and giving them a metaphorical interpretation in order to give expression to their psycho-spiritual and philosophical thoughts. The names of Indian months and seasons can be taken for example. Twelve months of the Indian year have been named according to their climatic conditions and the corresponding changes in nature or ecological environment. Sikh theology, rooted as it is in eco-theology, picks up each month, identifies and describes its atmospheric or environmental conditions briefly and then makes it a metaphor for expressing the corresponding psycho-spiritual state of a devotee in Gurbani verse. Like some other medieval Indian saints, Sikh Gurus have also used the traditional literary poetic mode known as *Baran Mahan* (narrative of twelve months) to compose their sacred verses in this genre. There are two sets of *Baran Mahan* verses included in the sacred Sikh scripture one composed by the first Sikh Guru, Guru Nanak Dev ji in *Raag Tukhari* (p. 1007-1010) and the other composed by the fifth Sikh Guru, Guru Arjan Dev in *Raag Majh* (p. 133-136). With small variations here and there, each month of Bikrami Calendar in both these verses represents as much a state of nature as the state of mind of a spiritual seeker.

The first month of Chet/Chaitra (March-April) represents nature at its beautiful best as it is the climax of spring (Basant) season with abundance of greenery, thick foliage, blossoming flowers and bird songs in abundance. It is a month of joy and saturation for the winged and other species in nature. Similarly for a spiritual seeker visualizing himself decked as bride, it is a period of union with the Divine Lord after prolonged waiting and expectation.

The second month of Vaisakh/Vaisākha (April-May) in nature is a month of fulfillment as the ripened Rabi crop is ready to be harvested. Similarly vaisakh in spiritual domain is the period of consolidation and relishing the fruit of meditational hard work. It is a period of bliss and fulfillment for a devotee.

The third month of Jeth /Jayesth (May-June) being the hottest month of the year, everything in nature seems to succumb to the sun's heat. But a devotee, saturated with the elixir-like sacred name of the Divine, feels at home and at peace even in the midst of extreme discomfort caused by the excessive summer heat.

Similarly, in the fourth month of Asard /Āshāda (June-July) as the whole earth suffers bearing the brunt of sun's heat and all round desolation, human beings, bereft of spiritual kinship with the divine, are bound to suffer like the earth. On the other hand, those aligned with the remembrance of the Divine Name remain immune from the pangs of spiritual isolation.

The fifth month of Sawan/Shraavana (July-August) with skies overcast with dark clouds, spells of pouring rain, and dry, parched earth covered with green shoots and sprouting vegetation, as the human bride longs for a union with her worldly spouse gone abroad, a spiritual devotee also yearns for a communion with the Divine. Heavy downpour from the skies makes the pangs of separation more poignant.

The sixth month of Bhadon/Bhādra (August-Sept) is marked by a stuffy, suffocating, sultry and humid climate resulting in physical discomfort and feeling of congestion. With plenty of poisonous insects and foul smell of stagnant waters, this month evokes images of existence in an imaginary hell. But a devotee does not suffer from any such feelings of desolation provided he is endowed with the Divine grace.

In the seventh month of Assu/Ashwina (Sept-Oct) as the weather starts cooling down and humidity levels decline, there is an all round sense of comfort and well-being. Earth's moisture content is getting favorable for sowing crops. As human activity picks up to make new investments for a better livelihood, it is an equally favorable time for more spiritual investment in the spiritual domain as well.

The eighth month of Kathak/Kartika (Oct-Nov) is the month of harvesting the earlier sown kharif crop and sowing of the new Rabi Crop. As the yield is directly proportional to the farmer's efforts and his planned sowing of the new crop based on his past experience, the ultimate quality of human life is also the result of deeds performed in the past together with the vision for the future. Good moral deeds performed in complete submission to the Divine Will lead to Spiritual fulfillment.

The ninth month of Maghar/Agrahayana (Nov-Dec) is a season of warmth and modest climate. It is the best season to meditate and make efforts to seek communion with the Divine. It is a month of harmonious blend of heat and cold. Human body and soul feel at peace with the feeling of Divine Bliss.

The tenth month of Poh/Pausha (December –January) is the coldest month in the northern part of India, as Jeth/Jayesth, the third month in the Bikrami Calendar, is the hottest month. As everything in nature seems to succumb to the excessive cold in this month, it dries the sap from all vegetation in this autumnal phase of nature. During both these extremes of nature as the whole human/ worldly activity ceases to exist, those engaged in spiritual pursuit remain unaffected from these fluctuations of nature since they have the protective umbrella of Divine grace. The well-springs of their spiritual life keep them rejuvenated.

The eleventh month of Magh/Māgha (Jan-Feb) is the month of revival of human activity and is considered auspicious for going on a pilgrimage to the sacred places/ shrines in the company of the pious and the saintly. However in Sikh theology, spiritual pilgrimage is internal rather than external as ablutions in the sacred rivers wash and clean the human body only. Since Sikh Guru's stress is always on the purification of human mind and thoughts rather than the human body, it is best achieved through continuous remembrance and meditation on the sacred name of the Divine. Performance of good moral deeds in all humility and meditation in this auspicious month are most rewarding.

Falgun/ Phalguna (February-March) being the last month of

the Bikrami calendar is the climax of all human activity round the year. It gives a sense of satisfaction and fulfillment. In the spiritual domain, the meditative hard work put in during the past eleven months have come to fruition. Its reward is in the form of a feeling or sense of bliss experienced by a spiritual devotee. It is reflected in realization of the Divine presence in every object of nature. It would be appropriate to quote this verse from *Baran Mahan* in *Raag Majh* to communicate this rare experience:

Of Phalgun know: Bliss abounding have those
To whom the Lord, true Friend, manifests Himself.
The holy who with God are associated,
In His grace to them has He granted union.
By such union come all joys to the loving wife in the couch bedecked,
All sorrow banished.
Fulfilled is the blessed woman's wish
In finding the Divine King as mate;
Her bridesmaids sing prothalamions of joy,
Lilting the song celestial.
None the Lord's equal by the eyes is seen,
None like Him.
This life and the next has He blessed,
And the innumerable attributes?
Those falling at Thy feet liberation have found.
Of Phalgun know: Ever laud Him who is above all desire.[15]

In addition to the metaphorical interpretation of these twelve divisions of time and their climatic flavor, Sikh Gurus have given spiritual interpretation of the four Indian seasons as well in their Gurbani verses such as the Spring, Summer, Autumn and Winter in their verses composed in *Raag Basant, Ragh Malhar, Raag Mali Gaura, Raag Bihagra, Raag Tukhari* etc. In these verses, after taking a cue from the visible appearance and temperamental mood of nature and overall environmental ambience in summer,rain,winter, spring or autumn season and giving it a suitable expression, a paradigmatic shift is gradually made from the physical to the spiritual plane to express the spiritual cravings, joys and sorrows of a seeker of truth and exhortations are made to seek inspiration from the cosmic laws of nature.

Thus, the spontaneously, effortlessly changing seasonal rhythm in nature and its harmonious reflection evoke a similar response in the Sikh Gurus, engaged in a spiritual pursuit and inspires them to give expression to nature's seasonal symphony as well as their psycho-spiritual states of mind. This close affinity between the intricacies of eco theology and Sikh theology makes these two approaches integrated into each other. In other words, a close observation of the rainbow -like spectrum of natural phenomena and understanding of its cosmic laws become a launching pad for founders of Sikh religion to take flights of spiritual imagination leading to their communion with the Divine and lay down the guidelines of Sikh theology.

III

Apart from the close affinity between the nature's seasonal rhythm and graphic presentation of Sikh spiritual spectrum, Sikh theology highlights all human instincts, impulses, feelings and thoughts which dehumanize as well as elevate human beings in their life's journey and determine their degraded or morally uplifted state through the use of similes and metaphors borrowed from nature and its vast variety of flora and fauna as well as biodiversity. This imagery is so rich, vast and appropriate that it becomes a most appropriate medium of expression for expressing almost every human instinct. Before we bring out the one to one correspondence between the natural object picked up and the intended human instinct to be expressed, it will be appropriate to catalog some of the prominent human vices and virtues which Sikh theology highlights and records. Human vices in the negative list are like lust, anger, greed, worldly, familial attachments, pride, tendency to grab what belongs to others, encroaching upon other's right, indulgence in slander, calumny, violence, double dealing, disguise or keeping false appearance. On the positive side, are human virtues of love, detachment, urge and desperate craving for communion with the Divine, cultivation of virtues of contentment, patience, steadfastness, humility and sense of fulfillment, performance of good deeds and enlightenment. Nature's biodiversity provides the widest framework of reference for the expression of human feelings and thoughts as Sikh Gurus were intimately connected to nature. Their Sikh followers, majority of whom have been engaged in agriculture since the early stage of their history, also remain closely in touch with the earth and nature. So Gurbani verses communicate human feelings and thoughts through the use of similes and metaphors from nature. Excessive carnal desire or lust in human body, beyond a legitimate cathartic purgation of an irresistible natural biological attraction towards the opposite sex partly for procreation through a marital relationship leads to degeneration of both human body and mind and soul.

Similarly, feelings of anger, rashness of temper and human tendency to flare up at the slightest provocation has a debilitating effect upon the human body. Both excessive lust and anger are corrosive for the human body as borax melts the gold. A Gurbani verse states:

Lust and wrath disintegrate the body,
As borax gold.[16]
Kaliyuga is the vat, lust the wine; the mind the boozer.
With wrath is the cup by attachment filled;
Pride the Cup-bearer.[17]

Human greed, indiscrete craving for acquisition of material wealth through means fair and foul, indulgence in corruption even at the cost of one's reputation and moral character and willful violation of rule of law has been squarely condemned in Sikh Gurbani and theology. A human being, falling a victim to excessive greed is worst than a mad dog stricken with rabies:

Man like a rabid dog in ten directions runs.

The avaricious man, of discrimination bereft, grabs things, righteously and unrighteously.[18]

Another verse compares a greedy person to a nomadic hunter with a sharp edged dagger leading a pack of dogs consisting of a male dog and two female dogs (bitches) symbolic of human greed and craving desire to amass more and more wealth day and night and grabbing even what belongs to others.

By my side is a hound and two bitches,
That each morning raise terrible howl,
The dagger of falsehood and robbed carrion with me I carry,
Know Lord-Creator, a low-caste nomad am I.[19]

Man's attachment to one's family, wife and offsprings to the complete exclusion of one's spiritual bond with the Divine creator and complete ignorance about the moral nature of human life, its temporariness and inevitable termination with the coming of death has been compared to a fish carelessly swimming in the water unaware of the fishing net cast around with every chance of being caught unaware. Human beings entangled in the lustful enticements of flesh and physical attraction of the female spouse remain ignorant of death and his spiritual destination:

Like to the fish living in water,
That forgetful of the net, instrument of death,
For pleasure of palate the iron hook it swallows;
Even thus is man bound by attachment to gold and woman.[20]

Arrogance, egoistic domination over others and narcissistic tendency to be self-centered is another human vice which has been highlighted in Sikh theology and Gurbani verses through the use of appropriate similes and parallelism from nature. Egocentric persons have been termed as Manmukh (self-oriented) in contrast to the idealistic persons termed as Gurmukhs (God oriented) The former remain entangled in verbal duals and continuous strife and become notorious for their bad reputation like the smell of garlic:

Saith Kabir: The materialist is foul like bit of garlic
Which even though you consume on top of a root,
Will yet become apparent.[21]

Even a shit-eating pig is better than an egoistic and self-centred person says saint Kabir:

Even the pig is better than the misbeliever,
As it keeps the village clean,
As the writched misbeliever dies, none his name mentions.[22]

Thus, all these human vices recorded in Sikh Theology have been illustrated through the employment of similes and metaphors taken from appropriate species mainly from the animal kingdom. In one of the important verses written in semi-sanskrit Gurmukhi script called *Sahaskriti* human world and life have been projected through the metaphor of a thick forest infested with animals like dogs, jackals and asses symbolizing human greed and wild temperament. It is a dwelling place of five smugglers symbolizing five human vices of lust, anger, greed, worldly attachments and egoistic pride which are forever on the lookout to rob human beings who are unaware of their disguised presence. The world also is a seamless river of fire which can only be crossed with Divine grace. It runs as follows:

Man in the forest of the world abides, wherein those related to him,
Abide like dog, jackal, ass.
Hard is this spot, wherein the mind by wine of attachment is intoxicated,
And in it live the five irreclaimable thieves.
In attachment and fear does man wander,
With the tormenting, hard noose round his neck,
In this world is unextinguishable fire of desire,
And the terrible ocean, with shore inaccessible, hard to cross,
Saith Nanak: In holy company to the Lord the devoted;
By seeking shelter with the Divine feet by His grace shalt thou be saved.[23]

It is pertinent to point out here that in Sikh theology and Gurbani verses most of the human vices and other human weaknesses have been depicted through the imagery of beastly diminution from the animal kingdom while most of the human virtues have been represented through the images of birds, from the world of winged species (aviation). Repeated use of images of dog, jackal, snake, ass, elephant, pig, fish as similes and metaphors highlights one or other human weakness or vice in different contexts. On the other hand, rainbird, Cuckoo, swan, sea gulls have been used to represent human virtue of detachment, desperate spiritual craving for communion with the Divine, human soul's flight from human body and human faith in Divine protection and grace. The only exception to this rule from the general pattern are the images of dog and fish as dog also stands for loyalty besides being a symbol of human greed and fish out of water represents human predicament of inescapable death without Divine union besides being a symbol of the continuous restlessness of human mind.

Coming to the human virtues and their representation in Sikh theology, the foremost virtue is one of detachment even while living in the thick of worldly affairs. Sikh theology advocates a house holder's life contrary to asceticism and monasticism preached by the yogic creeds and renunciation or *vanprastha* in old age preached by Hinduism. Sikhism believes in the cultivation of detached outlook even while leading an active life of a householder. This display of detached outlook has been highlighted through images of a duck and a lotus flower both of which while rooted in water keep themselves out of it. Duck keeps her feathers dry even while swimming and lotus flower with its roots in mud and water keeps its head above water while it blossoms:

By remaining as the lotus untouched by water and the duck on the stream,
By concentrated fixing of the mind in the holy word,
By contemplation of the name,
Saith Nanak, is crossed the ocean of existence.[24]
God enlightened ever are immaculate
As the lotus growing in water is by it left untouched.[25]

Besides these similes and metaphors from nature symbolizing human virtues, there are two most prominent images of white swan and sandalwood tree (*chandan*) signifying human spiritual enlightenment and human perfection. We find repeated usage of the symbol of white swan for the description of a spiritually enlightened person as is evident from the references cited below:

The Pool and Swans from primal Time are to each other attuned,

Such is the Lord's Will,

Inside the Pool lie pearls and jewels that are the Swan's feed.[26]

Similarly, the sandalwood (*chandan*) is the richest symbol of human perfection as its fragrance is spread into the whole ambience around it as association with pious and spiritually enlightened person uplift others in his company:

In union with the holy Preceptor, true friend,

The Lord's exalted merits have we low ones sung,

On us like neem tree abiding by sandalwood, qualities of sandalwood are bestowed.[27]

In company with sandalwood is changed some tree –

That tree as sandalwood has ended.[28]

Living a life of contentment, austerity and within one's means without envying anybody else's affluence is valued in Sikhism:

Farid, eat thy dry crust of bread; take simple cold water;

Envy not the delicacies another is enjoying.[29]

Spiritual and mental enlightenment is the highest virtue. It is the climax of all human activity as a tree laden with fruit is the end of early germination, growth and flowering. Spiritual enlightenment wipes out even past Karmas and leads to human emancipation.

To bear fruit is vegetation in bloom,

As appears fruit, do flowers disappear,

For enlightenment is involvement in action,
As appears enlightenment, is the effect of action annulled.[30]

Water has a similar relationship between the Rainbird (*Babeeha* and the first rain drop from the sky). Both swan and rain bird in Sikh theology and Gurbani verses are symbols of human seekers of truth and spiritual enlightenment.

My heart for sight of the holy Preceptor yearns,
And like the Chatrik [Rain bird] Wails,
My thirst goes not, nor comes peace,
Without sight of that beloved, devotee of God.[31]

There are numerous other allusions to other birds like *chakvi* (ruddy shelduck), sparrow, pigeon, parrot, peacock, hawk, falcon, vulture to represent various human psychic instincts.

Thus, nature, with all of its biodiversity from animal, bird and vegetational segments is the storehouse of richest imagery for the Sikh theology to project its major tenets of philosophy to be followed by its believers / followers.

IV

In addition to the close affinity between nature and Sikh theology, some developments in Sikh history, Sikh architecture, Sikh practices, rituals and ceremonies also draw inspiration from nature and have their roots in the composite, and closely integrated ecology and nature. Some of the Sikh Gurus during their pontification and religious missionary activities initiated digging of wells, ponds for drinking water in the arid zones of Punjab and planted mangroves around the Sikh shrines built on the banks of these water bodies. Besides the Golden Temple located in the center of the pool of water at Amritsar, the other major Sikh shrines at Taran Tarn and Muktsar are also located near the water bodies.

The Sikh architecture has also imbibed some of the ecological features of fresh air, sunny, bright ambience and openness of space. A standard Sikh Gurdwara building is spacious with four doors opening in four directions and a dome with a pinnacle pointing towards the sky. The four entrances opening in four directions, besides being symbolic of the universal outlook of Sikhism indicating free unhindered access to everyone irrespective of caste, creed color and gender, also signifies nature's openness and spaciousness. Sikh shrines have never faced any stampede due to congestion nor ever barred the entry of any one on the basis of difference of religion, caste or gender. Sikhism has imbibed its catholicity of outlook partly from the integrated nature of ecology and partly from the universal outlook of Sikh Guru's teachings.

The Sikh practice of running daily free community kitchen (*Langar*) by every Sikh Gurdwara and now by some Sikh organizations, especially during the occurrence of some natural or manmade calamities such as the present day Corona Virus pandemic all over the globe has also its roots in Divinely created nature dispensing its bounties to its created specious without any discrimination. Partaking of food prepared and served free, sitting in a line together in *Langar* without difference of social status is a derivative corollary from Nature's benevolence. Most of the Sikh rituals associated with birth, betrothal, weddings and death ceremonies are without any claptrap of religious jargon and begin and end with a simple traditional Sikh prayer with the recitation of sacred verses in between suitable to the occasion. Last rites of the departed person's body include a traditional Sikh prayer followed by the recitation of *Sohila* (celebratory verses) including the Guru Nanak's *Aarti* verse celebrating the natures' magnificence and beauty of nature.

Sikhism does not believe in good or bad omens, auspiciousness or ill effects of particular days, months, occasions, and moments since it considers all units of time as part of nature's grand design. Majority of Sikh weddings called Anand Ka Raj ceremony and prayer meetings for the departed soul take place on Sundays or any other day convenient to the concerned families. There is neither any search for an auspicious moment for any *Lagan* or *Mahoorat* for fixing a wedding nor any matching of horoscopes of the prospective wedding couple. With faith in God's benevolence and prayer for Divine grace,Sikhs launch on their family or business ventures. Sikh farmers undertake sowing of their crops when the climatic conditions are favorable with a prayer on their lips. Sikhism since its inception, believes in gender equality and recognizes the indispensability of male female relationship. The collection of Guru Nanak's verse in *Asa Di var* highlights the equality of women and their indispensable need in human life:

From women is man born, inside her is he conceived;
To Women is man engaged, and woman he marries.
With woman is man's companionship.
From Woman originate new generations.[32]

Sikhism rejects any superstition attached to female body after giving birth to a child and her solitary isolation or confinement for a fixed period. It considers child birth as a natural process. Sikhism does not believe in the Sati tradition / system where a married woman was mandated to burn-herself on the funeral pyre of her deceased husband. On the other hand, Sikhism believes in the practice of widow marriage without the attachment of any stigma to a widowed female. Neither do Sikh women undertake fasts (*karvachauth*) for the longevity of their male spouses nor do they feed any Brahmins or observe any other ceremony like *shradh* for their dead ancestors.

There are plenty of Sikh / Punjabi folk songs, sayings, maxims and proverbs associated with agriculture which broadly refer to changing seasons, suitability or adversity of climatic conditions for carrying on various agricultural activities. Communicating these rustic usages in a foreign language such as English would dilute their real flavor and essence. Some of the festivals like Vaisakhi, Lohri and Basant are also associated with the changing phases of nature and celebrated with fervor.

Thus, every aspect of Sikhism including its spiritual, mystical and conceptual theorization of the Divine Cosmic power; the expression of its spiritual insights, state of Sikh devotees mind and spirit and its reflection through the use of symbols and images from nature as seasonal changing rhythm and biodiversity together with its rituals, practices, ceremonies, architecture and folk songs has its genesis in nature and its cosmic laws being visualized and studied as eco-theology. In other words, Sikh theology and eco-theology are inseparable. Sikh theology is a derivational corollary of eco-theological laws. Sikh theology besides observing and recording the operation of cosmic laws makes a metaphorical interpretation of these laws to lay down the tenets of Sikh theology.

References

1. Guru Nanak: Japuji, Sri Guru Granth Sahib, [SGGS] p. 1 translated by Gurbachan Singh Talib, Publication Bureau, Punjabi University, Patiala, hereafter referred to as GST, Vol 1, p. 1 *–Ikoankaar Sathnaam Karathaa Purakh Nirabho Niravair Akaal Moorath Ajoonee Saibhan Gurprasaadh||*

2. Guru Nanak: Japuji, pauri 1, Sri Guru Granth Sahib, p. 1, GST, Vol I, P. 1-2.,

3. Guru Nanak: Raga Asa, Asa Di War, Sri Guru Granth Sahib, p. 464 GST, Vol II, p. 984,

4. Georges Henry Joseph Edourd Lemaitre: Theory of expansion of the universe, Big Bang theory, Lemaitre Coordinates 1931 - en.wikipedia.org/wiki/georges_lemenitric.

5. Guru Nanak: Japuji, pauri 16, Sri Guru Granth Sahib, p. 3, GST, Vol I, p. 8.

6. Guru Nanak, Japuji, Pauri 16, Sri Guru Granth Sahib, p. 3, GST, Vol I, p. 8,

7. Guru Nanak: Raag Maru sohila,, Sri Guru Granth Sahib, p. 1035. GST, Vol III, p. 2114.

8. Hawking Stephen: *A Brief History of Time: From the Big Bang to Black Holes*, published by Bantam Books, 1988. In a Brief history of Time, Hawking writes in non-technical terms

about the structure, origin, development and eventual fate of the universe. He talks about basic concepts like space, and time basic building blocks that make up the universe (such as quarks) and the fundamental force that govern it such as gravity) – en.wikipedi_org/wiki/a Brief History of Times.

9. Collins Francis: The language of God: A scientist presents evidence for Belief, Free Press, 2006, ISBN – 07432-8639-1. Collins is an American physician – genetist noted for his discoveries of disease and genes…. In this book, he explains atheistic evolution, Collins raises arguments for the idea of God, drawing from Science and philosophy. He cites many famous thinkers, most prevalently C.S. Lewis, as well as St. Angustine, Stephen Hawking, Charles Darwin, Theodosins Dobzhansky ? and others. http:// en.wikipedia.org/wiki/ language of god.

10. Guru Nanak: Japuji, Pauri 34, Sri Guru Granth Sahib, p. 7, GST, I, p. 19-20.

11. Guru nanak: Rang Asa, Asi Di Var, Solk M. 1, Sri Guru Granth Sahib, p. 473. GST, Vol II, p. 1003

12. Guru Nanak: Japuji, Sloka, Sri Guru Granth Sahib, p. 8, GST, Vol 1. p. 22

13. Guru Nanak: Dhanasari Mohalla 1, Sri Guru Granth Sahib, p. 663 GST, Vol II, p. 1388.

14. During Tagore's father Debendra Nath Tagore's visit to Amritsar he had collected this verse of Guru Nanak, which he translated into Bengali and printed it got it set to music by his on Jyotindernath and Rabinder Nath Tagore must have sung it at Brahmo Festivals. The arti motif of this song may have inspired Tagore to write a song "Tuharo arti kari cantra tapan (Moon & Sun) in 1884.(Courtesy: http://www. mainstreamweekly.net/article5261.html)

15. Guru Arjan Dev: Majh Mohalla 5, Baran Mahan, SGGS, p. 136; GST, Vol 1. p. 276.
16. Guru Nanak: Ramkali Mahala 1, Dakhani Onkar, SGGS, p. 932, GST, Vol. III, p. 1908.
17. Guru Nanak: Salok Mardana, SGGS, p. 553, GST, Vol II, p. 1169
18. Guru Arjan Dev: Sri Rag, M. 5, SGGS, p. 50; GST, Vol 1, p. 105.
19. Guru Nanak: Sri Raag, M. 1, SGGS 24, GST, Vol 1,p. 55.
20. Namdev: Sarang Bani Namdeo Ji ki, SGGS, p. 1252; GST, Vol IV, p. 2524,
21. Kabir: Salokas 17, SGGS, p. 1365, GST, Vol IV, p. 2730,
22. Kabir Saloka 143, SGGS, p. 1372; GST, VOL. IV, p. 2742
23. Guru Arjun Dev; Salok SahasKriti, M. 5, SGGS, p. 1360; GST, Vol IV, p. 2719
24. Guru Nanak; Ramkali, Mahalla 1, Sidh Gosht, SGGS, p. 938; GST, Vol III, p. 1922-23
25. Guru Arjan Dev: Sukhmani M. 5, SGGS, p. 272; GST, Vol I, p. 563
26. Guru Nanak: Salok, Rag Ramkali, SGGS, p. 956; GST, Vol III. p. 1962
27. Guru Ram Das: Rag Nat Narayan, SGGS, p. 976; GST, Vol III, p. 2002
28. Guru Arjan Dev: Raga Bhairon, Ast Padian, SGGS, p. 1158; GST, Vol IV. 2346
29. Farid, Slok, SGGS, p. 1379, GST, Vol IV, p. 2755.

30. Ravidas, Raag Bhairon, SGGS, p. 1167, GST Vol IV, p. 2326
31. Guru Arjan Dev, Majh Mohalla, Chaupaday Ghar 1, SGGS, p. 96, GST, Vol 1, p. 200
32. Guru Nanak: Salok, Asa di Var, Slok 2, SGGS, p. 473; GST, Vol II. p. 1004

Chapter 6

Nature in Gurbani: An Aesthetic Perspective

Dr. Ambalicka Sood Jacob

Andhretta, a small hamlet in Himachal Pradesh is known for three acclaimed personalities in the field of Art and Literature. They are Madame Norah Richards, Sr. Sobha Singh and artist B.C. Sanyal besides Sr. Gurcharan Singh and Mansimran Singh under whose auspices the *Andhretta* Pottery Centre was established . The connect is seen strongly through the above personalities, that of Mother Nature and *Gurus' Bani.* They are synonymous to the very core- Air is the *Guru,* Water the Father and the Earth the Great Mother. These words of Guru Nanak Dev *Ji* are the great truism, especially during the times of 'Nature-deficit disorder' and the pervasive climate change we experience in the current times.

The *Sri Guru Granth Sahib* makes a vivid mention of Mother Nature in multifarious forms. The two words '*Waho-Waho* 'refer to the appreciation of the moment of realization that unveils the mystiques of Nature, self-realization and an inexplicable experience of light, 'enlightenment'. The portrayal of Nature in Sikh Scripture is not alone to marvel at Nature but for being a part of it. It is not for any material gain. Guru Nanak Dev *ji,* the First Guru referred to it as *Qudret* (the word is of Arabic origin).

Through His *Udasis,* Guru Nanakji professe being one with Nature is a way to attain infinity. Out of 31 *Ragas* in *Raga Asa De Vaar,* the emphasis is on Nature. Nature, like God Almighty, is infinite and beyond comprehension. The humans create their surroundings as a reflection of their inner state. The spirit of humility and prayers are two ways in which we become part of Nature and respect others. The History of the Gurus, unfolds stories enshrining the love for animals, birds, trees, vegetation, rivers, mountains and sky. Ecological balance is attained when all have equal rights of life and sustenance.

In Judeo-Christian Religion, the relationship of Man and Nature is of dominance where all have been delivered to Man for the convenience of the species. The first book of Moses, commonly called Genesis[1] (1:3) mentions 'And God said Let there be light and there was light.' This light became the source of inspiration. The remaining of the days of the week brought into existence other aspects of Nature over which the Man was positioned as the superior of all beings. The protection of all came under his/her purview. In *Gurbani,* in awe begin the words '*Baliharikudratvaseya tera aantnaajayedasya'*. It means broadly that the Creative force of the Divine is beyond human comprehension as His grace is limitless and infinite and this realization fills us with humility and gratitude.

The importance of the article is to sensitize the reader to the very temper of the Artist, *Yogi* and Nature and how it is depicted, perceived and presented. The artist supposedly is an instrument in the hands of the spirit and flows with the whisperings of the nature. This intervention of the spirit is referred to in art as the Ultimate Truth. It is similar to the aesthetic experience that each artist undergoes. It is not taught, many a time it is not understood and at others, it causes a sense of wonder- 'Have I done this?' The experience is comparable to that of the experience of a *Yogi* or the

---

1 American Bible Society; *The Holy Bible;* (International Council of Religious Education.; 1929), 01.

one in penance irrespective of the religion and practice. A spectator who has been to the *Dhauladhar* ranges will understand how the moods of nature change with the delightful play of the Sun's beams on the snow-clad mountains. The intricate relationship of one to the other is realized here when time just seemingly stops. And in perfect discipline of the mind, one realizes the futility of thoughts that distract from the truly cherishable parts of our lives. The beautiful moments of our own lives are unveiled amidst pristine natural surroundings. The most important aspect is of '*chit*', '*chinta*', '*chitram*', '*chitera*' and '*chitrakar*' all implore the mind and in its turn the heart. Answers are disclosed to one who is keen to listen to Mother Nature, since human being is a part of the whole ultimately.

The aspect of '*Aarti*' in *Gurbani* refers to the shedding away of all superstitions and rituals in the adoration of the Lord. In Sikh Religion, *Aarti*i is a means to unite with the Ultimate. There is darkness and the Light, both come together. It is quite different from Hindu way of recital. It is more of a *Kirtan* where *shabads* from Guru Nanak Dev *ji* and *Bhagats* are recited. It is the Divine Wisdom on which focus is laid and it is in the form of *Guru Granth Sahib* The bowing before the Holy *Granth* is a mark of respect to the Divine Knowledge in the spirit of'*Guru ManyoGranth*', where the Guru is regarded as manifest in the Scripture and not to a physical form. The Name of the Lord resounds incessantly through day and night. The complete Universe comes together each moment and displays the adoration of the Lord through its glow and vibration. This vibration is understood by each individual without requiring an explanation. It is through deeds that a person is recognized and not by the façade. '*Gaganmeinthal, ravichanddeepak ...kaise aarti hoiyebhavkhandanateri aarti.*' *Shabad* or the word of God, recital, music and chanting all are various ways of concentrating and meditation. The moments of experiences differ vividly one from the other. The trance built thence takes one beyond their selves to assess Nature and its manifold paths. The prayer of an artist is of a unique kind, embedded in keen perspective and it is attained in solitude. The five senses of our body and the five elements of nature play important role in the life of human beings. For an artist or *yogi* these five elements are more important as they are sensitive to the surroundings. Earth, Sky, Water, Air and Fire are serving significant relationship. '*Pawan Guru Paani Pita Mata Dharti...*' These verses from *Gurbani* means that water serves as the Father, Earth the Mother, and Air as the Guru. Nature is a part of our existence.

If we concentrate upon the fact we will find that we have all the five elements present in us through emotions of sweetness, anger, envy, jealousy and love. The emotions of joy, grief, anger and frustration can be understood by the theory of the nine *rasas*. One realizes that the most difficult is the *rasa* of *Karuna* that descends upon the parched land as rain. For the artist, raindrops are the drops of *amrita* that freely flow to accord an immortal life. The experience of these raindrops is like the strings of the stringed instrument being pulled by the master musician. It is an experience that a person attains when he is quietly moving amidst sprawled-out Nature. Perhaps it is a similar experience traversed by the artist that is a moment of celebration of the musician after winding up his melodious song in front of the audience and is yet unsure of the applause awaiting him. Meditation and spirituality too lead one to experience these feelings. The first hand experience at the completion of the art work is a joy for the artist and the thought is reciprocated by the words from *Gurbani*- '*kareaasankardithachau*' that means, after creating such a beautiful world even God sat down and was thrilled to watch what He had created.

In the Holy Bible; Genesis (1:31) 'And God saw everything that He had made, and behold, it was very good' reciprocates the very thought of the artist. If what the artist experiences and executes upon the canvas with complete concentration is good, s/he experiences ecstasy. Nature around, is replete with beauty in every form but it has no permanence. In *Andhretta*,one is in close proximity to Nature. The droplets of morning dew upon the green leaves are carried as pearls upon their surface, the billowing shapes of the clouds dance and rejoice along with the birds in the sky. They playfully flutter along the wings of the birds, the soft eyes of the calf, the smile of a young child, the running brooks and flow of soft rapids with temples made to adorn and worship. It would be quite pertinent to say here that 'In the *Guru Granth Sahib,* we are not being introduced to magic or fearless worship of Nature but the stress is being laid on the essence of nature,'[2] basically being one with Nature.

One of the essential elements in the *Guru Granth Sahib,*that has been dealt with is liberation of the self from the bondage of ego. They are referred to as the five *vikaras* –lust, greed, jealousy, ego and anger. The *Guru* has elaborated the disbelief in image worship and rituals that are following form-based notions. God is formless, shapeless, omnipresent and omnipotent. Thus the need arises to liberate ourselves from the multifarious gods and goddesses we are so acquainted with from the reference of polytheistic religions. The sensation is created by the sound called *Nada. Anhadanāda* is the resounding of the music in the space but this space has nothing to do with the *kal*(time) we are dwelling in. The resounding of the music needs not to have lyrics, or regulated academic training but they are the structural play of sounds vibrating in the Universe. Though relying upon them for devotional expression, articulations in Sikhism are to be free from the formal and iconographical formulations that have been profoundly presented in the various *Rāgas,* some of which are enumerated below. The tradition is long-drawn. The simple and plaintive things are most eloquent in their own right. The in-depth understanding of the *Rāga*s would enable one to know how importantly nature plays a balancing act in Space. The orders in which the 31 *Rāga*s[3] appear in the *Adi-Granth* are:

---

2 Dr. Gopal Singh; *Shri Guru Granth Sahib De SahitakVisheshta* Library Religious studies, Punjabi University, Patiala.1990.

3 Ambalicka Sood Jacob*; Musical Modes in Visual Forms- A Journey through the Creative Minds*; (New Bhartiya Book Corporation, Delhi.; 2012), 126-134.

RāgaŚri: it creates love for truth. ŚriRāga is sung in extreme weather conditions. The emotions are in their prime and the mind and the heart settle down at this juncture to relieve the pain of psyche and the body.

RāgaMajh: *Majh* word evolves from the *Majha* region of Punjab showing the pastoral life of the people with simple desires of the mind. It depicts the separation from the beloved.

RāgaGaurī: The variations are *GaurīPurbi, Bairāgan, Gaureri, Deepki, Majh* and *ceti. GaurīRāga* is an old *Rāga* and varies from region to region from where it had evolved. *GaurīRāgini* is considered as a *Rāgini* to ŚriRāga but in the *Guru Granth Sahib* it is referred as *Rāga,* the ultimate cry for meeting the Almighty. It is a *Rāga* that depicts the *Guru*. Nature, is depicted as life as a whole till death and *Atman* (soul) seeking *Mukti*, the final relief from the circle of life and death.

RāgaAśā: This *Rāga* is indicative of hope and patience. It is the *Rāga* of the early morning. It is essentially sung in the winter months at dawn. The insight is slowly built believing in Him and having a positive ambience,It gives more confidence by synchronizing the moments before the sunrise or even after the sunset.

Rāga Gujri: This *Rāga* has a folk appeal and is a traditional and a regional *Rāga* of the *Gujri* tribe. It has in fact evolved from the folk songs of the *Gujjars*. It is linked with the *Rāga Deepak* as its *Rāgini.* It is normally sung at dusk time when the cattle are returning home and the rhythm is natural of the home coming. The song springs from the heart, resting with the Lord and offering thanks for providing enough feed to the cattle for the satiation of the mind, stomach and the body.

Rāga Dev Gandhari: It is a *Rāga* of the evening. It is referred to as *Rāgini Todi.* It is bejeweled with fragrance and abandonment to pleasure. It is like the fragrant foot of God, the ultimate resting place. It is the reflection of those moments that a person pining for knowledge spends with his Guru.

RāgaBihagra: The *Rāga* is sung at night time,the effect of North Indian music rules prime on the *Rāga Bihagra.* It is reciprocating the state of melancholy. The fear of separation is washed away and the mind is at constant ease.

RāgaVadhans: means to be possessed by God. The *Rāga* is inspired from the popular folk songs. The essential element is to control our humanly and physical pleasures. The control is basically on all our outbursts whether it is of the tongue, mind, desire and lust for the ultimate union with the God Almighty. Fear and illusion disappear from our minds and even death does not harm though songs of death are also sung in this *Rāga.*

RāgaSorath: *RāgaSorath* is sung in the evening time. It bespeaks of union with God. These are the moments of contemplation and thoughtlessness. This *Rāga* is apt for building the concentration of the mind with reverberations of truth. It is the *Rāga* of darkness. It is to defy all the restrictions curbing the materialistic desires of the heart. This *Rāga* creates light in darkness.

RāgaDhanāsari: This Raga highlights richness of the heart. This is the *Rāga* of Northern region in India, specifically Punjab. It is like an impressionable image seen for the very first time. It reflects the birth and the fresh hope of living. The clarity is achieved in the scintillating stars, if the darkness around them is deep, so is reflected in this *Rāga. RāgaDhanāsari* helps the devotee to find his path. The blindfold from the eyes of the student is removed by the *Guru.*

RāgaJaitŚri: *RāgaJaitŚri* is sung for celebration. It reciprocates calmness in life. It relaxes one and makes one understand that the treasure lies in the name of God and not in the collection of worldly objects. It is a request to God from the grieved heart, a call from desperation to enlivening the mind and filling it with Supreme energy. The *Rāga* is played in the winter season.

RāgaTodi: It is a meticulous *Rāga* and sung at the time when the fields are ripe and ready for harvesting. The evening time is the time to play this melodious *Rāga.* It is like the magic weaved by the *vīnā* or the stringed instrument. The *Rāga* takes the spectator away from all humanly bondage in a world of purity.

RāgaBairari: It is a *Rāga* of the late afternoon when the Sun is receding but yet not having lost its sheen. It is an old *Rāga* but popular among the genre. This *Rāga* is associated with *RāgaTodi, Triveni* and *Deskara.* It is ornamented and decked up like the bride and is replete with the blessings of God. It is a constant praise to God irrespective of the circumstances.

RāgaTilang: *RāgaTilang* is the *Rāga* of happiness and is played in the evening. It is a sharp upsurge in the sequence of notes. The inexplicable feeling of finding something and losing something is intrinsically felt.

RāgaSuhi: It is a *Rāga* of expectation. It is either sung early in the morning or in the afternoon. *Suhi* is the *Rāgini* of *Rāga Suha.* It is the *Rāga* of desire and richness of the heart. The *Rāga Suhi* rejoices all sorts of celebrations in the lifetime of human as if savored the taste of the Divine in admiring the *Anhatanada.*

RāgaBilāwal: It is an old and a prevalent *Rāga* popularly sung in the morning time. It is a *Rāga* of happiness and is also referred to as *Vilāvali* or *Velavali*, many a time known as the *Rāgini* of *HīndolRāga.*

RāgaGound: *GoundBilaval* in its variation praises God Almighty. It is a complicated *Rāga*, can be sung any time at day or night when it rains and pours heavily. It is sung in combination of *RāgaDhanāsari, Malhār* and *Bilaval.* This *Rāga* has deep roots in Indian Tradition.

Rāga RamKāli: *DakhniRamKāli* is its variation and the one who sings it, God resides in his heart. It is a melodious *Rāga* very popularly played by the genre. *RāgaRamaKāli* is an early morning *Rāga* reciprocating the flow of the rivers. The mood is of the heralding of clouds. The rains will pour upon the dry land, quenching the thirst of the soil. It is a popular *Rāga* of the *yogis*.

Rāga Nat-Nārāyana: There is a deep mystery inside each human being. Our actions and behavior are dependent upon certain *Bhėdas*. The mind is craving for meeting the Lord. *Rāga Nat-Nārāyana* speaks of the Truth. The peace in the mind will be reflected on the face of the being when the inner light is aglow similar to performance of the Lord of Dance- Śiva.

Rāga Mali Gaura: bespeaks the love for God in heart. It is a *Rāga* of solitude and sadness. It is played in the afternoon. There is a need to bring under control the 5 *vikaras* to get relieved from the human bondages.

Rāga Maru: *Maru Dakhani* is the variation. *Maru Rāga* is a complicated *Rāga*. It is *Rāga* of death. The body is to be totally detached from life and the pleasures therein. The feeling that is evoked here is a sentiment of a wanderer or a nomad. The flight in the *Rāga* is similar to the feeling of the bird that flies high in the air beyond the clouds and the moments within the reach of the human perception.

RāgaTukhari: The association of the *Rāga* is to Punjab. It is a combination of the new and the old *Rāgas*. It encapsulates the *Baramaha*- the saga of twelve seasons thereby releasing energy into the monotonous lifestyle. It is a mood of a *yogi*. It is the experience of the joy of meeting the Almighty and as an after-effect release of mighty energy. The ancient texts highlight that *RāgaTukhari* was the name, given to the Himalayan Mountain.

RāgaKedara: inspires love for God. It is an evening *Rāga*. It is played to highlight an achievement. It was usually played when a battle was won or to rejoice in the celebration of victory. It represents the feeling of the fluttering of the flags in the sky.

RāgaBhairo: *This Rāga* is of the morning time. The *Rāga* has no place for the ego. It highlights dispelling of darkness.

Rāga Basant: *Basant Hīndol* is a variation of *Rāga Basant*. This is a seasonal *Rāga*. It is a perpetual mood. It is different from *AśāRāga*. Everything in the vicinity comes to life and blooms, reflect the energy. It is like the magic being woven by the Nature . *Basant Rāga* is very close to the celebratory sentiment of the *HīndolRāga*.

Rāga Sarang: It is a *Rāga* played in the evening. It is generally sung in the winters and represents happiness. The *Basant* and the *Saranga Rāgas* should not be sung at the same time. It is a taboo and is restricted at the time of *Basant*.

Rāga Malar: The emphatic stress on rain is laid in this *Rāga*. It is a seasonal phenomenon. It is sung at night during the rainy weather conditions. Nothing can satiate the human body other than the rain that pours down from the clouds loaded with droplets of myrrh.

RāgaKanra: The *Rāga* reciprocates the vibrations of the evening time. The sound of rain is synchronized to the falling of the utensils from the shelves. It is an extended vibration, something like the experience of the resonance of the tuning fork. The feeling is that of universal brotherhood.

RāgaKalyān: It is the *Rāga* of late evening or the first part of the night. It exudes happiness. The *GauraRāga* is followed by *KanraRāga* preceded by *RāgaKalyāna*.

RāgaPrabhati: It is a *Rāga* of the early morning. It is autumnal *Rāga,* the emotion is of joy. The highlight is on knowledge, concentration, wisdom and the positive energy that exuberates from playing the *Rāga*. Ancient musicians place it with *RāgaAśā* and *Bhairavī*. It reflects growth.

RāgaJaijaivanti: It is a morning *Rāga*. It is the moment of peace.

A variety of musical *Rāgas* symbolize various sentiments as well as myriad hues of Nature in the context of the seasons, the time of day, the weather and of the cycle of life and death.

Nature worship is one of the important aspects of worship in any religion. Nature inspires and forms a special bond between the Creator and the human justifying in becoming a Creator in his own right. 'Its confidence in the goodness of the man rests upon a sharp distinction between nature and reason.'[4] Its identification of reason and spirit obscures the fact that human freedom actually transcends the capacities which are usually considered as rational. The artist thus paints freely when he reaches this transcendental level in art through the faculty of the mind. S/he produces art and appreciates all things that are in aesthetic order. 'In making or enjoying art, people render themselves slightly independent of the outside world and obtain aesthetic satisfaction which may substitute for those that Nature fails to yield or compensates for the frustrations it inflicts.'[5] Art in fact gives pleasure, consoles the uneasiness as also tends to give semblance to the chaotic situations of the mind. In an age of violence and anxiety, there arises a need to look beyond self to have more of a considerate attitude towards the need of others. Hence the need to interact arises and thereby the culture and aesthetic sense come into play to balance Man and Nature.

The greatest of human capacities is to communicate. The visual art gives Man the means to go beyond the scope of words. The aesthetic level of human interaction with art, the artist and the Nature forms a unique language, a dialect, even a religion in its own right. The essence of communication could be realized

---

4 Daniel J. Bronstein; *Approaches to the philosophy of Religion;* Basic Problems of Philosophy; 1964.

5 Paul W. Pryser; *A dynamic psychology of Religion*; Sigmund Freud's analysis of mild narcosis.(Harper and Row; New York; 1968), 281.

through the quotation on the walls of Norah Richard's house that were mud plastered by her own hands 'Walls are my signatures and they wait for your gesture.'[6] The house of Norah serves as a shrine for artists singing praises of humanity and natural surroundings: The ripple in the shimmering brooks, the glittering sunlit streams replenished with perennial flow of chilled water from the snow-clad mountains, the torrents of rapids, gentle spray of water from the waterfall - all these, in solace, readily become part of the naturalistic environment being engulfed by the clouds above, the resounding sound of the flow of water by the side and the gathering mist in the mornings and the settling down of the dew in the evenings longing for Mother Nature. The Sun enlivens the sleeping *Dhauladhar* mountain ranges every morning and unveils from its womb the *Purusha-Prakriti*, male and female forms that appear in varying positions-sometimes lying and at others in half upright positions. The fleeting moments are so brief that one has to wait upon each second like an anxious creative photographer to capture the variant moods of nature.

Art has the capacity to touch every phase of human life by providing it that perspective which is unimaginable. The artist sets order to the structure of life and weaves intricate patterns into it. Man is filled with the urge to form harmony to bring order into this incongruous world. Art is a vent to the pent-up feelings that releases one from the clutches of not only frustrations but also unnecessary running after and collecting materialistic 'garbage' from the world. In the act of creation, the artist is so involved in the work, s/he is doing, that s/he is oblivious to the surroundings. The synthesis of intellect and emotion is possible on aesthetic level of experience. This piece of art might evoke a response from the spectator that is proportionately dependent upon the *rasik*- the onlooker, who if can reach the thoughts of the artist would call the symphony thus created as *raswandana* in other words complete communication.

---

6 Norah Richards; *Writer's Home*; *Andhretta*.Guest House, Punjabi University, Patiala.

The artist lives with the visual in his mind till the time it emerges through his subconscious mind and encapsulates the canvas. It is through this creation that the artist attains balance in his work termed as '*Catharsis*'. The artist creates a religion of her/his own and redefines Nature as per one's perspective. The sweetest music is well differentiated from the range of tones as is deciphered through the silent and the strident. The music and lyrics have a deep influence upon our psyche. In a similar manner, paintings, through their visual impact keep on playing their music even after they are away from our eyes. The impact is so deep that upon closing our eyes we can conjure up an image of what we had seen earlier. This spontaneity is present in the child that slowly is manicured in adolescence and is completely refined by adulthood to diminish when one gets older. The effort is to preserve this child-like spontaneity through the article and make an endeavor to bring Man, Nature and the spectator one step ahead in understanding one another and increase the sensitivity for a better ecological harmony. Many verses are closely linked to nature and the elements therein but the following 12 verses[7]emerge as a part of the harmony. The selected verses are to bring the vast ocean of Sikh Teachings within the purview of the article in order to study the interrelation of Nature, Meditation and Art. The Translations are as per the reference quoted while the experiences are personalized by the journey in *Andhretta* thus realizing Nature and the Text hand-in-hand:

- *Jiunjalmehejaluaaiyekhatana/*
  Teun jotisangh jot samana//

'As water comes and gets blended with water; so does His light blend with the Supreme Light. His coming and going ends and he attains rest.' This companionship is not in terms of the fish to water, of the water to its banks, the soil to the water, the pebbles and Life to Death.

---

7 Dr. Gopal Singh; *Shri Guru Granth Sahib De SahitakVisheshta* Library Religious studies, Punjabi University, Patiala.1990.

- *Tun dariya O dana beena/ meinmachalikaiseantlaha//*
  Jah jahdekha the the tun hai/ tujh se niksephuttmaran//

'Thou art the river, all knowing and all seeing. How can I, a fish find Thy limit? Wherever I look there Thou Art coming out of thee, I burst and die.' The universal chanting of the word '*Om*' vibrates. The life too enfolds the same formula where the roots ought to be strong in order to give a bold performance.

- *Kudratedesaekudratesunaiye/ Kudratebhausukhasaar//*

'By Thy power we see by Thy power we hear. And by Thy power we fear and have the essence of happiness.' The power that has been projected here is infused from within and has no external source. This communication is possible at the subconscious level.

- *Baleharekudaratvaseya/ Tera aantnajaiyelakeya.//*

'Sacrifice am I unto thee who abides in his Creation, Thy limit cannot be comprehended.' Seemingly the source of inspiration is the Sun rising above the horizon creating myriad hues. There is hope in the silver lining around the dark clouds. *Purush* and *Prakriti* appear yet to be in slumber and they are to be awaken at the beck of the rising Sun.

- *Gagan mein thal ravi chand deepak bane/Taarika mandal janak moti//*
  Dhuupumalaanalopawanchawarokare/
  Sagalbanraiphoolantjyoti//
  Kaise aarti hoiye/Bhavkhandanateri aarti//

'In the sky's salver, the Sun and the Moon are the lamps and the stars with their orbs are the studded pearls. The fragrance of sandalwood makes Thy incense wind Thy fan and all the vegetation Thine flowers. O! LuminousLord. What a beautiful worship with lamps is being performed! This is the present adoration, O! the destroyer of dread.' The floating clouds upon the sky, the mountain peaks with snow and the valley deep beneath seem to be uttering the verse. The morning walk through the woods is filled with the scented mountain air and the vibrations are replete with the luminous energy.

The moonbeams seem to caress the water and the little ripples created in the water with energy that is full of wholesomeness. The flowing water is the flow of life for the artist. The bamboos on the banks of the river are celebrating the whispering through their flutes and dancing to the tune in rhythm of the flowing water.

- *Jal thalmahialepooreya/ Suamisirjanhaar//*
  Anekbhantihoiyepasreya/ Nanak ekankaar//

'There is but one God. By the true Guru's Grace He is obtained. Lord, the Creator is in the water, on the Land and in the Sky. In manifold ways, one Lord has diffused Himself,O Nanak.' The furrows and the hills, the rocky texture and the fine winding roads of mud, the trees, whispering willows and the weeping branches of the tree stooping low to touch the soil and the paddy fields seem to reflect in the verse. The garden of Norah Richard's house has suddenly come to bloom and everything surrounding it glows in happiness. Wherever we find light we see there the fertility either of the mind or the heart. The two souls are coming together and there is the union of the *atman* and *parmatman.*

- *Teri kudrate too hee janhe/ Aur nadoo jajaane//*
  Jisnu kripaka rhe mere peaare/ Soae tuuj hae pachanae//

'No one knows the Omnipotent, No one can equal Thee. Only he enjoys the experience, whom You select and attach to Yourself.' Having talked to nature in its eloquent little voice, the nature seemingly responds to the calling, that is for sure. The evening breeze gently billows the tree, laden with flowers so as to drop a few crimson hued flowers on the ground.

- *Sabhmehejotehjotehhaisoyi/*
  Tis kai channanesabhmehechananhoiye//
  Guru sakhijotehpargatuhoiye/
  Jo tesbhave so aarti hoiye//

'Amongst all there is Light, that Light art Thou. By His Light the Light within all the souls shines. By Guru's teachings the Divine Light becomes manifest.' The light that shines from the background is the colour of being alive and smiling amidst the valley of *Andhretta*. The form emerges from the evening time when the Sun is to set and also from the morning light when the rays of the Sun gently wake all up. The meditation allows the artist to understand nature and reciprocate through intense emotions the knowledge of time and space.

- *Jah jhilemilekaardesanta/ Theaanhadsabadbajanta//*

'Where the dazzling light is seen, there plays the celestial strain.' The tree represents the cosmos that unfolds the birds, animals, insects, and many organisms in the womb. The Universe unfolds. A *yogi* in *Samadhi* as if he merges well with the vast mountain and the tree at the back. The roots of the tree have been dissected and shown in such a way that in its intrinsic range we are to unearth fish, birds, reptiles, and sea organisms. The depiction is of the dazzling light in the cosmos.

- *Panchshabaddhunkaardhune the baajeshabadneesaan/ Deep loahparhtaalteha khanda mandalhairaan//*

'The Lord is manifest in the 10th gate, where the celestial strain resounds, to the accomplishment of the sound of the Five musical instruments. Struck with wonder one sees all, the islands, Universe, under waters, continents and spheres there.' Each human being is an integral part of nature being made by integrating the five elements of nature -the Earth, Fire, Ether, Water and the Sky which reciprocate to the five senses in our body, the sense of touch on skin, taste on the tongue, sound in the ear, smell with the nose and sight of the eyes, asif a prism taking the white light and producing the vibrant rainbow. The five sides of the prism and their association to each organ of the body are thus depicted through the colours.The light that emerges forth enlightens everything in its wake and depicts the flower that though passes through many rough phases in life to wither but ultimately gives place to a ripe, sweet fruit.

- *Sabherutechangeeyan/ Jitesachaeseounehou//*

'All the seasons for which love for God, The true Lord is embraced are good. How benevolent would God be, come spring!' A social message for the coming generations to leave aside all tensions, failures and worries and to spread wings wide having firm roots planted in good soil with His Blessings. The stones are the hurdles, experienced in life but rendered powerless.

In Conclusion, *Andhretta* could be any place on the surface of the Earth. It is just that the author, like so many others such as her and the three esteemed artists of our times; found an inspiration to reflect upon Nature in the spectacular and ephemeral vistas of the majestic *Dhauladhars* and the quietude they offer; so conducive to the communion of the mind to Nature and to the creation of Art. Finding thus an in-woven linkage to Nature, natural elements and Art – especially that of the musical composer and lyricist– has been enshrined in the teachings of the *Gurus*, the *Adi Granth* of the Sikhs. The Earth and Sky,especially here are providers of space, energy and enthusiasm. The involvement of the artist, the subject matter and deep understanding are the prerequisites in the process of creation. The intersection of the *Guru Granth Sahib* and the teachings are for the betterment of the human being. The teachings relate to all the Universal brotherhood and kindness. It unfolds in a simple manner what is His will and what needs to be done while being born as a human. Life is temporary. By being close to the environment and Nature, just like an artist, we all are elevated, become creative,develop an abundant mindset and a harmonious ecological balance is attained thereby.

Bibliography

1. Daniel J. Bronstein*; Approaches to the philosophy of Religion;* Basic Problems of Philosophy; 1964.

2. Paul W. Pryser; *A dynamic psychology of Religion*; Sigmund Freud's analysis of mild narcosis.Harper and Row; New York; 1968.

3. Ambalicka Sood Jacob; *Musical Modes in Visual Forms- A Journey through the Creative Minds*; New Bhartiya Book Corporation, Delhi. 2012.

4. Dr. Gopal Singh; *Shri Guru Granth Sahib De SahitakVisheshta* Library Religious studies, Punjabi University, Patiala.1990.

5. American Bible Society; *The Holy Bible*; International Council of Religious Education. 1929.

Chapter 7

An Ecology of the Yogatantra and Alex Wayman

Prof. S.K. Pathak*

The Third *Dharmachakra-pravartana*

Attention may be invited to an important contribution of Alex Wayman, a doctorate of Columbia University, who endeavored to study –*Yoga* in the *Guhya samaja-tantra*: The Aracane Lore of Forty Verses. The *Guhyasamaja-tantra* GST is otherwise called as Tathagataguhyaka-sutra as that deals with the secret core of the effulgence of the phenomenal cosmic universe understandable by deep meditation *Yogatantra*. The text was published by Mm. H. P. Sastri from Baroda and reprinted by Mithila Institute. Its commentary of Chandrakirti named *Satkotivyakhya -tika* edited by my teacher Chintaharan Chakravorty was published by K.P. Jaysawal Research Institute, Patna, 1976.

A learner of *Yogatantra*,[1] whether of Buddhist *Tantra* or that of non-Buddhist *Tantra* becomes aware of means—*upaya* in balancing psycho-soma of the individual for cohesion with the universe. Ecology is not mere bio-environ balance of the animate origination and decay, 'Ecology of *Yogatantra*' may refer to

* Author is a renowned Professor having specialization in Indo-Tibetan and Sino-Indian Buddhist Studies, retired from Vishva Bharati, Shantiniketan (WB).

the positive measures of pacifying the psycho wavering of the functional mind for adjustment in balance with the vibrations of the phenomenal universe.

Alex Wayman and F:D Lessing translated Tibetan indigenous work *Rgyud sdevspyi'I rnam par gzhag pa rgyas par brjod* ascribed to Mkhas grub rje (cent. 17 A.D.) into English (1978) with its English naming *Introduction to the Buddhist Tantric Systems* (IBTS) in which three instances of the *Dharmacakrapravartana* by *Sakhyamuni* are referred.[2] Here, the third one is important in the context of the *Yogatantra* in the Buddist thought. An apparent contradiction occasionally rises when *the Lankaavatara-sutra* mentions that Buddha did not utter a word after his attainment of Bodhi till his demise *Parinirvana*.[3]

In fact, *Yogatantra* itself is appositioned there. The Buddha *Sakyamuni* did not use any meta-symbol in passing a dictum through letters, words by his vocal organs. He was in deep concentration- *samadhi* of the pure homely status of the universal mind: That assembly had been effulgent as multi-coloured rays came out of the phenomenal potentials of the universe. The Tibetan learned practitioner author Mkhas grub rie describes the last Wheel of *Dharma* with reference to the *Sandhinirmocana sutra*. The sutra holds the characteristics of the 'absolute certainty' *about the Truth don dam rnam par nges pa'i chos kyi khor lo*. The ITBS reads: The last promulgation, the Wheel of the Law which had a perfect and intensive analysis, was pronounced in such a place at *Vaishali* to the innumerable Bodhisattvas rightly stationed in any of the vehicles of candidates for the high goal (1978-47).

Yoga Tantra

In general, Yogatantra is the third course in practice and it varies in practice since its methods are pluralistic. In spite of the common object of the Tantra to extend human internal capacity with the external universe for rendering welfare of the movable or immovable beings, the Buddhists describe *tantra* as what unifies *prabandha*.[4] Accordingly, it holds three characters.

1. Causal unification of phenomena internal, external or both *hetu-tantra.*
2. Unification in their fruition to achieve the goal *phala-tantra.*
3. Unification of methodical cohesion by means to unify the internal with the external aspects of phenomena thoroughly upaya-tantra.

The commentary of the GST and that of the *Mahamaya-tantra* elaborate the characters of the Buddhist *Tantra.* The phenomenal causation and its effectuation are in the order of generation, whereas, the methodical cohesion for going in the process of unification becomes the order of the completion. In other words, a is inseparable from b, and b is inseparable from a, as the conventional reality of causation. Again, b is the conventional reality in effectuation, while ab the cause and the effect enter in the order of completion being inseparable one from another. That is, the inexplicable overall reality *sunyata* and the expiable reality in conventional manifestation *karuna-* compassion being functional *upaya,* enter in unification by psycho-ecological course of deep meditation *samadhi-yoga* and infinitum.

Ecology of Yoga Tantra

Candrakirti (c. 7th cent. A.D.) an exponent of *Nagaruna's Prajna* endeavored to trace the ecology of the *Yoga Tantra.* He composed forty verses to explain the underlying significance or arcanum of inseparable unification of *sunyata* and *karuna* i.e. *prajnopayayoga.* Alex Wayman in his analysis of the said *prajnopaya-yoga* concentrated on those forty verses of the *Satkoti vyakhya pradipadyotana* commentary ascribed to Candrakirti referred already.

Alex Wayman with his erudition in Sanskrit ventured to study Buddhism and Hinduism for the last five decades. He was attached to Columbia University (1967) as a Professor in Sanskrit and became Professor Emeritus (July 1997). He had an honorary degree from Nalanda University for academic contributions. His research in Indology may be classified in three categories (i) Hindu-Buddhist Studies, (ii) Buddhist Studies General, and (iii) Buddhist Tantric Studies (Appendix-A). He was a well-known leading scholar in Buddhism of the twentieth century. Particular mention may be made about his *Yoga* in the *Guhya-samaja-tantra* with a critical observation on the forty verses of *Candrakriti* translated into English with annotations from the Indo-Tibetan materials.

In the ecological observation of the *Yoga Tantra* the GHT is the *mula-tantra,* root *tantra* for the application. In respect to a practitioner it initiates with *Kriya-tantra*. Threefold distributions of the Buddhist tantra are given above. The *Tantra* texts preserved in Tibetan version of the *Kanjur* (*bhka'gyur*) had been arranged by Bu ston Rin chen grub (cent.13A.D.) in four successive orders *Anuttara-yog-tantra*, Yoga-Tantra,*Carya-tantra* and *kriya-tantra*.

The arrangement of the *Tantra rgyud'bum* by Bu ston begins with the seka initiation method. The initiation method is applicable in respect to each course of Tantra practice, namely *Kriya*, *Carya*, *Yog* and *Anittara yoga*, for becoming 'capable' *samartha*. In each course separate initiation is required. In respect to *Tantra* spiritually each initiation *seka* is a gateway for entrance in the Tantric psycho –spiritual eco. 'Eco' literally means home or abode. A *Tantra* practitioner becomes conversant in each course like *kriya*, *carya* etc. and avails spiritual bliss *ananda* towards the advancement of being awakened in this life. The Buddhist *Tantra*, therefore, leads to experience the psycho-spiritual homeliness of becoming the Buddha. In this regard the third course of *tantra* on meditation i.e. *yoga-tantra* is related to the deep concentration of the fickle mind *samyak amadhi*, as the first *Dharmacakrapravartana* referred.

The Noble Eightfold Path may be distributed in three courses in practices

i. *Sila*, Observance of moral precepts
   proper words *samyak vak*
   proper action *samyak karmanta*
   proper livelihood *samyak ajiva*.

ii. *Samdhi*, observance meditation is for the concentration of the functional mind, otherwise named *citta*. Proper exertion for concentration of the mind *samyak vyayama* proper mindfulness *samyak smrti* lead to the experience of proper equilibrium status by meditation *samyak samadhi*.

iii. *Prajna*, Intuitive Awareness in the deep mind, proper determination *Samyak samkalpa* and proper view *samyak dristi*.

The ecology of the *Tantric* spirituality is not divorced from the ethical purity. The symbol of *mandala* is one of the five Ms as practised by a *Vajracarya* exponent engaged in *Vajra* practice.[6] Vajra has several significance in the Buddhist *Tantra* to observe an adamantine vow for availing the objective. Five Ms in the Buddhist *Tantra* are *Mantra* meta – symbols to mutter, *mandala*, the psycho-ecosphere, *mudra* physical symbol that manifests in form, *murti* image effulgent in vision and *mahamudra* the great psycho-symbol to avail for unification. From the initiation a practitioner is to go through the status of joy and harmony. *Mantra, murti, mudra* and *mandala* lead to the equipoise of the wavering mind becoming *mahamudra* a seat of joy[7]. Candrakirti elaborates the symbol as Alex Wayman dealt in his Female energy and symbolism in the Buddhist *Tantra* (History of Religion, Vol II No. 1962). The infinite space *ambara* becomes the abode in which the excellent one always avails joy in the state of great bliss *mahasukha* in the equipoise of psychic equilibrium.

gehastasyambaram caiva yatra suncarate pravhunk /
Tatraiva ramate nityam mahasukha samadhina //

Alex Wayman contributed learned papers on the *mandala* of *Yoga Tantra.* Also Benoytosh Bhattacarya edited *Nispanna-yogavali* with twenty six *mandala*(s).[8] Multiplicity in enumeration *mandala* is significant in the *Tantra* with reference to multiple rays effulgent in the space. The GST refers to five *Tathagatas* with their respective *vajrayosit* the symbols in five manifestations out of multiple phenomena, sarvadharmanam sunyata. Those are radiant in the sphere of the light in infinite universe: Five Tathagatas are named:

Aksobhya: The unagitated space (sky) having vajra-bodhi of all *tathagatas* in spite of multiple oscillations.

Amitabha: of immeasurable effulgent radiance out of fire.

Vairvcana: Holding glittering radiance all around.

Ratnasambhava: Jewel like glow out of the light of knowledge.

Amoghasiddhi: Bright with the self-nature of *anahata* vibration.[9]

The GST identifies them with five aggregates. In the course of *Yoga Tantra* practice those are purified with fivefold *abhisambodhi.* That refers to the transmission from the conventional reality *samvrti satya* towards perfection. In respect of five *abhisambodhi* Alex Wayman and F.D. Lessing elaborately annotated while rendering Mkhas grub rje's work (ITBS).

The ecology of spiritual harmony, emphasized in the mental equilibrium and meditative concentration extends in spontaneity of radiance. The general tendency of allurement leading to ignorance *avidya* prompts *samsara vasana* with repeated birth and death. Moreover, ignorance *avidya* is the cause of being originated in three spheres of existence i.e. the sphere of desire, of forms and that of no-form *kamavacara, rupavacara, arupavacara,* respectively.

The GST *Yogatantra* text endeavours to lead a practitioner towards purification by five types of internal contemplations e.g. mirror—like ideation the ideation of equality, the ideation of discrimination, the ideation of duty bound procedure and lastly that of the *Dharmadhatu-nana* the potential knowledge of the *dharma* covering both essenceless *sunyata* – with phenomenal functioning *karuna*. That becomes *prajnyopaya-yoga.*[10]

The psycho – spiritual eco-harmony reaches by the *vajracarya* to experience the equity in the external and internal phenomena around. In the order of completion the practitioner may experience a harmonious unity in the midst of plurality through the spiritual sense-organs of vigor *viryendriya*, that of faith *sraddhendriya* etc. A practitioner experiences the spiritual bliss and submits the offering to the *Tathagata* for complacent harmony as *Candrakirti* states:

tattadindriya-margena visayam prapya sadhakah /
tathagatebhya saklam pritanaya nivedayed //

By the door of sense—organs a practitioner acquires objective knowledge that should be submitted as all offerings to the *Tathagatas* to cherish.

Alex Wayman summed them up in three columns in respect to five Tathagatas referred to in the GST.

Tathagata	Knowledge	Initiation
Aksobhya	Mirror like	Flask-Water
Ratnasambhava	Equality	Diadem
Amitabha	Discriminative	Diamond
Amogha – siddhi	Procedure of duty	Bell
Vairocana	*Dharma* realm	Name

In Indian *Yoga* traditions for balance of the human psycho-ecology with the external phenomena many sequences in procedure for cultivation of the human mind may be traced-such as

Yoga: sequence of two, In Buddhism a tendency of synthetic *Yoga* practice is observed and that may be decided in separate sequences.

1. *Sanimitta-Yoga*: Unification with motive or reason.
2. *Aniitta-Yoga*: Unification with no motive.

Yoga: Sequence of four.

1. *Yoga*: mental enterprise for unification of a part with whole (here the individual and the universe).
2. *Anu-yoga*: the follow up enterprise to be unified.
3. *Ati –yoga*: a super charge towards unification
4. Mahayoga: extensive experience in union corresponding to *sayuiyata*.

Yoga : Sequence of six.

In addition to the above four.

5. *Guhyayoga*: inexplicit interior unification.
6. *Sarvayoga*: total unification, wholesome oneness.

Procedures of Yoga:

	Six limbed: *Sadanga Yoga*	Eight limbed: *Astanga yoga*
1.	*Pratyahara* retreat	*yama-vrata* obligatory vows
2.	*dhyana* abstract Contemplation	*Niyama* disciplinary vows.
3.	*Pranayama* breath Suspension with mindfulness.	*asana* meditation postures.
4.	*dharana* breath Steadily with the objective.	*pranayama*
5.	anusmriti remembrance	*Pratyahara*
6.	*Samadhi*	*dharana*
7.		*dhyana*
8.		*samadhi*

In the *astangayoga* the unification of the individual soul with the Supreme soul is *yoga*. While in *Sadanayoga, shunyata* essencelessness of the object of meditation equates with the individual, that holds no substance or soul to discriminate.

Notes and References

1. *Vimala Prabha* commentary of *Kalacakratanta* defines *yogatantra* as the union of the wisdom with the means *prajnopayatmakam tantram yogatantram*. Here, the wisdom *prajna* is shunyat*a* and the means refers to the mental enterprise to hold the compassion karuna for all beings, sentient and insentient.

2.i. The first *Dharmacakrapravartana* (deliberation of the Wheel of *Dharma*, was held at Sarnath, Varanasi within about three months from the Buddha's Awakenment at *Bodhimanda*, near the *Niranjana* river (present day Bodhgaya) in presence of the five senior elders like *Mahakasyapa*.

ii. The second one was deliberated about thirteenth years after, the Awakenment in presence of the revered *Arhatas* and many celestial bodies on the Vulture's Peak *Grdhrakuta sikhara* near Rajgrha (present day Rajgir in Bihar).

iii. The Third deliberation on the Wheel of *Dharma* is said to be held at *Dhanyakataka* (identified with *Nagarjunakonda* near Amaravati) by the eighteenth year after his Awakenment in which *Bodhisattvas* and celestial bodies were present.

Mhas grub rje referred to a tradition what referred to Vaishali as the sacred seat of the Budha's third *Dharmacakrapravartana*.

3. Ed. B. Nanjio, Kyoto, 1934, Chap. II, 8-9.

4. Literally, the word *Tantra* suggests that which extends. It is derived from the Sanskrit verb – root tan which means to extend, to expand. A practitioner involved in doing such extension of his or her innate potential efficiency widely in multiple phenomenal spheres, particularly in three spheres accepted by the Buddhists here for keeping ecological balance of the animate and the inaminate worlds. The GST defines *tantra* as *prabandha* that binds and interacts thoroughly in the world as much as the practitioner efforts. Alex Wayman further examined three Vedic worlds in his paper published from *Adiyar Library Bulletin*, No 50. 1986 (Appendix A)

5. *A Catalogue of the Tibetan Tripitaka* (*Kanjur* and *Tanjur*) Tohoku University Collection, Kyoto, Japan, 1934, rgyerd section preserves the texts of the four *Tantra* in series.
6. Alex Wayman: *Buddhist Genesis* and *Tantra Traditions* Orient Expresses, 9.1.1962. *The Buddhist Tantras: Light on Indo-Tibetan Esoterism*, New York, 1973.
7. Alex Wayman: The significance of *Mantras*, from the *Vedas* down to Buddhist Tantric practice, *Adyar Libarary Bulletin*, XXXIX 1975, Buddhist Mandala in Palace Design *Ibid*, 1978.
8. Ascribed to Abhayakara Gupta (cent. 11-12 AD), edn. Gaekawad Oriental Series, LXI, XCI,CIX, 1932, 1947 respectively.
9. Alex Wayman: The *Tathagata* Chapter of Nagarjuna's *Mulamadhyamaka – Karika*1988 *Poets, Essayists and Writers* XXXVIII. Also *Yoga* in the *Guhya Samaja Tantra*, New Delhi, 1977.
10. Pathak, S. K. Ekayana Buddhayana, *Proc.* of *International Buddhist Conference*, Indosan Nipponji, Bodhgaya, 1982.
11. *Guhyasamaya-tantra-pradipodyatanatika Satkotivyakhya* ed. Cintaharan Chakravarti K. P. Jayaswal Research Institute, Patna, 1984, P. 15 lines 21-22. Alex Wayman in *The Arena Lore of Forty verses*, verse no. 21 explained.

Appendix –A

(*Important works of Alex Wayman*)

- Contributions regarding the thirty – two characteristic of Great Person, *Sino-Indian Studies*, Liebentbal Festscbrif, Visva Bharati, 1957.
- The Meaning of Unwisdom (*avidya*) *Poets Essayists & Writers* (*PEW*), 7:1-2, 1957.
- Studies in Yama and Mara, *Indo-Iranian Journal*, 3:1-2, 1959.

- The Twenty-one Praises of Tara, a Syncretism of Saivism and Buddhism, *Journal of the Bihar Research Society*, 45:1-4, 1959.
- The Sacittika and Acittika Bhumi and the Pratyekabuddhabhumi (Sanskrit Texts), *Journal of Indian and Buddhist Insight* (1984).
- Analysis of the Sravakabhumi Manuscript, University of California Publications in *Classical Philology*, Vol. 17, Berkeley, California, 1961.
- The Buddhist 'Not this, not this', *PEW*, 11:3, 1961.
- Buddhist Genesis and the Tantric Tradition, *Orient Extremus*, 9:1, 1962.
- Female Energy and Symbolism in Buddhist Tantra, History of Religion. Vol. 11, 1, 1962.
- The Yogacara Idealism, (A review article) *PEW*, 15:1, 1965.
- Climatic Times in Indian Mythology and Religion, History of Religious, 4:2, 1965.
- The Hindu-Buddhist Rite of Truth. An Interpretation, *Studies in Indian Linguistic*. Linguistic Society of India, Poona, 1968.
- Contributions to the Madhyamika School of Buddhism, (a review article) *Journal of American Oriental Studies* (JOAS), 89.1.1969.
- The Buddhist Theory of Vision, *Anjali: A Felicitation Volume* (Peradeniya;University of Ceylon, 1970): reprinted in Wayman, *Buddhist Insight* (1984).
- Buddhism, *Historia Religionum*, Vol. II, eds. E. Joneco and Geo Widengren Leiden: E. J. Brill, 1971).
- *The Buddhist Tantras: Light on Indo-Tibetan Esotericism* (Samuel Weiser New York, 1973.
- The Intermediate – State Dispute in *Buddhism, Buddhist Studies in Honor of I. B. Hornor, Ed.: L. Cousins, et. al.* (Dordrecht: D Reidel, 1974) : reprinted in Wayman, Buddhist Insight (1984).

- The Mirror as a Pan-Buddhist Metaphor – Simile, *History of Religions*, 13:4, 1974.
- Purification of Sin by Vision and Confession, *A Study of Klesa*, ed. G. H. Sasaki (Tokyo, 1975).
- The Significance of Mantras, from the Veda down to Buddhist Tantric Practice, *Adyar Library Bulletin*, XXXIX, 1975.
- Medition in Theravada and Mahisasaka. Studia Misionalia, Vol. 25, 1976.
- Secret of the Heart Sutra, Prajnaparamita and Related Systems. Ed. L. Lancaster (Berkeley: Berkeley Buddhist Series, 1977).
- *Yoga of the Guhyasamajatantra: The Arcane Lore of Forty Verses* (Delhi: Motilal Banarsidass, 1978).
- *Calming the Mind and Discerning the Real. From the Lam rim chen mo of Tsong-kha-pa* (New York: Columbia University Press, 1978); Indian edition, Delhi, 1979.
- Ancient Buddhist Monasticism, *Studia Missionalia,* Vol. 18, 1979.
- Yogacara and the Buddhist Logicians, *The Journal of the International Association of Buddhist Studies*, II: 1, 1979.
- The twenty Reifying Views (sakkayaditthi), *Studies in Pali and Buddhism,* ed. A. K. Narain (Delhi: B. R. Publishing Corpn. 1979); reprinted in Wayman, *Buddhist Insight* (1987).
- Buddha as a Savior, *Studia Missinnalia*, Vol. 29, 1980.
- Dependent Origination – the Indo – Tibetan Tradition, *Journal of Chinese Philosophy* 7, 1980: reprinted in Wayman, *Buddhist Insight* (1984).
- Nescience and Insight according to Asanga's Yogacarabhumi, Buddhist Studies in Honor of *Walpola Rahula* (London: Gordon Frazer, 1980); reprinted in Wayman, *Buddhist Insight* (1984).
- A report on the Aksayamatinirdesa-sutra, in *Studies in Indo-Asian Art and culture*, Vol. 6, ed. Lokesh Chandra (International Academy of Indian Culture, New Delhi, 1980).

- Some Accords with the Samkha Theory of Tanmatra, in *A corpus of Indian Studies* (Calcutta: Sanskrit Pustak Bhandar, 1980).
- The Samadhi lists of Aksayamatinirdesautra and the Mahavyupatti, *Acta Orientalia Academiae Scientiarum Hug,* XXXIV, 1:3, 1980.
- The Religious Meaning of Concrete Death in Buddhism, *Studia Missionalia*, Vol. 31, 1982
- A Study of the Vedantic and Buddhist Theory of Nama-Rupa, *In Indological and Buddhist Studies*, (Canberra: Faculty of Asian Studies, 1982).
- Eschatology in Buddhism, *Studia Missionalia*, Vol. 32, 1983.
- *Buddhist Insight*: Essays by Alex Eayman, Ed. George E. Elder (Delhi: Motital Banarsidass, 1984.
- The Interlineary – Type Commentary in Tibetan, *Tibetan and Buddhist Studies*, Ed. Lousi Ligeti, Vol. 2 (Budapest: Akademiai Kiado, 1984.
- The Metaphysics of Cooking in the Satyartha Prakash and in the Indian Tradition, *World Perspectives on Swami Dayanand Saraswati* by Ganga Ram Garg (New Delhi: Concept Publishing Company, 1984)
- Sakyamuni, Founder of Buddhism, *Studia Missionalia*, Vol. 33, 1984.
- *Chanting the Names of Manjusri,, translation of the Manjusrinama-Samgiti* (Boston: Shambala Publications, 1985).
- Nagarjuna: Moralist Reformer of Buddhism, *Studia Missionalia*, Vol. 34, 1985.
- The Gait (*gati*) and the Path (marga) – Reflections on the Horizontal, *JAOS*. 105:3, 1985.
- Some observations on dualistic mirror symbolism in Western Philosophy and in the Upanisads, *Aligarh Journal of Oriental Studies*, II, 1-2, (1985).

- The Vedic Three Worlds in Early and Later times, *Adyar Library Bullentin*, Vol. 50 (1986).
- The Guru in Buddhism, *Studia Missionalia*, Vol. 36, 1987.
- A Prajnaparamita Scripture within a Tantra, I *Sramana Vidya* (Sarnath, Varanasi, Central Institute of Higher Tibetan Studies, 1987.
- The Mathura Set of Asta-mangala (Eight Auspicious Symbols) in Early and Later times in *Mathura: The Cultural Heritage*, Ed. Doris Meth Srinivasan, et. al. (New Delhi American Institute of Indian Studies, 1988).
- The Tathagata Chapter of Nagarjuna's Mulla-madhyamaka-karika, *PEW*, XXXVIII:1, 1988.
- Vasubandhu – Teacher Extra-ordinary, *Studia Missionalia*, Vol. 37, 1988.
- Doctrinal Affiliation of the Buddhist Master Asanga, "*Amala-Prajna: Aspects of Buddhist Studies*, Ed N. H. Samtani and H.S. Prasad (Delhi, 1989).
- The negative-an prefix in Sanskrit, Ed. B.K. Mtilal and P. Bilimoria (Delhi, 1991).
- The position of Women in Buddhism, *Studia Missionalia*, Vol. 40, 1991.
- Wayman Alex and Wayman, Hideko, Trs. Srimaladevisin – handsutra: *The Lion's Roar of Queen Srimala: A Buddhist Scripture on the Tathagatagarbha Theory*, (New York: Columbia University Press, (1974); reprinted (Delhi, 1990). Wayman, Alex and Tajima, R, *The Enlightenment of Vairocana*, Book one: Study of the Vairocanabhisambodhi-tantre, by A Wayman; Book Two: *Study* of the Mahavairoana-sutra by R. Tajima (Delhi, Motilal Banarasidas, 1992). Wayman Alex Wayman Alex

Chapter 8

ENVIRONMENTAL CRISIS VIEWING FROM THE BUDDHIST PERSPECTIVE

Manjula Vibhasini Vithanapathirana

Introduction

The Buddha is perhaps, one of the earliest 'humanistic religious teachers 'to appear in the world. This humanistic concern of his is very clearly seen from a number of his early discourses (suttas). He purposely highlighted the transient condition that prevails in this world of human existence. He explained that this condition operates in a cycle process which does not have a clearly foreseeable beginning. The Buddha explains this in detail in a section of the *SamyuttaNikāya* (SN), elaborating the ever-recurring process of births and deaths the human beings are made to undergo in this cyclic process of their existence. It is this state of worldly existence that the Buddha referred to 'samsāra'.

Based on this understanding the Buddha concluded that this world of human or their samsāric existence is established in a state of constant turmoil, conflict which is an immensely undesirable and unsatisfactory state. He used this particular Pali language technical term '*dukkha*' to connote this undesirable state. This word '*dukkha*' is generally rendered into English as 'suffering'.

This rendering however, does not quite exactly bring out the deep and varying numerous connotations by the Pali term ‘dukkha’. However, it should be borne in mind that ‘dukkha’ should not be taken to connote a pessimistic idea. It is better to consider as connoting ‘realistic’ nature of this cyclic existence.

It is this realistic understanding of the true nature of human existence that made the Buddha direct his main concern to explain what ‘dukkha’ means, how it arises, how it should be faced, handled and managed and also finally how it could be overcome and reach a state of mental appeasement, putting an end to this miserable and dampening mental state. This supreme state of mental peace and bliss is referred to in Buddhism as Nibbāna / Nirvana connoting the ‘summumbonum’ the Buddhist practice attainable by following the Noble Eightfold path.

Occurrence of Environmental Problem in Samsaric Life

All sober, sane and sensitive people of the world will totally endorse the Buddha’s observation of samsara given above. This is because the emotion of suffering (dukkha) makes its presence felt in varying shapes, modes and intensities making all affected as also concerned about the looming threats that lay hidden in day to day affairs of life.

Besides recurrent and devastating wars, constant insurrections, terrorist uprisings, youth unrest, develop very often into nerve-wrecking proportions that is quite monstrous in nature. It is on top of such dreadful threats, at present takes place very often, very unexpectedly environmental crisis that completely and ruthlessly shatters people, destroys their lives, their properties and everything they hold near and dear.

Such environmental crisis includes unexpected torrential down pours, floods, earth slips, earth quakes, tsunamis etc. resulting also in the rapid rising of sea levels that consequently swallows up vast coastal regions ruthlessly robbing and sucking the lives and property of the people. Countries lying below sea-level very often have to live on pins at times of extreme weather. They lead, tend to forget the miseries they suffer due to natural calamities and over and over again succumb to the same fate. They hardly make any serious effort to gear themselves to take the best precautionary steps to protect themselves.

Urgent Need of Remedial Measures

For the remedial measures, at least to minimize the dreadful effects of the calamities, people are not committed and united in using the knowledge they have derived through the advancement of science and technology, instead they engage in holding endless meetings, seminars etc. postponing the imminent need of making more concerted practical solution. Even the recently held summit in Indonesia well demonstrate this squabble that prevails over environmental issues between developed countries and developing countries. These squabbles are more about safeguarding personal interests than about finding solutions to the problems as a whole.

Aren't There Any Remedies?

It is this point that I feel, that we are not helpless and totally lost. What comes to the aid of humankind is the benign advice and teachings we have been fortunate to inherit. The humankind has been blessed with a host of humanistic religious teachers and being a Buddhist, the relevant teachings of the Buddha come to my mind and my view as the most assured medium of intervention.

Effective Applicability of Buddhist Proposals

The distorted vision is the major cause that leads to the escalation of numerous environmental problems. The preliminary remedial measure that should be taken is to straighten the views. Religions in different ways attempt to correct the vision of the people and try to make them see in a correct perspective of the nature of their life and the world in which they live in. Religions attempt to inculcate in their followers a world-view to make them incline to follow certain norms that are conducive to personal and collective well-being for peace, harmony and happiness. All religions: theistic, non-theistic, monistic, pluralistic, aim at bringing about the well-being and happiness of the followers. In this regard Buddhism plays a very important role, specially concerning the environmental problems. It is seen that a basic premise accepted by Buddhism is that the environment has a great impact on man. Hence, in the MahāmangalaSutta of the Suttanipāta (stanza no.260) there is a clear assertion of the importance of the environment in which one lives. Based on its central teaching of Dependent Origination (paiccasamuppāda) Buddhism upholds that environment and man are inter-related and interdependent. Therefore, they mutually impact upon each other. The man and environment are, hence, products of dependent origination (paiccasamuppanna).

This interdependent nature of man and environment is very well explained in the AggaññaSutta, the sutta no. 27 of the Dīghanikāya,(DN) 'A collection of Long Discourses' of Tipitaka. It describes how the environment influences man's physical appearance and how man's responses to the environment brought about changes in the environment. The relation between man and environment is so close that scholars have rightly observed that the current crisis is not a crisis of the environment, rather a symptom of a deeper human crisis that raises fundamental questions about the values we uphold and the kind of lives we lead, basic issues of ethics, religion and philosophy.

The observation is quite noteworthy, for it brings out the fact that it is man's undue intervention that has created the present environmental crisis. If the present environmental crisis is mirroring a psychological crisis in man, then a religion like Buddhism has the power of intervening and controlling this crisis. This is because, perhaps, of all religions, Buddhism is the most psychological one. Hence, it is noteworthy to pay heed to Professor O. H. de A Wijesekera's observation.

"It is no exaggeration to claim that of all the religions it is Buddhism that gives the greatest importance to mind in its scheme of deliverance. That is to say, Buddhism is the most psychological of religions. Even ethics and logic in Buddhism are studied from the psychological standpoint. This remains a fundamental characteristic of Buddhism throughout all stages of its historical development."

As Buddhism upholds that all man's deeds are preceded by the mind guiding and regulating all affairs of life, placing it in the right path is the ultimate cure to all our environmental problems. This cure is undoubtedly very effective and hence, the Buddha attempted to induce all to commit themselves totally to follow the spiritual path he put forward, wherein mind-culture plays a very prominent role. The Buddha's initial call was for many to enter the path and follow it 'full time'. However, this happened to be too much an idealistic approach for solving man's predicament. It is seen that soon the Buddha offered, on the constant urging of the masses themselves to phase out this commitment, laid more stress on the culture of virtues, especially when the path is followed by the laity.

Buddha's Simple Advice Regarding Care and Conservation of Environment

In this mode of practice of the path, Buddhism was able to address many issues that immediately impacted the day to day life of the people, and among them the protection as well as the conservation of the environment is one major aspect. This, however, does not mean that the protection and conservation of the environment were not included in the life of clergy. In fact, as the Buddha himself and also his disciples lived close to nature, caring and protecting nature, it was given serious consideration. The Theravada TipitakaVinaya contains specific rules in this regard. The Bhikkhunivibhanga also contains many such rules. Thus, it is said that water should not be spoiled by defecating, urinating or even spitting into water. Similarly, in Vattakandhakāya in the CullavaggaPāli it is clearly laid down how to preserve the cleanliness of the water. Therein is given a rule prohibiting the setting-up of residences near places where there is water for drinking and general use. This measure was adapted to prevent the spoiling of water. The Buddha willingly acceded to the request made to follow the observance of Vassa, the three-month annual Retreat observed by Theravada practitioners. Taking place during the rainy season, Vassa lasts for three lunar months.

The VinayaMahāvagga in VinayaPitaka (Basket of the Discipline) (VinayaPitaka PTS. P.137) says: that monks should refrain from walking about during the rainy season damaging the growth of fresh greenery. This was to protect the new vegetation that crop-up with the fall of rain. The Buddha prescribed the observance of vassa to help the growth of the new greenery. This shows not only the concern of the Indian masses about the protection of the environment, but also the Buddha's sensitivity to such environmental issues. The significance attached to such issues is further seen when one notes the precept which regulates the practice of loitering about in this period, encourages abstinence from destroying all kinds of plant life and vegetation (see SāmmaññaphalaSutta of the DhganikayaSutta No. 02). The two terms Bijagāma and Bhutagāma are used to refer to all plant life.

There are many other precepts and rules meant to be observed by the bhikkhus for the purpose of protecting and conserving the environment. Further, it is seen that the Buddha urged and encouraged monks to lead lives close to nature, in forests, under trees and in caves. The Thera-thergathā (stanzas no. 601-602) bears evidence to the deep appreciation of natural beauty displayed by enlightened members of the sangha. The poems of serene joy uttered by SankiccaThera is a case in point:

> *"Crags where clear water lies, a rocky world,*
> *Haunted by black-faced apes and timid deer,*
> *Where cloaked in watery moss the rocks stand,*
> *Those are highlands of my hearts delight,*
> *I've dwelt in forests and in mountain caves*
> *In rocky gorges and haunts remote*
> *And where the creatures of the wild do roam"*

Songs of appreciation uttered by Tālaputo, Vañgisa and host of other enlightened elders are eloquent evidence to show how closely and happily the Buddhist clergy lived close to nature enjoying its beauty and its cooling serenity.

Such a way of living was imbibed into them through Buddhism. It not only made use of nature to refine the nature of humans, but also did inculcate in its followers feeling and care for nature, promoting and making them harmonize with nature, enriching both their own lives and the life of nature itself. It is the Buddha himself that set the example to the rest. The AriyapariyesanaSutta describes the attention be paid to the environment when he describes how he selected the spot for his final striving. This is said to be recorded in his own words. It reads in English as follows:

> "Still in search, bhikkuhus, of what is wholesome seeking the supreme state of sublime peace, wandered by stages through the Magadhan country until eventually I arrived at Senānigama near Uruwela. There are I saw and agreeable piece of ground, a delightful grove with a clear-flowing river with pleasing smooth banks and nearby village for alms resort"M.I, 167; Middle Length Sayings, P. 259)

New Ethic for Environment Care, Protection and Conservation

Through profound understanding and also deep personal experience the Buddha, whenever he found the occasion, did his best to inculcate in listeners an environmentally friendly attitude. Through his discourses he constantly kindled the awareness in his listeners regarding their responsibility to protect and conserve nature. To do this efficiently he linked the protection and conservation of the environment with ethics. In fact, he developed a new ethic for environmental protection and conservation. The VanaropāSutta of the Samyuttanikaya (S.I, 33) is a good example for this. In this sutta Buddha says:

"For whom does merit always increase
Both by day and by night?
Who are the people going to heaven?
Established in the Dhamma, endowed with virtue?"
"Those who set up a park or a grove
The people who construct a bridge
A place to drink and a well
Those who give a residence"
"For them merit always increases,
Both by day and by night
Those are the people going to heaven

Established in Dhamma, endowed with virtue"(Bhikkhu Bodhi, The Connected Discourse of the Buddha, pp 122-123)

The linkage brought about by the Buddha between virtuous living and protection of the environment culminating in social service did contribute much to induce people to be quite concerned about the environment. Besides, this Buddha linked folk beliefs also to imbibe in his followers respect for the environment. Thus, he adapted the folk belief which held that trees and mountains etc. serve as residences for a class of deities. This made people become cautious when deciding to cut down trees and even cause deforestation. In this manner trees, mountains and even rivers were considered as sacred shrines, thus encouraging people not merely to protect them, but even to conserve them.

Trees and groves have been closely linked with the life of monks, especially with the Buddha. He attained enlightenment under the 'asvattha' tree, which later came to be called as the Bodhi tree. The VinayaMahāvagga (Vin. I, 1) says that the Buddha spent his first week under the bodhi tree, enjoying the bliss of freedom (vimuttisukhampatisanvedi). In the Jatakanidāna (J.I, 77) the belief develops that the Buddha cast unblinking gaze one whole week at the bodhi-tree. This led to a belief that trees should be considered with gratitude, for they are of much use to beings. Thus, the Petavatthu says that it amounts to betrayal of friendship, if one were to cut even a branch of a tree that has provided shade to him.

Rukkhapañha of the Milindapañha elaborately explains how useful the trees are for people. It says that trees offer fruits and decorate the environment with flowers; flowers help us to understand the evanescent nature of life. "pupphammilāyathiyathāidam me kāyotathāyāthivināsabhāvam" just as the flower withers away, similarly body too gets destroyed; trees provide shade without making any discrimination to friends and foes, thus truly teaching the value of friendliness.

Buddhism induced people to protect and conserve the environment, making it a part of their virtuous living. Virtue or sila is the foundation of the whole Buddhist practice consisting of the threefold training (tisiksha) of sila (virtue) samādhi (mental culture) and paññā (development of wisdom). Sila cannot be observed if one fails to protect the environment and also conserves it for the benefit of others. To observe sila is to conduct oneself well, and the Buddhist teaching is that those who conduct themselves well will attain heaven. The Vanaropa Sutta already cited also endorses this view. Protecting and conserving nature can even lead one to attain the state of the king of gods, the Sakka. This belief is recorded in the KulāvakaJataka (Jataka No. 31).

Advice to Political Leadership

Buddhism did not stop at making protection and conservation limited to day to day ethical living of the people. Buddha tried to incorporate it as an important feature in the political philosophy, making it essential for exemplary good governance. Thus, in the KūtadantaSutta (Dighanikāya, I, 141) he said that mass scale religious sacrifices which were a common feature of the government policy at that time should be conducted in a way that would not be harmful to either flora and fauna. Thus, this sutta explains why the King should give up the destructive ostentatious religious rituals necessitating cutting of large numbers of trees and killing of large numbers of cattle, goats etc. Buddhism clearly saw how counter-productive such bloody and destructive religious rituals were for the progress of the society. Hence, he admonished the rulers to perform religious rituals where no bulls to be slain; no goats, no sheep, no cocks and pigs or other animals would be slaughtered; no trees to cut down for sacrificial posits, no grass to be mown for sacrificial purposes, no forced labor to be used to perform various tasks (D.I.141 ff).

In fact the Buddha included this as an essential item in good governance. CakkavattishanādaSutta (D. III, 61 f) lays down as the first norm - a Universal monarch (rājācakkavatti) should invariably comply with this norm, says that such a ruler depending this Dhamma, honoring it, reversing it, cherishing it, paying homage to it and venerating it, having the Dhamma as the badge, the banner, the master, should establish guard, ward and protection for his own household, troops, nobles, vassals, brahmins and householders, town and country folk, ascetic and brahmins as also beasts and birds.

The mention of beasts and birds on par with humans shows the importance attached to protection and conservation of nature, of all flora and fauna. From pre-Buddhist times itself, establishment of sanctuaries (of MigadayaKalandakanivāpa) was a part of Indian green-policy. Emperor Asoka attempted to put into practice these norms and went even to the extent of establishing hospitals for animals, perhaps for the first time in the history of mankind. This was followed by the well-known Sri Lankan King Buddhdasa (340 AC-368 AC).

The AdhamikkaSutta of the Anguttaranikāya (A. II 74 pp), the sad plight of the subjects when rulers are not paying heed to protection and conservation of nature- explains how consequently the whole country gets engulfed in all sorts of disasters and calamities. Seeing the importance of rulers' adherence to righteousness, it says that when they are prone to immorality (ya sminsamayerājānoadhammikohonti), then corruption seeps down the officialdom and compel the readiness of ordinary people resorting all kinds of corruption and exploitative practices. Callous disregard of nature, selfish exploitation of it is a part of these corrupt practices, This unrighteous practice (adhammacariyā), improper conduct (visamcariyā) on the part of the persons in authority affect even the natural forces, the courses of the sun and the moon. From this also it is clear that such corrupt practices have exploitation of nature as its cause, for such acts affect the normal functioning of natural forces like the appearance of the sun and the moon.

This is further proved when one examines the other ill-effects that arise from this. When the orderly movements of the sun and the moon are interrupted, the whole seasonal patterns get affected, with rain not falling at the proper time and sunshine failing to appear when needed. This affects agricultural productivity. Food will not only be scarce and decrease in quantity, but also will be of low quality as it is not being properly nurtured by maturing and ripening. Consumption of such low-quality food will naturally affect the health condition of the people. The text Anguttaranikāya says that those who sustain on such low quality food will be of short life span, bad complexion, weak and much afflicted with diseases (appāyukācahontidubbannācadubbalācabevahātādhaka). For a translation see Bhikkhu Bodhi's "The Numerical Discourses of the Buddha, p.4.5 f)

This is a very strong positive reminder to the political leadership regarding how their ethical living will have repercussions in the country and the subjects and also how political leadership has a great responsibility in the protection and conservation of nature and environment. The oft-chanted prayer which reads:

"Devovassatukālena
Sassasampattihetuca
phitobhavithulokoca
rājābhavatudhammiko"

This contains the wish: "May the clouds (gods) rain in time, may the harvest be bountiful, may people be prosperous and the ruler be righteous. The suggestion is that for all other conditions to get fulfilled, the rulers have to be righteous. The rulers have to set an example. This further is said: Anguttaranikaya (loccit) says that when cattle are crossing a farm, if the chief bull goes crookedly all others go crookedly, because their leader has gone crookedly. The pali stanza is as follows:

Gunnamcetaramānānamjimhamgacchatipungavo
Anbbetejimhamgacchantinettijimhagati sati
Gunnamcetaramānānamujumgacchatipungavo
Anbbeteujugacchantinetteujugati sati

Conclusion

From the foregoing discussion what becomes clear is that Buddhism is greatly concerned about ecology, its influence on the wellbeing and happiness of people and the country; Buddhism considers environmental crisis as a part and parcel of man's predicament, his dukkha. This dukkha is not a condition imposed by some other power, whatever it may be, but it is one's own creation, the result of man's imbalanced, unrefined unrighteous conduct (visamacariyā/ adhammacariyā). This way it relates this to ethics or sila, virtuous way of living.

To lead the followers to the virtuous way of life,the Buddha in his numerous discourses presented admonitions, including inducements. He himself set the example for others to follow a life that could be led in harmony with nature and the natural environment. The Buddha very emphatically pointed out the responsibility of the political authorities in appearing to solve such grave problem.

He pointed out both the psychological and material causes that propel man to unethical living, forcing him to resort to unscrupulous means of exploiting nature and natural resources. In very graphic accounts he highlighted the correlation between decline of basic human ethics and environmental crisis. His immediate remedy for this environmental crisis was to establish the man in virtue (sila), to lead life according to the ethical teaching on a firm ethical base which would make him abstain from destroying the environment and natural resources for quick but temporary gain. To further strengthen this ethical foundation the Buddha warned the followers about the dreadful pitfalls, found in the way of ostentatious living.

His message to all is to live in harmony with nature, enjoying its bountiful generosity. In the same vein he warns one and all of the dreadful consequences that would follow the exploitation of nature.

All primary references if not mentioned otherwise are to texts published by the Pali Text Society, London.

References

- Bodhi, Bhikkhu, *2017. The Suttanipata: An Ancient Collection of the Buddha›s Discourses and Its Canonical Commentaries.* Wisdom Publications.
- Rhys Davids, T. W., and J. Estlin Carpenter. The DighaNikaya Vol III, Pali Text Society
- De Silva, Padmasiri, 2002.Buddhism Ethics and Society: The Conflicts and Dilemmas of Our Times, Monash University Press.
- Wijesekera, O. H. De A, 1994. Buddhist Vedic Studies: A miscellany, Delhi, Motilal Banarsidass.

Chapter 9

Jain Religious Practice and Ecology*

Christopher Key Chapple

Introduction

The Jain premise that individual life forms pervade the earth down to the elemental level, paired with the requirement that all harm to life be minimized, predisposes Jainism to a friendliness toward life that lends to what in modern times is referred to as environmental ethics. Because all environments are suffused with life and because life must be honored, Jainism implicitly affirms the basic ideas of ecological ethics and although a bit more complex, of bioethics. Actions taken by Jain persons, in order to recognize and abide by the teachings of *ahimsā*, must take into consideration the desire on the part of any life form to flourish. This sentiment is expressed in the oldest surviving Jain text as follows:

> All breathing, existing, living, sentient beings should not be slain, nor treated with violence, nor abused, nor tormented, nor driven away. This is the pure, unchangeable, eternal law (Jacobi, 1968, 36).

---

* Adapted from the website of the Forum on Religion and Ecology: https://fore.yale.edu/World-Religions/Jainism/Overview-Essay

Harm to any life form causes the karma that obstructs one's energy and consciousness and happiness to densify. Such actions must be avoided.

Environmental or ecological concerns did not enter the modern Indian awareness until the 1984 Union Carbide industrial accident in Bhopal that took thousands of lives. Other similar disasters have prompted a reconsideration in recent years of the prevailing post-independenceNehruvian drive to industrialize India with little concern for impact on local economies. Though some concerns had been expressed by Gandhi and others regarding pollution of local water sources, this was not seen to be part of the broad systemic problems that have been revealed since the Bhopal disaster. Since that time, numerous campaigns have been aimed at cleaning India's rivers, improving air quality, and ensuring the integrity and vitality of the soil. Leaders within these movements include M. C. Mehta who campaigned successfully for the transition to less-polluting compressed natural gas auto-rickshaws and taxis in Delhi and other cities and Vandana Shiva, whose work on behalf of organic agriculture has reached millions of farmers throughout the subcontinent. Because of Jain involvement with numerous businesses, various attempts have been made to infuse business ethics with an ecological sensibility. This article will explore Jain involvement with select businesses at both the theoretical and practical level, examining the writings and work of the late jurist L. M. Singhvi, the late religious leader AcaryaTulsi, educator and activist Satish Kumar, contemporary ethicist Atul Shah, and Chairman of the Indian Green Building Council, late Prem C. Jain.

It is now well recognized that India stands first in the world for polluted cities whose air and water have become quite foul. Litter abounds throughout India. Sewage treatment is woefully inadequate and simply absent from most towns and cities. Industrial and human waste effluent flows into rivers and streams. Particulate matter rising from dung, cooking fires and transport vehicles, turn Indian skies gray and choke the population. The World Health Organization has ranked Delhi's air as the most polluted on the planet. More than 600,000 premature deaths yearly are estimated to occur due to pollution in India.[1]

At a conference convened at Harvard University's Center for the Study of World Religions in 1998, scholars and activists engaged in a robust conversation about the prospects for a Jain contribution to the contemporary issue of pollution and its mitigation. At the conference, everyone agreed that the situation is dire and unprecedented. This is true, of all historic religions no religion confronted the social sin of ecological imbalance incurred by the human hand as seen in the past century. However, each religion developed a moral code to guide human actions. At the conference, many Jain leaders lifted up the premises and practices of their faith as a torch to light the way out of the current predicament. In particular, Nathmal Tatia suggested that "By strengthening themselves to resist the various temptations put forth by technology and consumer mentality, Jains can perhaps provide an example for living lightly on the planet earth" (Tatia 2002:16). Padmanabh S. Jaini cited two examples of Jain innovation in regard to reducing coal pollution and mitigating malaria, stating that "the Jain response to development issues must be mindful of traditional Jain teachings on nonviolence and non-possessiveness" (Jaini 2002: 153). SadhviShilapi, citing the work on Jain nuns in Bihar to encourage the planting of trees and the adoption of a vegetarian diet, stated that "Wants should be reduced, desires curbed, and consumption levels kept within reasonable limits" (Shilapi 2002:164).

Two scholars at the Harvard conference raised the measured counterpoint that the evidence does not always indicate that Jain vow-based decision making leads to environmentally friendly practice. John Cort pointed out that the Jain focus on one's liberation from the world (*mokṣa-mārga*) might downplay "the sociobiological contexts in which Jain live and in which any Jain environmental praxis will be located." (Cort 2002: 70). Cort also raised the issue that reforestation is sometimes deleterious to those who support themselves by collecting fodder. Paul Dundas noted that Jain acts of worship generally involve the construction of temples and offerings of flowers and other substances, deemed by some Jains to be acts of violence. Dundas, having quoted AbhayadevaSūri, Haribhadra, and Yaśovijaya, writes that digging the earth to create wells and temples, clearly an act of violence, constitutes "a lesser evil... outweighed by the greater goods of water made available to human beings and worship offered to the Jinas" (Dundas 2002: 109). Simply put, Jains throughout history have advanced an instrumentalist argument in regard to natural resources. If a greater good can be achieved, a little violence is acceptable and even deemed to be necessary. Though he does not state it directly, Dundas implies that this position constitutes an ethical slippery slope. Such justifications arise from the same anthropocentrism that caused the current ecological crises. When man becomes the holder of all things, harm to nature and the environment cannot be avoided.

It must be noted, however, that the Jain approach to environmental ethics rests on premises radically different from those presented in the prophetic, monotheistic religions. The Jain position also differs from the views of Hinduism and Buddhism. Rather than assenting to the notion that the world was created by a benevolent presiding deity, Jainism holds that the world has always been present and will exist forevermore. Rather than following an externally imposed moral code, practitioners of the Jain faith are taught the benefits of self-initiated virtuous action,performed not for the sake of sheer obedience but for the purposes of self-improvement and purification. In contrast to Hinduism, Jainism does not advocate sacrificial activity such as killing animals to propitiate wrathful deities. Jainism does not posit an underlying unifying state of consciousness such as Brahman but insists upon the individual integrity of each and every soul, from beginningless time into an infinite future. Unlike Buddhism, Jainism posits the reality of a Self or Soul that holds the potential to attain its unique state of freedom. Buddhism teaches emptiness of self and other; Jainism teaches about a universe filled with innumerable living souls.

Jain Physics and Metaphysics

The Jain approach to the natural world is simultaneously respectful as well as cautious, and above all driven by moral concerns. First, according to Jain ontology, the world is suffused with life forces (*jiva*) that merit protection. Hence, the lives contained in particles of earth, drops of water, rays of light, gusts of wind, as well as micro-organisms, plants, and animals must be acknowledged and to the greatest extent possible, not to be harmed. Each has entered its particular form due to the materiality of karma. One must exert caution because each harmful action causes the karma surrounding one's own soul to thicken and darken, obscuring the radiant consciousness of the soul and blocking its ascent to freedom. The Jain universe, thus conceived, becomes a moral universe. In order to advance toward freedom, one must develop impeccable adherence to the moral code in order to purge all impedimentary karmas.

Physics and metaphysics, matter and spirit stand intertwined in the Jain worldview. The tradition posits only four forces that do not possess life: matter or *pudgala* which can manifest as karma, time, space, and movement. Aside from these, all beings, including elemental realities and plants, possess consciousness, energy, and an innate state of bliss. The following passage from the ĀcārāṅgaSūtra, the oldest extant Jain text (ca. 350 BCE), gives an idea of how the Jains regard life to pervade all aspects of the natural world:

> As the nature of (human beings) is to be born and grow old, so is the nature of plants is to be born and grow old.... As (humans) fall sick when cut, also that (tree) falls sick when cut; as (the human) needs food, so that (plant) needs food; as the (human) will decay, so that (plant) will decay; as the human is not eternal, so that (plant) is not eternal.... As this is changing, so that is changing. One who injures plants does not comprehend and renounce sinful acts. The one who does not injure plants comprehends and renounces sinful acts. Knowing (those plants), a wise person would not act sinfully

> toward plants, nor cause others to act so, nor allow others to do so. The one who knows the causes of sin relating to plants is called a reward-knowing sage (Jacobi, 1968, 10-11).

In regard to not harming plant life, Jain monks and nuns avoid brushing up against any form of vegetation, knowing the harm that might be felt by the leaves and stems.

The Jain practice of avoidance of harm to plants, whether invasive or native, differs from Hindu forms of reverence toward plants. David Haberman has written about the affection for trees felt by Hindus in Varanasi, which he sees as continuous with "tree worship worldwide: trees have not only been commonly thought of as animate beings but also as powerful divine beings who when approached in a respectful manner offer in return life-enhancing benefits to human beings" (Haberman, 2013, 57). In the Jaina context, the presence of spirit (jīva) within the tree would be acknowledged, though the primary concern in avoidance of harm to the tree would not necessarily be for the sake of the tree, but for protecting oneself from the inflow of negative karmas that would occur if one were to harm the tree. It is also important to keep in mind that it is possible for a soul embodied in one of the elements, in a plant, or in a tree to attain a human birth in the next life and enter the path toward freedom from all karmic constraints.

In the coding of a pan-ethical universe, Jainism, particularly in the *Tattvārthasūtra* (fifth century CE) of Umāsvati, each life form stands within a hierarchy of ascent from elemental beings, microbes, and plants, said to possess the sense of touch; worms, which add the sense of taste; crawling bugs which add smell; flying insects which add sight; and the array of mammals, reptiles, fish, and amphibians who can also hear and think. Life constantly moves from one form to the next. A virtuous human may even take birth in a heavenly realm, while a person of dissipation may endure torture in one of the seven hells. The nature of one's next birth depends upon action performed in the immediate past body. The human birth stands supreme, being the only domain through which one can perform the necessary karmic purgations to attain freedom, a state at the edge of the universe untouched by the effects of karma, known as the place of freedom or the Siddha Loka.

Jain Vows as Moral Foundation

According to Jainism, regardless of one's station in life, choices made by the individual determine future circumstance. If one has earned the good fortune of human birth, a golden opportunity looms: to consciously and purposively commit to the spiritual path of pursuing a life shaped by religiously inspired vows. A creative rethinking of these vows might be useful when thinking about strategies, personal and social, to address pressing environmental issues such as resource management and adoption of environmentally friendly technology.

The Jain vows applicable to both lay persons and monastics but in varying degrees of intensity, include a set of five greater vows (*mahāvrata*) and a set of twelve lesser vows (*anuvrata*). ĀcārāṅgaSūtra lists five forms of intensity for each of the five great vows, summarized as follows: In the observance of nonviolence (*ahimsā*), a monk (*nirgrantha*) must be "careful in his walk;" guard against any thought that "produces cutting or splitting or division and dissension, quarrels, faults, and pains, injures living beings, or kills creatures;" not engage in speech that is "sinful and blamable;" be "careful in lying down his utensils of begging" so as to not "hurt or displace or injure or kill all sorts of living beings," and must not "eat or drink without inspecting his food and drink" for the same reason (*AS* II:15.i.1-5, Jacobi, 1968, 203-204). From an ecological perspective, Jain advocacy for vegetarianism aligns with the environmentalists' desire for humans to eat lower on the food chain, which uses less water, requires less land, and has been proven to improve general health.

The second vow, holding to truth (*satya*), requires the five following qualifications: speaking only after deliberation, not speaking from a place of anger, not speaking out of greed, not speaking due to fear, and not speaking for the purpose of ridicule. Part of any social movement requires "speaking truth to power." To the extent that identifying the risks of global warming requires good science and a recognition of its fundamental facts, truthfulness plays an essential role in naming difficulties that must be addressed.

The third vow, not stealing (*asteya*), entails the pronouncement that "I shall neither take myself what is not given nor cause others to take it, nor consent to their taking it" (*AS* II.15.iii.). Because a monk's livelihood depends upon gathering alms, five further qualifications are given: thoughtfulness about where to ask for food, receipt of permission to do so from one's supervisory director, moving onto a new place after a fixed period of time in order to not become a burden, always asking permission to visit a new place, and consulting with other monks about the duration of stay. From the perspective of resource allocation, it is a well-known fact that with the sense of entitlement that borders on arrogance the consumers in the developed world arrogate for themselves a disproportionate amount of energy, water and access to food, resulting in waste.

The fourth vow involves restraint from sexual thought and activity. Acknowledging the range of ways in which sexual desire can manifest, the ĀcārāṅgaSūtra proclaims: "I renounce all sexual pleasures, either with gods or humans or animals" (*AS* II.15.iv). In terms of the environmental concerns that arise with population growth, clearly the most problematic form of sexual expression would be unprotected intercourse between men and women. By pointing out the benefits of family planning and slowly reducing the rate of population growth worldwide, this Jain vow can be reconstrued in an eco-friendly manner.

The fifth vow, nonpossession (*aparigraha*) requires the monk or nun to renounce all attachments. The basic monastic vows restrict the postulant to a bare minimum of possessions, generally a change of robes, a begging bowl, and small satchel for carrying books for members of the Svetambara orders. Male monks of Digambara communities eventually renounce even clothing. The

ĀcārāṅgaSūtra mandates that the senses must be controlled in each of their five expressions. One must vow "not be attached to, nor delighted with, nor desiring of, nor infatuated by, nor covetous of, nor disturbed by the agreeable or disagreeable sounds" (*AS* II.15.v). The same is said of seeing, that if one "sees agreeable and disagreeable forms or colors, one should not be attached." This formula repeats for smelling, tasting, and touching. When translated into advice for human behavior writ large, this vow throws down the gauntlet in regard to consumerism. By suggesting that happiness cannot be found through the enjoyment of external sense pleasures, Jain ethics confront the entire process of acquisitiveness, which lies at the heart of the global economy. By renouncing attachment to "stuff," being a reversal,that potentially can undo the root cause of environmental imbalance: complicity in consumer culture.

At the very start of the *TattvārthaSūtra* (ca. 4th century C.E.), the central manual for Jain faith and practice, the author Umasvati asserts the need for right outlook, right knowledge, and right action in order to enter the path to freedom (*samyakdarś*ana, *jñāna*, *caritra*: *mokṣamārga*, I:1). From an ecological view, this would entail, in sequence, an epiphany that nature is important and is in peril, the knowledge of what has caused the current dire circumstance and what can be done as remedy to the situation, followed by undertaking corrective action. This threefold process has indeed been enacted by several Jain leaders in the past few decades, showing the adaptability and ingenuity of faith leaders, monastic and lay.

Moral Conscience in Indian History

There has been historical precedent for Jain leadership in the moral sphere of larger society within India. They campaigned (along with the Buddhists) against the Brāhmanical rituals that involve animal sacrifice, with some success. The Jains became particularly influential during the period of approximately 700 to 1200 in two kingdoms, Karnataka in the south where the Digambara community rose to prominence and Gujarat in the west, largely Svetambara in persuasion. King Kumarapala of Gujarat (ruled 1143-1175 CE) converted to Jainism under the tutelage of the great scholar and Svetambara monk Hemacandra (1089-1172). Kumarapala enacted Jain-friendly legislation and financed public work projects including Jain temple construction. The Jains were also influential at the Mughal court. In 1587, the SvetambaraJain teacher HiravijayaSuri (1527-95 CE) so impressed Emperor Akbar that a decree was issued banning the slaughter of animals in the empire during the week-long Jaina celebration of Paryusan, a time of fasting, forgiveness and reconciliation held every September (Dundas, 1992, 126). In regard to environmental activism in the modern era, two Jain figures have made significant contributions to moral philosophy including environmental advocacy in India: AcaryaTulsi (1914-1997) and L. M. Singhvi (1931-2007). The work of these two leaders will be considered in the section that follows, along with the work taken up by three contemporary figures, Satish Kumar, Atul Shah, and Prem Jain.

AcaryaTulsi, Religious Exemplar (1914-1997)

AcaryaTulsi was born into a large family in Ladnun, Rajasthan, during British colonial rule. He entered the SvetambaraTerapanthi order of Jain monks at the age of eleven after meeting AcaryaKalugani, its eighth leader. This movement, established by AcaryaBhikshu in the 18th century, started as a more austere branch of the SthanakvasiSvetambaras, renowned for their eschewal of all images that are generally used as part of worship. The year of separation came in 1759 when Bhikshu broke all formal ties and brought six fellow monks with him to establish a new self-initiated order (Dundas, 1992, 219). In many ways, this proved to be a Protestant movement, with Bhikshu decrying the notion that anyone can earn merit through donation. According to AcaryaBhikshu, only strict adherence to the rules of nonviolence can guarantee spiritual progress. From the onset, the Terapanthi pioneered education for Jain nuns, who previously were not given the opportunity for study afforded to men.

Tulsi was elevated to leadership of the order at the age of

22 and presided for many decades over a dynamic period of growth. The numbers of monks, nuns, and lay followers increased within the Terapanthi community. A new order of Samanis was established, allowing women in particular to postpone their final vows. Samanis have established learning and meditation centers in London, Florida, New Jersey, and Texas. AcaryaTulsi established Jain VishwaBharati on a hundred acre campus in his home town of Ladnun in 1970, that obtained the status of a deemed university in 1991.

Tulsi turned his attention in 1949 toward a campaign known as the Anuvrat Movement. He saw that newly independent India needed a moral compass for guidance and he distilled and reinterpreted the standard Jaina precepts for contemporary times. Whereas the first ten vows expound upon general ethical concerns (no killing, no unprovoked attacks, no agitation, unity, tolerance, honesty, simplicity, good government, self control in regard to sex and substances), the eleventh vow proclaims: "I will strive to minimize environmental pollution (no cutting of trees; no wastage of water)" (Vibha, 2012). By the late 1990s, this precept took form of a graduate degree offered at Jain VishwaBharati on environmental protection.

When I interviewed AcharyaTulsi in 1989 and asked him about environmental ethics, he smiled and pointing to few items that he owned:- his clothes, few books, a broom and a begging bowl he commented that this was the model for environmental ethics: Learning to do with less. With fewer possessions, one inflicts less harm to the environment (Chapple, 1993). On face value, this response seemed at the time a bit too easy and obvious. However, upon deeper reflection, this suggestion to consume less served as a cultural and historical critique and a gentle assertion of the timeless nature of Jain values.

Some years later, while working with Vandna Shiva in the forest near Dehra Dun, AcharyaTulsi's wisdom dawned in a new way. I had accompanied a group of learning students to BijaVidyapeeth, Vandana Shiva's organic farm dedicated to studying and teaching eco-friendly methods. She has been urged to create this training center on the urging of Satish Kumar, the former Jain monk and life-long advocate for simple living. We learned seven forms of composting, weeded the herb garden, helped preparing meals, and wandered with local villagers and forest dwellers. The lifestyle for the locals was remarkable in its non-reliance on technology of any form beyond fire. The trip took place in the winter. The forest people gathered at night around a campfire near the lean-to shelters where they slept. During the day they lopped low hanging limbs to feed their goats and foraged deep into the forest. The children played imaginative games all day long while helping their parents. On the one hand, the group from the United States felt the contrast between our western global privilege and the hardscrabble subsistence life of these nomads. On the other hand, their presence gave us strange solace: Even if the structures that maintain the current global economy collapse, these people will survive and thrive. Though they have not renounced the world in any sense of the word and perhaps would welcome greater modern conveniences and comforts, these forest dwellers offer some hope that a simple life like that advocated by AcharyaTulsi still exists.

L. M. Singhvi, Barrister (1931-2007)

Member of a mixed Hindu-Jaina family, L. M. Singhvi rose to prominence in the fields of law and government. He served as High Commissioner (Ambassador) from India to Great Britain in the 1990s and as a member of India's Parliament for many years, in the LokSabha (Lower House of Representatives) from 1962 to 1967 and in the RajyaSabha (Upper House; approx. Senate) from 1998 to 2004. He was tireless in his advocacy of Jain causes. He presented the Jain Declaration on Nature to Prince Philip in 1990 on the occasion of Jainism's participation in the World Wildlife Fund Network on Conservation and Religion. It was reprinted in 2002 as the appendix to the book *Jainism and Ecology*. The Declaration outlines the core principles of Jainism, reframing them as dialogue partners in the emerging discourse on religion and ecology.

The Declaration states that Jainism presents an ecological philosophy and consequently summarizes various aspects of the faith in light of its particular attention to nature. The first part discusses Jain teachings on nonviolence, interdependence, recognition of multiple perspectives, emphasis on equanimity, and commitment to compassion, empathy, and charity. The second section provides a synopsis of Jain biological categories as delineated earlier in this chapter. The third and final part highlight the Jain Code of Conduct as exemplary for bringing about environment justice. Key aspects include the restatement of the five Jain vows (described earlier in this chapter), the history of Jain kindness to animals, the Jaina advocacy of vegetarianism, the teachings on restraint and avoidance of waste, and finally, the value of charity in the tradition (Chapple, 2002, 217-224).

Decidedly more complex than AcaryaTulsi's eleven Anuvrats, this Declaration demonstrates the philosophical commitment of the Jain community not only to regard life but to advocate for sustaining and protecting life in all its forms. By asserting the presence of conscious life within soil, rivers, fires, and wind as well as within the overly self-obsessed human realm, Jainism calls for an expansion of view, a broadening of horizon that can serve as an antidote to the damning anthropocentrism that has characterized most of human philosophical endeavors. When Singhvi writes about compassion and empathy, he intends not to limit one's scope to the merely human but to include all the animals and plants and the elements . His work demonstrates a commitment to link Jainism with an ecologically friendly philosophy. Singhvi claims a link between nonviolence and environmentalism, claiming that "waste and creating pollution are acts of violence" (Chapple, 2002, p. 224).

Satish Kumar, Contemporary Ethicist (b. 1936)

Satish Kumar, who served as a Jain TherapanthiSvetambara monk for nine years before joining the BhūDān movement of VinobhaBhave and subsequently founded Schumacher College in southwest England, has long championed the social engagement of Jain values with public life. He edited *Resurgence*, the leading journal for ecological spirituality in Britain, for several decades, contributing himself many pieces on how the Jain value of simplicity intersects with ecological values. At Schumacher College, which Satish Kumar co-founded in 1990, spirituality and ecology are taught in tandem, inspired in large part by the nature-friendly aspects of Jain thought and practice.

Satish Kumar makes direct parallels between Jain philosophy and ecology. He cites Mahavira who "forbade riding on animals" and "taught his disciples that the earth has soul, water has soul, fire has soul, air has soul, and of course all plants and animals have souls" (Kumar, 2002, 184). For him, the Jain vows convey the restraint necessary to encourage a balanced ecological lifestyle.

Gandhian principles have deeply influenced the life and work of Satish Kumar. During his years in Vinoba Bhave's ashram, he chanted twice daily Gandhi's eleven exhortations to live the good life, which Kumar has translated as follows:

> Nonviolence, truth, nonstealing,
> Sacred sex, non-consumerism,
> Physical work, avoidance of bad taste,
> Fearlessness, respect for all religions,
> Local economy, and respect for all beings,
> These eleven principles should be followed with
> Humility, care, and commitment (Kumar 1999, p. 285).

Respect for all beings (*sparśabhāvanā*), the eleventh principle, inspired Satish Kumar to write that this idea "requires a deep respect for all species and acceptance of the intrinsic value of all beings" as well as to provide a critique of "human colonialism, every expanding over the territories of nonhuman species," noting that "we need to learn to rejoice in the beauty and the mystery of existence as it is and not look at it as a source for economic activity" (p. 305). Satish Kumar's work has influenced thousands who have studied with him in England and who have read the journal *Resurgence* and his autobiography.

Atul Shah, Academic and Theoretician (b. 1973)

Dr. Atul Shah, professor at Sussex University in England, makes links between the world of business and environmental ethics in his book *Jainism and Ethical Finance: A Timeless Business Model*. He notes that "Crucially, the concept of 'society' extends beyond human communities to other species and ecosystems" and that "Jain philosophy recognizes an intimate link between spiritual practice and consciousness of the natural world. Shah goes on to state that "the conduct of economics has been too anthropocentric" and laments pollution of the air, seas and soil on a global scale; the unplanned expansion of cities to the detriment of quality of life; as well as the unfolding crisis associated with climatic instability and the growing encroachments on the habitats of other species, threatening their survival and denying them the dignity they deserve.

He suggests that the environmentalism "converges with the Jain belief in the connectedness of all forms of life and the need for us to remember these connections in both our individual and collective decision making" (Shah and Rankin, 2017, 3).

Spiritual practice in the Jain observance of nonviolence holds ramifications beyond a concern for human well-being. "Arbitrary interference with nature can injure or even eliminate ecosystems, species and organisms on which we depend for our survival" (Shah and Rankin, 2017, 31). Shah advocates careful consideration taking into account unseen possibilities that might cause harm.

One example cited by Shah is Jain Irrigation, a global Jain business. It educates farmers about sustainable agricultural practices and helps them market their produce. This company places "significant investment… in research and development to ensure efficient land use, mammal waste and sustainable productivity and harvesting" (Shah and Rankin, 2017, 97). This contrasts starkly with the approach used by Monsanto, an American corporation that through patents and monopolization of seed, fertilizer, insecticides, and herbicides, has destroyed many family farms in India through its "aggressive financialisation." In contrast, the farmers within the Jain Irrigation network are "supported and nurtured rather than exploited and squeezed" (Shah and Rankin, 2017, 97). Additionally, in response to the issue of worldwide climate instability, Jain Irrigation is working intensely at expanding solar operations to meet India's growing demand for electricity (Bhandari, 2016-2017).

Prem C. Jain, Chairman of the Indian Green Building Council (1936-2018)

Dr. Prem C. Jain received his Ph.D. in civil engineering from the University of Minnesota in the late 1950s and worked with Carrier Air Conditioning in Syracuse, New York, in the early 1960s. He brought his knowledge and expertise to India and helped contributing to the modernization of India through various undertakings, including AECOM, a corporation that has been "involved in designing and completing 56 LEED certified projects, over 5,000 kilometers of highways, 300 kilometers of metro and 14 sea ports" as well as Smart Cities program emphasizing sustainable development. He chairs the Indian Green Building Council and in an interview held in June, 2017, shared his enthusiasm for energy efficiency for the protection and enhancement of life in all forms.

Prem Jain was graduated from HiraLal Jain Senior Secondary School in Old Delhi's Sadar Bazar before taking up university studies. He returned to the school as a trustee in 2010 and worked for making this historic school, now serving underprivileged families of various religions, an example of best use of appropriate technology. A water catchment system has been installed on the roof, as well as solar panels that help with basic electricity needs. In an interview on June 28, 2017, he said that for him, all the elements of the world, earth, water, fire, air, and space, comprise divinity, Bhagavan. Attentiveness to this divinity comprises a universal faith, with "no Hindu, no Muslim, no Christian." He analyzes the word as follows: "*Bh* for the earth, *ga* for the sky, *va* for Vayu which means air, *a* for Agni, and *na* for water." The five great elements (*pañca-mahā-bhūta*) comprise the common ground for all experience.

Jain described the first major eco-friendly building that he undertook during the Reagan era in the city of Hyderabad. Microsoft had chosen this area of the country partly because it was free from earthquakes. During the construction of this complex in the 1980s, it was a leading example of the implementation of green building technology. In a personal interview with Jain, he predicts eventually we will go away from the coal. I am hoping that five years down the line, we will not have to use firepower. We will put in a lot of solar; solar has become very inexpensive now. When I started, the general cost was very high. Now it's very affordable. Solar plant is less in cost than of a coal plant. Then the petrol will eventually be replaced by natural gas. So there is a good chance that five to seven years down the line we will stop polluting. That is the situation. We must get more clean, with all the carbon absorbed. I can say that my grandchildren will have much cleaner air than we have today.

Prem Jain's optimism arises from his faith in a universal sense of connectivity, grounded in the Jain ethic of nonviolence and the Jain cosmology that sees life in all elements, all beings.

Each of the five figures profiled above are deeply engaged with the process of reflective, constructive environmental ethics. Though not blind to the benefits of modern industrialization, they advocate a return to a simpler lifestyle with reverence for life in all its forms rather than blind pursuit of wealth and comfort at any cost.

The Jain Declaration on the Climate Crisis

JAINA (Jain Associations in North America), an amalgam of temples, study groups, and religious and lay leaders, issued declaration on October 17, 2019 that supplements and updates the 1990 Jain Declaration on Nature described above. Drafted by the JAINA Ahimsak Eco-Vegan Committee, the name of the committee itself reflects the face of forward-looking change within the Jain community, many of whom have now taken up the cause of eschewing milk and dairy in favor of a vegan diet. Informed by science, this declaration cites the data on fossil fuel and animal agriculture-related emissions. The amount of CO2 in the atmposphere has increased from 280 parts per million (PPM) in pre-industrial times, to over 415 PPM in 2019. The results are stark: we are in the sixth major extinction event; climate change has resulted in increased human mortality from malnutrition, malaria, diarrhea, and heat stress; sea levels are rising, hurricanes are more destructive, forests are more susceptible to fire; air pollution has adversely affected human health; the range of mosquito borne diseases such as Malaria, Dengue, and Zika has increased. The document cites the need for Jains to reconsider their food sources, the transportation choices, and overall patterns of consumption. Individual Jains are asked to consider nine specific lifestyle changes: 1) calculate one's carbon imprint; 2) abstain from meat, eggs, and dairy products; 3) minimize food waste; 4) walk and bike when possible; 5) use hybrid or fully electric vehicles when essential; 6) reduce air travel; 7) live in smaller homes; 8) buy fewer consumer goods; 9) "consider how our work or business can benefit the climate for all living beings." The document ends with two calls-to-action. The first asks the Jain community to "green" its temples by engaging in renewable energy use and eliminating the use of plastics. The second calls for business and government leaders to adopt policies for regenerative agriculture, to "remove subsidies for the meat and dairy industries… and for fossil fuels," to encourage government support for public transportation, to ban plastics and deforestation, and, finally, to "support practices and vetted technologies to actively remove CO2 from the atmosphere."

This document extends a call to action for the more than four million Jains worldwide.[2]

Conclusion

In addition to their advocacy of a vegetarian diet, protests against animal sacrifice, and charities for schools and hospitals, Jains have been investing in eco-friendly businesses such as solar power generation and other forms of appropriate technology. The

Jain faith offers a multivalent, multi-life perspective on the nature and purpose of the world. According to Jain teachings, we live in a moral universe, governed by the laws of cause and effect. Moral agency requires paying attention and giving reverence to the natural world. Mahāvīra advocated the protection of trees, positing that any harm done to nature will immediate constrain and impede the soul. Adherents to the Jain faith have produced a biological inquiry that reveals the inter-connectedness of all life forms. With this insight comes great moral obligation. Knowing that life depends upon other forms of life, the Jains urge human beings never to take more than what is absolutely needed and be careful and loving in all ways.All people can be reminded of the sanctity of life, the moral voice of Jainism at the face of today's world of over-consumption and rapacious use of resources.

Bibliography

1. Chapple, C., ed. *Jainism and Ecology: Nonviolence in the Web of Life,* Cambridge, MA: Center for the Study of World Religions, Harvard University Press, 2002.
2. Chapple, C, *Nonviolence to Animals, Earth, and Self in Asian Traditions,* Albany: State University of New York Press, 1993.
3. John C. Cort, J. "Green Jainism?" in *Jainism and Ecology*, 2002.
4. Cort, J., *Jains in the World: Religious Values and Ideology in India,* New York: Oxford University Press, 2001.
5. Dundas, P., *The Jains,* London: Routledge, 1992.
6. Dundas, P., "The Limits of Jain Environmental Ethic" in *Jainism and Ecology,* 2002.
7. Economist.https://www.economist.com/asia/2016/01/16/particular-about-particulates
8. Frazer, J.,*The Golden Bough: A History of Myth and Religion*, London: Chancellor Press, 1994, first published 1922.
9. Haberman, D., *People Trees: Worship of Trees in Northern India*, New York: Oxford University Press, 2013.

10. Jacobi, H. trans., ĀcārāṅgaSūtra, *Jaina Sutras in Two Parts. Part One: the ĀkārāṅgaSūtra; The KalpaSūtra*, New York: Dover, 1968, first published 1884.

11. Jaini, P.S. "Ecology, Economics, and Development in Jainism" in Jainism and Ecology, 2002.

12. Kumar, S., "Jain Ecology," in Christopher C. ed., *Jainism and Ecology: Nonviolence in the Web of Life*, Cambridge, MA: Center for the Study of World Religions, Harvard University Press, 2002.

13. Kumar, S. *Path Without Destination: An Autobiography*. New York: Eagle Brook, William Morrow and Company, 1999.

14. Shah, A. and Rankin A., *Jainism and Ethical Finance: A Timeless Business Model*, New York: Routledge, 2017.

15. Shilapi, S. "Environmental and Ecological Teachings of Mahavira" in *Jainism and Ecology*, 2002.

16. Singhvi, L.M. "The Jain Declaration on Nature." In *Jainism and Ecology*, 2002.

17. Tatia, N., trans.,*That Which Is TattvārthaSūtra, A Classic Jain Manual for Understanding the True Nature of Reality.* San Francisco: HarperCollins, 1994.

T18. atia, N. "The Jain Worldview and Ecology" in *Jainism and Ecology: Nonviolence in the Web of Life*, edited by Christopher Key Chapple (Cambridge, Massachusetts: Center for the Study of World Religions, Harvard University Press, 2002).

19. Vibha, M., *Acharya Shree Tulsi: A Legend of Humanity*, New Delhi: AcharyaTulsiJanamShatabdiSamarohSamiti, 2012.

20. https://www.economist.com/asia/2016/01/16/particular-about-particulates

21. https://cdn.ymaws.com/www.jaina.org/resource/resmgr/jaindeclarationonclimatechange/Update_Jain_Declaration_on_C.pdf

Chapter 10

Jainism and the Nature – A Canonical Perspective

Jagat Ram Bhattacharyya*

Karma theory is a unique identity of Jainism in propounding the message of self-restraint in a straight way. Theist schools of Philosophies advocate that the life of human beings is for karma, in contrast with those of heavenly beings and hellish beings, as they have the life of enjoyment and suffering respectively. And those, the consequences of karma, are accumulated only in a mundane life. So self-restraint, in one sense, is the means of violence free life, which holds the practical mission of the ideology of 'live and let live'. Jainism staunchly believes in an existential mode of life in which all living beings hold equal importance. This is one of the prime sources of ecotheology. The ethical doctrines preached in both the schools of Jainism (Śvetāmbara and Digambara) are recorded in the canonical treatises. The seed of philosophy is preserved in the canons in a dormant state. Be it the Śvetāmbara canons starting from the Ācārāṅga, Sthānāṅga, Bhagavatīsūtra, Uttarādhyayana and Daśavaikālika and so on or the Digambara philosophical treatises of Kundakunda, Vaṭṭakera and the like, the sole teaching is focally framed on self-restraint. This very important act of life leads to the path of

* Professor, Department of Sanskrit, Pali&Prakrit, Bhasa-Bhavana, VisvaBharati University, Santiniketan (INDIA)
E-mail: jagatrb@gmail.com

emancipation through the purification of one's physical, mental, emotional and spiritual beings. Co-existential ethos is the pivotal point that Jainism cherishes for its candid approach towards ethical doctrines. It not only advocates preventing violence from physical level, but from the vocal and the mental states also. The very first canon of the Śvetāmbara sect, the Ācārāṅgasūtra starts with the self-introspection and prevention of weapons. It teaches the violence-free life in a subtle way. Jainism preaches "parasparopagrahaḥjīvānām'' inter-dependency to each other, from one-sensed being to the five-sensed creatures. It pleads for the universal kinship, beyond the knot of human relation. It warns the killer that there is no difference between him and the victim in a real sense. In the event of eco theological studies, Jainism can show the path of tranquility, peace and bliss in human life.

Non-possessiveness is one of the vital dictums of Jain ethics. Though this is strictly followed by an ascetic, this rule, for the laities, is applied in a flexible manner. And the term used for it is limitation of desire. Where there is the condition of possession, there is the condition of extortion of Mother Nature. A Jain monk (henceforth it will include the term nun), while begging alms from the householders are prescribed to take food as per his need for the time. The ethics does not allow him to preserve it. So a monk is allowed to take less food from many families that are not in a food crisis. It has been expressed metaphorically compared with a black-bee that procures honey from many flowers without causing them harm[1]. A monk who maintains this norm is called a sāhu[2]. He will never be selective in begging for food. It may be tasteless or dry. But a self-restraint one will always be indifferent[3].

The earliest Jain canon is the Ācārāṅgasūtra. Though it begins with the renunciation of weapons and is directly related with the non-violence, the very first doctrine of the five-great vows and preaches to be free from indulging violent acts to all beings, it concerns the preservation of nature in other ways. The jīva, according to its karma, is tied with the cycle of birth and death. All the actions through mind, speech and body lead the jīva in the bondage of karma. Primarily the jīvas are classified by four categories – the heavenly being, the hellish being, human and the sub-human. The state of heavenly being and hellish being are the fruits of virtuous deeds and sinful deeds respectively in intensive nature. The heavenly beings enjoy while the hellish beings suffer as per their karma to the fullest extent having no capacity in eradication of pre-accumulated karma through penance. The sub-humans are in the state of partial sufferings and having power of partial penance. The humans are only in the category of jīva having the strength of eradication of pre-accumulated karma, be it virtuous or vicious. Jain ethical doctrine preaches three kararaṇas and three yogas. The fundamental principle of that intent has been dormant in the Ācārāṅgasūtra. The doer says 'akarissaṃcahaṃ, kāravesucahaṃ, karaoyāvisamṇuṇṇebhavissāmi' (I had acted, I had caused others to act, and I had approved of others' indulgence in action; I act, I cause others to act, I approve of others' actions; I shall act, I shall cause others to act, and I shall approve of others' actions). This spirit of thought has been spreaded over the later canons and philosophical doctrine in the name of karaṇa. The same doctrine has been seemed to be developed in subsequent canonical treatises[4] as—"jāvajjīvāeṇakaremi, ṇakāravemi, karaṃtaṃ pi ṇasamaṇujāṇāmimaṇasāvayasākāyasā" [In my whole life through mind, speech and body neither I shall do (any act), nor I shall cause other to do, nor even shall I approve others indulging in actions]. The same vow has been committed in case of other great vows, such as retention from indulging falsehood, stealing, incontinence and possessiveness. Here it is to be noted that the phenomenal nature of non-violence is refraining oneself from indulging violent acts through mind, speech and body. The Tattvārthasūtra says kāya-vāṅ-manaḥkarma yogaḥ[5]. It means the operation of the body, speech and mind is action (yoga). In case of an ascetic these are maintained strictly through their arduous practice of penance. These are, in other ways, practised by a laity in a lenient way.

Jainism prescribes for the application of philosophy in human life. It teaches gradual progress from the worldly life to the spiritual life. The fundamental entity is of two, the soul and the matter. Except the soul everything is under the category of matter. The bondage of the soul with the matter is eternal. The soul can only be realized in the state of its association with the matter, that is, the body. The emancipated soul being free from the matter enjoys its own state of knowledge and bliss. The karmic matter in its subtlest form remains stuck with the soul even in the penultimate stage of emancipation. This karma is manifested in our activities in a gross form. The karma, be it meritorious or sinful, binds the soul and consequently prevents the soul from being liberated. Jainism prescribes for shedding off of karma through penance and austerity for letting the soul be liberated. But in mundane life, in its practical aspects, meritorious karma is allowed. And in this view, a person should always be very careful that his action through mind, speech and body does not cause harm to any living being. Here the Daśavaikālikasūtra teaches us through the style of question and answer- how to walk, how to stand, how to sit, how to lie down, how to eat, how to speak and so on, so that a person be free from indulging violence to the living beings. The answer is all should be performed with utmost care and vigilance.

> *kahaṃ care kahaṃciṭṭhekahamāsekahaṃsae|*
> *kahaṃbhuṃjaṃtobhāsaṃtopaavaṃkammaṃnabaṃdhaī*
> || *4.7*||
> *jayaṃ care jayaṃciṭṭhejayamāsejayaṃsae|*
> *jayaṃbhuṃjaṃtobhaasaṃtopāvaṃkammaṃnabaṃdhaī*
> || *4.8*||

In Jainism, the worldly souls are classified as mobile and immobile. These are again categorized in terms of senses. The earth-bodied beings, the water-bodied beings, and the plant-bodied beings are sensed beings but the fire-bodied beings and air-bodied beings are counted as mobile beings in some respect. On the other hand, there are mobile beings which are numbered from two sensed to five sensed beings. The beings with two or more senses are genuinely mobile creatures. In the SvopajñaBhāṣyaṬīkā by Siddhasenagaṇi of the Śvetāmbara sect[6] it is mentioned that the fire-bodied and the air-bodied beings do not move on their own accord and for that reason they cannot be considered as belonging to the class of mobile creatures. In the Sarvārthasiddhi the element of vitality is added to explain the nature of all beings[7], however many senses they have. There are ten vitalities of the mobile creatures and these are —

1. Sense of touch
2. Body
3. Respiration
4. Lifespan
5. Sense of taste
6. Faculty of speech
7. Sense of smell
8. Sense of sight
9. Sense of hearing
10. Rationality.

The following chart gives the number of vitalities of sentient beings according to the number of senses they possess —

Beings	Vitalities
One-sensed	1-4
Two-sensed	1-6
Three-sensed	1-7
Four-sensed	1-8
Five-sensed non-rational	1-9
Five-sensed rational	1-10

Jainism advocates that in terms of existence all beings are equal and have the right to live unharmed. But it is a hard truth that living is based on inter-dependency. It is conditional that one should sacrifice one's life for the sake of others' living. So it is there in Jainism that injury (violence) is defined as – pramatyayogātprāṇavyaporaṇaṃhiṃsā (TS. 7.13). It means, taking life away out of passion is violence. The passion means the powerful emotions of anger, pride, deceit and greed. This violence is of two types, dravyahiṃsā and bhāvahiṃsā. Dravyahiṃsā is such an act of violence (or killing) which is perpetrated to a living being (insect etc) by an ascetic who is in the state of non-remissness and which is of the inevitable category or is impossible to avert[8]. It is supported by the commentary of Haribhadra on the Daśavaikālikasūtra —

> *yāpunaradyavyatonabhāvataḥsākhvalīryādisamitasy-asādhoḥkāraṇegacchataiti (24).*

In the OghaNiryukti 748.749 the same idea has been echoed.

> *uccāliammipāeiriyāsamiassasaṃkamaṭṭhāe/*
> *vāvajjejjākuliṃgīmarijjataṃjogamāsajjā//*
> *nayatassatannimitto, baṃdhosuhumo*
> *vi desiosamae/*
> *aṇavajjo u paogeṇasavvabhāveṇa so jamhā//*

Bhāvahiṃsā is the Psychical violence. It is the mental resolve to kill or injure any living being. It can be understood with the example that if any person misunderstands a string to be a snake in the dim light and cuts it in the motive in killing is the psychical violence. It is justified by the statement of Haribhadra in his commentary on the Daśavakālikasūtra as —

> jahākevi purpose maṃdamaṃdappagāsappadesesaṃṭhiaṃis ivaliyakāyaṃrajjuṃpāsittāesaahittitavvaha-pariṇāmapariṇae ṇikaḍḍhiyāsipatteduaṃduaṃchiṃdijjāesābhāvaohiṃsānada vao (24.25).

Dying of a living one is a natural and inevitable consequence in this loka (cosmic space). So a natural death is not violence. The Jain concept of violence is unique in its nature. A self-restraint one, being ever-vigilant in non-violence cannot accumulate sin, though by chance he causes an injury to a living being. On the contrary, a person with remissness becomes responsible for such an act and accumulates sin for that.

Human beings are (apparently) the most powerful creatures on this earth. So the activities, be it meritorious or sinful, the human is the doer and enjoyer or sufferer. Humans having distinguishing and judgemental ability, can discriminate the consequences of both the acts. In the Tattvārthasūtra (5.21) Umāsvātī has propounded the ideal concept of coexistence parasparopagrahojīvānām – Jīvas (Living beings) render service to one another. This is the natural function of the soul. It influences each other without discriminating the favourable or unfavourable result, good or bad, beneficial or harmful. Jīva cannot exist alone and independent. Interdependency is a must in the case of Jīvas. By virtue of their existence they share their pleasure and pain with others. As partners in good and evil acts they are jointly responsible. But they must bear the karmic results individually for the part they play. They create a common environment and live together in weal and woe.

Jain canons, in case of propounding non-violence emphasize the protection of nature, especially the sentient beings. Interestingly, according to Jainism the vital elements of nature are sentients. The earth, the water, the air and even the fire are sentient. So a person should be very careful in protecting their sentient identity. Until now modern science does not conform to the sensibility of these elements, at least for protecting nature in its own form the concept of Jainism on this issue should be well-appreciated. The earliest Jain canon, Ācārāṅgasūtra endorses this matter in a significant manner. Just as consciousness of man born without some or other sense organs, that is, who is blind, deaf, dumb, crippled etc from birth, is not manifest, the consciousness of the beings of earth-body is also not manifest. Such a man born with physical impairment, experiences pain when is struck or slain with a weapon[10] (and so also the beings of the earth-body). The same explanation has been given in the case of other one-sensed immobile beings, such as, the water, fire, air and vegetation. There are many references in the Jain canons where the dialogues between Bhagavān Mahāvīra and his Chief disciple Indrabhūti Gautama are mentioned- Questions raised by Gautama and solutions are given by Mahāvīra. Although the respiratory system of a wounded man is clearly visible that cannot be realized by one-sensed immobile beings, Mahāvīra confirms that their respiratory system is not perceptible to them. But they have their own system of respiration. Like a man in a swoon, the beings of earth-body and the likes do not manifest consciousness. This occurs due to the slumber producing karma, technically said as styānardhi. Mahāvīra continues[11] that a man in swoon may be unconscious externally or internally. Internal swoon means the internal unconsciousness, that is, inner numbness. In such cases nothing is felt or experienced. But in case of external swoon, the external unconsciousness is lost. And the inner consciousness still remains active. So there is the experience of pain. They experience pain through inner consciousness on being struck or cut. At the time when these one sensed-beings are attacked by the external forces they experience terrible pain. He exemplifies it as an old feeble man is hit on the head by a strong young man. The pain of this living being is excruciating. Gautama has raised many questions on the consciousness and activities of one-sensed beings and BhagavānMahāvīra answered in such a way that the concept of non-violence can be established in its subtlest form —

Gautama – jīvāṇaṃbhaṃte !kiṃkāmī? bhogī?

Mahāvīra – Goyamā! soïṃdiya-cakkhiṃdiyāiṃpaḍuccakāmī, ghāṇiṃdiya-jibbhiṃdiya-phāsiṃdiyāiṃpaḍuccabhogī/ se teṇaṭṭheṇaṃGoyamā! evaṃvuccaïjīvākaamī vi bhogī vi// Goyamā! puḍhavikāiyāṇokāmī, bhogī/... Goyamā! phāsiṃdiyapaḍucca / se teṇaṭṭheṇaṃjāvabhogī//

One-sensed immobile beings only by touch can feel pleasure or pain. This teaching of Mahāvīra, if it is practised in a minimal state of responsibility, the ecosystem of nature will be compatible and sustainable for the creatures. Philosophy, especially the ethical doctrines always act as the guiding force of human life. It teaches harmonizing the gross with the subtle, a link between the manifested world and the consciousness. Humans with their wisdom exert for it from the time immemorial and paying constant effort in the quest of the self, the consciousness. BhagavānMahāvīra experienced the truth of the soul and matter. The apparent feature of a soul with one-sense had been realized in its sensuous form thousands of years ago. Not only in Jainism, but in other Philosophies also, respect to nature has always been a pivotal point.

An ascetic is ever vigilant in prohibiting the accumulation of karma whereas the laities in laxity attach themselves with different types of karma, technically it is called karmādāna. It is the occupation involving great bondage of karma. It comes through undertaking materialistic dealings like business and industry etc. In this way of life one earns livelihood involving great violence and great possession that lead to bondage of karma[12]. There is a mention of fifteen types of karmādāna in Jain canonical treatises, such as, iṃgāla-kamma (business of preparing and trading coal), vaṇa-kamma (forest-clearing), sāḍī-kamma (cart manufacturing), bhāḍī-kamma (a work done on hire by beasts of burden etc.), phoḍī-kamma (the act of digging ground etc.), daṃta-vāṇijja (ivory trade), lakkha-vāṇijja (trading in lac, a kind of gum), rasa-vāṇijja (wine-traffic), visa-vāṇijja (dealing in poison), kesa-vāṇijja (dealing in the animals having fur), jaṃtapīlaṇa-kamma (occupation of turning an oil-mill etc.), nillaṃchaṇa-kamma (the profession of castrating a bull etc.), davaggī-dāvaṇayā (setting fire to a mountain etc.), sara-daha-talāga-parisosaṇayā (drying of lake, deep fountain and pond), asatījaṇa-posaṇayā (maintenance of maid-servants, prostitutes etc.). The aforesaid prohibition of business, though apparently meant for the spiritual act, had great impact in restoration of nature, directly related to human life.

The canonical treatises prescribe some norms of the life that a man can realize as an ideal state of being. Continence is the tool of self-realization that leads to the path of purification. A harmonious coexistence with nature is the means of self-realization in its rudimentary stage. So spirituality means the fullness that does not overlook even the phenomenal world. Like that of five great vows (mahāvratas) – hiṃsā'nṛtasteyā'brahmaparigrahebhyo viratirvratam[13], such as, Non-violence, Truth, Non-stealing, Chastity and Non-possession, prescribed for an ascetic, a lay-devotee observes twelve small vows (anuvratas) in his life. A monk has to observe the vows in a perfect and flawless mode whereas some relaxations have been approved in observing those vows for a lay-devotee. In maintaining those five vows in a relaxed manner, a lay-devotee has to observe other seven supplementary vows of the anuvratas[14] called śikṣāvratas[15]. And again these śikṣāvratas are divided into three guṇavratas and four śikṣāvratas. So a laity has to observe twelve small vows[16] of righteousness in his life that directly or indirectly foster nature with harmonious coexistence. The teaching methodology of Jainism is quite interesting. Knowing the bad effect of an act is very important and then it is easy to renounce that act. So it is often mentioned 'jāṇiavvāṇasamāyariavvā' (to be known and not to be performed). Renouncing violence, falsehood, theft, sexual indulgence and possession are important, renouncing the partial transgression of non-violence etc are also known to be sinful act. The twelve vows negate the partial transgression of positive actions, such as, Non-violence, Truth, Non-stealing, Celibacy and Non-possession. Partial transgression is based on knowledge, faith and conduct. So jñānāticāra means the transgression of the conduct quâ knowledge, darśanācāra, that is, conduct quâ faith and cāritrācāra, conduct quâ abstinence[17]. The Sthānāṅgasūtra, explains four types of non-observance of vows, such as, atikrama (resolve to transgress), vyatikrama (an attempt to indulge in transgression), aticāra (partial transgression) and anācāra (transgression of discipline by fully indulging in the prohibited act). In all cases violation occurs through knowledge, faith and conduct.

For a lay-devotee partial transgression of the vow of the sthūlaprāṇātipāta-viramaṇa (abstinence from causing gross injury to living being) is said to be of five kinds, and these are bandha – tying cattles and servants tightly with rope and causing them pain[18]; badha—killing or beating domestic animals and servants[19]; chavicceda—cutting off limbs of animals etc[20]; atibhāra – putting excessive loads on animals and servants[21] and bhakta-pānāvyuccheda—In case of domestic animals and cattles, not to supply nourishments, that is, grass, water etc and incase of servants etc, to withdraw due remuneration of the employees, i.e. his livelihood due to anger and ill will[22]. In the Lāṭīsaṃhitā it is said —

narāṇāṃgomahiṣyāditiraścāṃvāpramādataḥ/
tṛṇādyannādipātānāṃnirodhovratadoṣakṛt//4.171//

The partial transgression in observing abstinence from falsehood in a gross sense is of five kinds[23], such as, mithyopadeśa (wrong instruction), rahasyābhyākhyāna (divulging secrets), kūṭalekhakriyā (forging documents), nyāsāpahāra (misappropriating funds entrusted to one's care) and sākāramantrabheda[24] (disclosing confidential deliberations).

The partial transgression in observing abstinence from stealing in a gross sense is of five kinds[25] such as, stenaprayoga (abetting theft), tadāhṛtādāna (dealing in stolen goods), viruddharājyātikrama (evading customs in foreign lands), hīnādhika-mānonmāna (misrepresenting the weight of goods one is buying or selling) and pratirūpaka-vyavahāra (dealing in counterfeit goods).

In case of (partial) celibacy to be observed by a householder, Jain scriptures prescribe a very interesting solution that a lay-devotee can do, that is,having the only wife/spouse in life-so partial transgression in abstaining from sexual intercourse with any woman/ man other than one's spouse. In the Uvāsagadasā while taking a vow for maintaining the sexual relation with his only wife (svadārasantoṣavrata), Ānanda takes a vow that he will not be indulged with any other woman except his wife Śivānandā[26]. Abstaining from violation of this act is of five kinds, such as, paravivāhakaraṇa (matchmaking), itvaraparigṛhītā (promiscuity), aparigṛhītāgamana (sex with whore), anaṅgakrīḍā (unnatural sexual practices) and tīvrakāmābhiniveśa (intense sexual passion)[27]. An ideal householder should abstain from these types of activities that attract the sin for violating the svadārasantoṣa-vrata.

The great vow non-possession has been leniently observed by a laity is icchā-parimāṇavrata (limitation of desire). The laity puts voluntary restrictions upon his desire for possessions. This vow should be maintained very carefully and a laity should be vigilant in observing this vow. The transgression is of five kinds that a lay-devotee should always avoid possession of tillable land and buildings, silver and gold, livestock and grain, male and female slaves and of base metals, earthware and wooden furnitures[28]. This dictum mentions five types of transgressions of the small vow to abstain from possessiveness[29]. A lay-devotee should limit his desire on the aforesaid possession . Apart from these vows, a lay-devotee has to observe other seven small vows, called as (three) Guṇavratas and (four) Śikṣāvratas. Under this category of seven small vows the laity is advised to be self restrained in many ways. Some of these are – not to go beyond the limits of the set area upwards, downwards, horizontally. He should not add the set area and he should not forget the vow he has observed for. This is the vow to refrain from movement beyond a limited area. He should not be indulged in erotic talk, erotic gesture, garrulity, unmindful deeds beyond the set limit and excessive use of the consumer goods. This supplementary vow is to refrain from wanton destruction of the environment. He should be aloof from sinful conduct strictly in the avowed period. He, on the sacred days at least, should observe fast. So no vow should be observed unmindfully or disrespectfully. In order to avoid hurting and killing small animals and creatures he should be ever vigilant in cleaning and sweeping the place. So there are many restrictions in the life of a lay-devotee to deal with an ideal life that leads to the path of purification of heart and soul.

The origin of the vocal and physical action is the mind. So the ideological concept lies on the philosophy and consequently the applied form of those concepts are manifested through the actions. Jain Philosophy believes human life is the most precious life in terms of the purification of the soul from karmic matter. And that can be accomplished through penance and that is, to live a self-restrained life. And hence, the dictum '(Living beings) render service to one another' becomes materialized.

[**Key words** – jīva, mahāvrata, aṇuvrata, yoga, karaṇa, bandha, atibhāra, svadārasantoṣa-vrata]

Notes and References

1. jahādumassapupphesubhamaroāviaïrasaṃ/ nayapuppha-ṃkilāmei so yapīṇeiappayaṃ// Dasaveyāliya1.2.
2. Dasav.1.5.
3. ṇāṇāpiṇḍarayāṇāmaukkhitta-caragādīpiṃḍassaabhiggaha-viseseṇaṇāṇāvidhesuratā, ahavaaaṃta-paṃtāīsunāṇāvihesub hoyaṇesuratā, ṇatesuaraïkareṃti, Jinadāsa-cūrṇi, p.69.
4. paḍhamaṃbhaṃte!mahavvaepāṇāivāyāoveramaṇaṃ: savvaṃbhaṃte! pāṇāivāyaṃpaccakkhāmi – se suhumaṃvāvāyaraṃvātasaṃvāthāvaraṃvā, neva-sayaṃpāṇeaïvāejjāpāṇeaïvāyaṃte vi aṇṇeṇasamaṇu-jāṇe jjājāvajjīvāetivihaṃtiviheṇaṃmaṇeṇaṃvāyāe-kāeṇaṃna-kareminakāravemikaraṃtaṃ pi annaṃnasamaṇujāṇāmi – 4.11.
5. Tattvārthasūtra 6.1.
6. 2 vols, Seth DevchandLalbhai Jain Pustakoddhāra Fund, series nos.67 &76.
7. That which is : in the explanation of the sūtras from General edition of Tattvārthasūtra and the variant reading found in the Sarvārthasiddhi while narrating the sūtra for the mobile beings. The general sūtra says – tejo-vāyūdvīndriyādayaścatrasāḥ. And the Sarvārthasiddhi explains thus by the sūtra is dvīndriyādayastrasāḥ.
8. Jain Pāribhāṣikaśabdakośa.
9. Tattvārthasūtra,Kailash Chandra Shastri p.148.
10. appageaṃdhamabbhe, appegeaṃdhamacche 1.28.
11. Bhagavatīsūtra 19 – 35.
12. kammādāṇāiṃ ’tikammāṇi — jñāvaraṇādīnyādīy ante yaistānikarmādānāniBhag. 8.242 vṛtti.
13. Tattvārthasūtra.7.1.

14. aṇuvrato'gārī. TS 7.15.

15. samaṇovāsagāṇaṃpaṃcāṇuvvatiesattasikkhāvatie-duvālasvidhesāvagadhammepaṇṇatte. Sthān.9.62.

16. digdeśanārtha-daṇḍaviratisāmāyika-pauṣadhopavāsopabhoga-paribhoga-parimāṇā'tithi-saṃvibhāgavrata-sampannaśca TS 7.16.

17. tividheaïyārepaṇṇatte, taṃjahā – ṇāṇaaïyāre, daṃsaṇaaïyāre, cārittaaïyāre Sthā.3.442.

18. bandhedvipadādīnāṃrajjādīnāṃsaṃyamanam. Uvās. ṭīkā p.25.

19. 'vahe' ttiyaṣṭyādibhistāḍanam . Uvās. ṭīkā. P.25.

20. 'chaviccheetti' śarīrāvacchedaḥ. Uvās. ṭīkā.p.25.

21. 'aïbhāre' ttiatibhārāropaṇaṃtathāvidha-śaktivikalānāṃmahābhārāropaṇam. Uvās.ṭīkā. p.25.

22. bhattapāṇavocchee' ttiaśana-pānīyādyapradānam. Uvās. Vṛ.1.32, p.10.

23. tayāṇaṃtaraṃcaṇaṃthūlagassamusāvāya-veramaṇa ssapaṃcaaïyārājāṇiyavvāṇasamāyariavvā, taṃjahā – sahasābbhakkhāṇe, rahasābbhakkhāṇe, sadāra-maṃtabhee, mosovaese, kūḍalehakaraṇe. Uvās.1.25.

24. mithyopadeśa-rahasyābhyākhyāna-kūṭalekhakriyā-nyāsāpahāra-sākāramantrabhedāḥ. TS.7.21.

25. thūlayaṃadiṇṇādāṇaṃpaccakkhāiUvās. 1.26], [stennaprayoga-tadāhṛtādāna-viruddharājyātikrama-hīnādhikamānonmāna-pratirūpakavyavahāra TS7.22.

26. nannatthaekkāesivanandāebhāriyāe, avasesaṃsavvaṃmeh-uṇavihiṃpaccakkhāmi. Uvās. 1.27.

27. paravivāhakaraṇê-tvaraparigṛhītâ-parigṛhītāgamaṇânaṅgakrīḍā-tīvrakāmābhiniveśaḥ. TS 7.22.

28. kṣetra-vāstu-hiraṇya-suvarṇa-dhana-dhānya-dāsī-dāsa-kupyapramāṇātikramaḥ. TS.7.24.

29. aparimiya-pariggahaṃsamaṇovāsaopaccakkhāïicchāparimāṇaṃuvasaṃpajjaï. ĀvaśyakaPariśiṣṭa p.22.

Books Consulted

1. Ācārāṅga-bhāṣyam. 1994. AcharyaMahāprajña. Jain VishvaBharati Institute, Ladnun.
2. Dasaveāliaṃ. 1974. Vācanā-pramukhaĀcāryaTulasī. Edited and commented by Muni Nathmal. Jain VishvaBharati, Ladnun.
3. Dharmāmṛtaanagāra of Ashadhara.1977. Edited by Kailash Chandra Shastri and Jyoti Prasad Jain, BharatiyaGyanpith, Delhi.
4. Dravyasaṃgraha of Nemicandra. 1986. Edited by SaratchandraGhosal. ChandraprabhaDigambarMandir Trust. Bombay.
5. Dharmāmṛtasāgāra of Ashadhara. !944. Edited by Kailash Chandra Shastri and Jyoti Prasad Jain, BharatiyaGyanpith, Delhi.
6. Early Jainism. 1978. KK Dixit and DalsukhMalvania. LD Institute. Ahmedabad.
7. Environmental Ethics. 2006. S M Jain. PrakritBharati Academy. Jaipur.
8. History of Prakrit Literature. 2014. Jagdish Chandra Jain, ChaukhambhaVidyabhawan, Varanasi.
9. Jainism and Metaphilosophy. 1991. S Gopalan. Satguru Publications. Delhi.
10. Religion and Philosophy of the Jainas. 1993. Virchand R Gandhi. Edited by Nagin J Shah. Jain International, Ahmedabad.

11. Sthānāṅgasūtra.Aṃgasuttāṇi (part I) VS 2031 (1974). Vācanā-pramukhaĀcāryaTulasī, Edited by Muni Nathmal. Jain VishvaBharati, Ladnun.

12. Tattvārthasūtra of Umāsvāti. 2009. Annotator Pt. SukhlalSanghvi. Edited by Mohan Lal Mehta, JamnaLal Jain. ParshvanathVidyapith. Varanasi.

13. Tattvārthasūtra (That Which Is) of Umāsvāti. 1994. English Translation with an Introduction by NathmalTatia.Harpar Collins Publishers.

14. Uttarajjhayaṇāṇi. 2000. Vācanā-pramukhaĀcāryaTulasī. Edited and annotated by ĀcāryaMahāprajña. JainaVishvaBharati. Ladnun.

15. Uvāsagadasāo. Aṃgasuttāṇi (part III). 1992. Vācanā-pramukhaĀcāryaTulasī, Edited by YuvācāryaMahāprajña. JainaVishvaBharati. Ladnun.

Chapter 11

THE ESSENCE OF ECO-THEOLOGY IN JAINISM

Dr. Namrata Kothari

Nature and human beings are close to each other for mutual existence and sustenance. The mutual interdependence, relationship between nature, humans, plants and animals has always been discussed in the history of human civilization at different periods, in different religions of the world. Jainism is one among other ancient religions of the world, highlighting this issue. Jain thinkers at length discussed how one could protect the environment and save oneself, nation, society and all creatures from natural disaster, through non-violence and non-possession. This Chapter attempts to illuminate how Jainism has addressed questions of ecology and environment and created a consciousness regarding the interconnectedness and interdependence of all In the 1st or 3rd century A.D. Umasvamiin Tattavartha Sutra wrote :

Parasparopagrahojivanamsoul renders service to one another.[1] (5.21).

"Just as in a human body one cannot separate the life of the

1 Brown,Kerry and Sharma, Sima (ed.), *That which is the TattvarthaSutra,Sutra,* Umasvati trans by NathmalTantia, (San Franciso:Harper Collins,1994), pp.xx.

lungs from the life of the stomach or the life of the brain, similarly one cannot separate the life of human beings from the life of the trees, the insects or the seas"[2].

In fact, it stresses the philosophy of ecological harmony and non-violence on which the doctrines and ethics of Jainism are based. We have to understand that Jainism as a religion protects the damage done to the environment leading to the conception of eco-theology, where[1]religion cares for the environment would be beneficial to all.

In the last five decades, under the influence of materialistic desires, humans have become involved in an unnatural treatment of their environment, as they ignore ecological values opening the way to a myriad of problems. There is rampant growth of materialism, consumerism, industrial production, growth of arms and armaments, creation of chemical, nuclear and biological weapons in Western societies, the indiscriminate pattern of consumption in many countries and growth of population in developing countries in more recent years, in non-western societies as well, rating serious problems for the maintenance of the quality of human environment.

- The first casualties are the forests, grasslands and farm lands, which have suffered from extreme pressures of urbanization.
- The second casualty is seen in the water pollution i.e. lakes, rivers and oceans, by the disposal of factory wastes and chemicals. It is so high that many lakes and rivers no longer support fish and other forms of life.
- The third casualty is the virtual exhaustion of our non-renewable resources, including many of the minerals, sources of energy like petrol and other products.

---

2 Rajotte, Freda with Breuilly,Elizabeth, "What Is the Crisis?" in Breuilly,Elizabeth and Palmer, Martin '(eds.)', *Christianity and Ecology,*(London : Cassel, 1992), p.8

Friedrich Engels was right when he wrote in "*The Part Played by labor in the Transition from Ape to Man*". "Let us not, however, flatter ourselves over much on account of our human victories over nature, for each such victory nature takes its revenge on us"[3].

Given these environmental hazards, Mahavira's understanding, dating back to nearly 2500 years, becomes greatly relevant. An equality of all forms of life and reverence for all of them is his central teaching. He said, "As you want to live, do so to others". Herein 'others' he included not only all living beings that can move, but also the existence of earth, air, water and vegetation. This is reflected in some passages of Jain texts like *Sutrakritanga Sutra* and *Dasavaikalika Sutra* as under :-

Some learn sciences which teach the destruction of living beings, others study spells for killing all sorts of creatures.(4)[4]

> A cruel man does cruel acts and is thereby involved in other cruelties, but sinful undertakings will in the end bring about misery (7)
>
> Bhante !
>
> Desist I from past violence to water bodies
>
> I decry, I denounce
>
> Dedicate I my soulV.19 (S)[5]

Misconception About Jain Environmental Ethics

Statements that environmental religious tradition is inherent in Jainism or Jainism has always placed the philosophy of ecological harmony are largely incorrect as statements, and such

---

3 Jain, Bhagchandra 'Bhaskar' Ecology and Spirituality in the Jain tradition, in Chapple, Christopher Key, *Jainism and Ecology*, p. 170.

4 Muller,F.Max,(ed.), *The Sacred Books of the East,* trans by Various Oriental Scholars, Gaina Sutra, Sutrakritanga Sutra - H. Jacobi, VII. 4 & 7 p.298.

5 *Dasavaikalika Sutra* - trans R. C. LalwaniMotilalBanariadass, Delhi, 1973 p. 41

misstatements will hinder more than help the development of a Jain environmental ethic. There is no Jain environmental ethic, environmentalism is a relatively new episteme globally. It has developed out of a set of physical, technological and increasingly moral and intellectual demands of the past several centuries. Therefore, environmentalism raises a new set of questions and issues, considering relevant in Jainism. The external pressures of environmental crises have resulted in the beginning of efforts by Jains to explore their own tradition within the new epistemological framework of environmentalism. For meeting the ecological crisis each faith has something to offer and Jainism is not an exception. Jainism with its intricate theories of philosophy about life and its practices, designed to preserve and protect life, provides interesting insights into refining the lifestyle which is friendly to environmental values.

Ecology is increasingly becoming a focus of the Jain community because of the emphasis on non-violence (*ahimsa*) of all living beings. The representatives of the Jain community presented a Declaration of Nature on 23 October 1990 at Buckingham Palace, thus joining the World Wide Fund for Nature (WWF) Network on Conservation and Religion[6]. They also presented a Statement on Ecology and Faith at the Alliance of Religious and Conservation (ARC) in the 1992 UN Conference on Environment and Development (Earth Summit) at Rio de Janeiro.

Jains represent in an effort to meet the ecological challenges in this world, as it advances along the path of economic development and industrialization. They are in favour of adopting a program to raise public awareness of the responsibility of individuals, groups and all forms. The Jain VishvaBharati Institute, founded in 1970, in Ladnun, Rajasthan by Late AcaryaTulsi offers a program in Ecology and Environmental Science[7]. Moreover, being guided by their principles of religion they are undertaking

6 Chapple,*Jainism and ecology*, p. 14.

7 Jaini,Padmanabh S, "Ecology, Economic and development in Jainism", in Chapple,Christopher Key, '(ed.)'Jainism and Ecology (Cambridge: Harvard University,2002),p. 14

projects aimed at addressing social and environmental problems. They also initiate programmes for conserving nature at pilgrimage sites e.g., the Greening of Palitana project at Shatrunjaya, Gujrat, Shravanabelgola in Karnataka, so that the pilgrims will be motivated to take back with them the environmental message as an ethical mandate of their faith.

Spirituality is essentially an individual effort and it is created by the individual on the basis of discipline and practice. Jainism reconciles the parts of reality with the whole by means of a relativistic approach. In *Acaranga Sutra* (an ancient Jain text), it is said, "One who knows one comes to know all. One who knows all, knows one."

Je eke janaitesavvejanai, je savvejanaite eke janai[8]

From an ecological perspective, spiritual relationship can be understood with the help of some basic principles of Jainism :

(1) Do not injure any creature

(2) Do not command any creature

(3) Do not own any creature

(4) Do not employ one as a servant[9].

Jain ecology is based on equality: each life form must be respected. The term ecology within Jainism might be *sarvodayavada*, or a concern for lifting all forms of life. Samantabhadra (3rd C C.E), a prominent Jain philosopher said that this is the fundamental principle of Jainism.

"Jam icchasiappanatto, jam canamicchasiappananto
Tam iccaparassaviya, ettiyamjina sasanam"[10]

---

8 Bhagchandra Jain 'Bhaskar', 'Ecology and spirituality in the Jaintradition,p.171.

9 Yuvacarya,Mahaprajna,(ed.), *AyarangaSutta* English trans. by Muni Mahendra Kumar, (New Delhi : Today and Tommorrow, 1981), p. 175.(See also Ayaranga 1.4.23 p. 193).

10 Varni,SamkalakaJinendra, *SamanaSutta* (Ravadi : Agama Prakashan, 1996, Gatha 24, p. 7.

"Because one sees others as not different from oneself, an ecological view can arise that sees sanctity in all other persons as well as in plants and animals"[11].

Jainism holds that the entire world, including plants, trees, birds, animals, water, and so forth, have life. So it is our main duty to protect and preserve all these. Jainism does so philosophically by accepting the principle of interdependence between nature and animals. From the ecological perspective, we should understand that in Jainism souls are divided into two broad classes : world being, further divided into mobile and immobile being and liberated souls[12].

The table given below gives the number of vitalities for life-forms classed according to the number of senses they possess[13].

BEINGS	VITALITIES
One - Sensed	(1) - (4)
Two - Sensed	(1) - (6)
Three - Sensed	(1) - (7)
Four - Sensed	(1) - (8)
Five - Sensed non-rational	(1) - (9)
Five - Sensed Rational	(1) - (10)

The following table shows the varieties of elemental bodies, plants, animals, humans, internals and gods, and the number of senses they posses[14].

11 Jain,BhagchandraBhaskar, *Ecology and Spirituality in Jain tradition* p. 171.

12 Umasvati, *Tathvartha Sutra : That Which Is*, p. 40.

13 Ibid., p.43

14 Ibid., pp.45,46

Number of senses	Being
One Sense (Touch)	earth, water, fire, air and plant bodied.
Two Senses (Touch & taste)	worms, leeches, mollusca (oysters, mussels, snails etc.) curculionidae, vermes
Three Senses (Touch, taste & smell)	Some mini beasts such as ants, fleas, plant-lice, cotton-seed insects, termites, centipedes
Four Senses (Touch, taste, Smell & sight)	Some mini beasts such as wasps, flies, gnates, mosquitoes, butterflies, moths, scorpions etc.
Five Senses (Touch, taste, smell, sight & hearing)	Larger animals such as fish, birds and quadrupeds, humans, infernal and gods.

Mahavira proclaimed that anyone who neglects the existence of earth, water, air and vegetation neglects his own existence, which is essentially bound up with them. *Acaranga Sutra,* explains how one can do violence against earth, air, water, fire and vegetations. Plowing, digging, excretions and other violations of the earth fall into the category of violence towards the earth-bodied beings.

Similarly, according to Jainism, water bodies contain beings[15]. This is also proved by contemporary science, which demonstrates the existence of multiple microorganisms in water. The *Niryukti* enumerates some actions which kill the beings in water, like drawing water from a well, straining it, and washing clothes.

There are several types of water-bodied beings[16], like dew,

15 Jaina Sutras Part I Akaranga Sutra, translated by various oriental scholars and ed. by F. Max Muller *The Sacred Books of the East*, MotilalBanarsidass Pub, Delhi, 1994, Lecture 1, Lesson 3, pp.5 and 6.

16 Jain,Kailashchandra and Pannalal (eds.), *Mulacara*, (Delhi: BharatiyaJnanapeeth, 1984), Gatha 210.

hail, snow and brine which live below and above the earth in wells, tanks, pits, oceans and lakes. Fire-bodied beings are also to be saved by the follower of non-violence i.e., not to extinguish fire by throwing sand or water on it. Similarly, air-bodied beings can be killed by electrical fans and even by palm fans[17].

There is a lively discussion in Jain literature on how plants and other beings can and should be saved by a Jain. It shows the deep concern that Mahavira had for ecology, which consists of a balance between plants, animals and humans. This further avoids harm to water, air, fire and all forms of life and minimizes the evils of modernity like pollution, deforestation, consumerism, technological advancement at the cost of nature in order to balance the community and ecosystem.

However, this does not mean that Mahavira was not conscious of the fact that our existence involves violence of one kind or the other. Even his disciples asked him, "According to your philosophy of teaching, whatever we do, whether it be eating, drinking, walking, sitting or even breathing, we are committing violent acts, interfering with nature, destroying the environment". Mahavira said, "If you are aware of all your actions, and are careful about what you do in relation to other living things, you will develop spirituality and be in perfect harmony with natural world.[18]"

From the angle of the livingness of all things as articulated by Mahavira, Jainism developed the theory of *Karma* to explain the existence of various life forms. According to Jain karma theory, each life form will go through the cycle of birth and rebirth, till it attains spiritual liberation (*Kevala*).

It defines the scope of modern ecology as it stresses the fundamental principle that all aspects of nature belong together and are bound in physical as well as metaphysical relationship. Therefore, life is viewed as a gift of oneness, accommodation

17 Bhagchandra Jain 'Bhaskar' *Ecology and Spirituality in Jain Tradition*, p. 175.

18 Sadhvi, Shilapi, *The Environmental and Ecological Teachings of Tirthankara Mahavira*, p. 161

and cooperation in a universe teeming with interdependent constituents.

The Jain Declaration on nature is broadly divided into three main parts viz;

I. The Jain teachings

II. The Jain cosmology and

III. The Jain Code of conduct.

(I) Jain Teachings

Jainism recommends two types of vows :

(1) The *mahavrata* or the great vows followed by members of monastic orders (monks & nuns)

(2) The *anuvrata* or the small vows followed by the laity (common man)

The vows are abstinence from violence, falsehood, stealing, carnality and possessiveness. The former refers to commitment to complete abstinence, observed absolutely and without relaxation. The latter refers to a commitment to partial abstinence according to one's capacity[19].

In principle, monks and nuns are not involved in environmental damage in any respect because of the vows of *mahavrata*. Only the laity are responsible for ecological problems caused by overpopulation, too much competition, over indulgence based on deliberate exploitation of nature. Therefore, *anuvrata* is recommended to restrain the lay person from developing those inclinations leading to such problems. Due to their (Jainism) perception of the "livingness of the world"[20], Jains hold aloft for the ideals of the environmental movement. The Jain vows can easily be interpreted in an ecological fashion, which are as under:

---

19 Umasvati, *TathvarthaSutra : That Which Is*, p.140.

20 Chapple,Christopher Key, *Introduction to Hinduism – Hinduism, Jainismand Ecology* – www.rediff.com

Ahimsa (Non-Violence):

Broadly speaking, *ahimsa* means avoidance of harmful thought, speech and action. It also frees one from any sort of ill-will and refuses to entertain any kind of negative thought. It means abstaining from contact with sights of brutality and activities that cause pain and disharmony. Further, accepting the vegetarian diet. The *anuvrata* movement started by Acarya Tulsi in India and the Vegetarian movement amply speak about the significance of *ahimsa*. The full application of *ahimsa*, however, involves applying it not just to human beings but also to other beings like air, water, earth, plants, animals etc. It restrains the self from the violence of body, speech and mind – against all living forms. It also suggests to adapt oneself to the growth of technological world. Non-violence suggests love and protection of life and environment, and thus creates an atmosphere of dialogue between man and nature, peace among all living beings, protection of forests, endangered species, river, air, water from pollution.A rational maxim designed to govern all of one's actions is a universal law in Jainism .

In the 20th century the most famous proponent of non-violence was Gandhiji, who was deeply influenced by Jainism and combined love and non-violence. To him, non-violence does not simply mean non- killing. *Ahimsa* and truth, according to Gandhi, are so intertwined that it is practically not possible to separate them. The positive form of *ahimsa* includes "truth and fearlessness ...... The practice of ahimsa calls forth the greatest courage"[21]. Gandhiji carried this philosophy to the Indian people and it helped immensely in gaining India's Independence from the British yoke. His criticism of man's greed of over consumption displays his far sightedness with ecological wisdom, much ahead of its time. Therefore, *Ahimsa* is "live and love" more than "live and let live", the first of the five fundamental principles of Jain ecology.Nature is not secondary to serve man and to fulfill his aspirations but it is a co-habitat. Hence the slogan like 'save life' and 'save the forest' is not a mere jargon but an ecological assertion of *ahimsa*

---

21 Bose,Nirmal Kumar(ed.), *Selections from Gandhi*, (Ahmedabad: Navajivan Publishing House, 1957), p. 154.

and a manifestation of anger at ruthless destruction of life and environment. Therefore, by following only one of the main pillars in Jain philosophy '*ahimsa*', the suggestive eco-friendly spirit, one can save the nature from the clutches of Western modernity.

(b) Truth (*Satya*)

It means accepting the reality as it is and being truthful to it. It means "do not lie" do not have any illusion about yourself and face the truth with fearlessness. It also means avoidance of manipulation. Being truthful means humble and open to new discoveries, yet there is no ultimate final truth. "Truth is what is: we accept what is as it is, speak of it as it is, and live it as it is.[22]" It is eco-friendly in the sense that in the garb of modernity, technological advancement we have an illusion that man is superior to nature and able to control it,which, in reality is not the fact,rather he is controlled by nature. If one is true to oneself then he realizes the importance of nature in life and tries to do minimum harm to nature thereby preserve and protect it.

(c) Stealing (*Asteya*)

This means refraining from amassing goods or services beyond one's requirement. It is difficult to know what is our essential needs, so Jain ecology requires that we assess, examine and question, day by day, what is our need and what is our greed. If one draws in excess from nature than his essential need, one is stealing from nature. Thus, clearing an entire forest would be seen as a violation of nature's rights and an act of theft. Similarly, extraction from society in the form of food, cloth, shelter in excess means depriving other people which therefore, is a kind of theft .If one uses natural resources at a great speed, which leads to extinction, then one is stealing from future generations.

(d) Celibacy (*Brahmacharya*)

This principle is closely related to the conduct of sexual

---

22 Jaini,Padmanabh S, *Ecology, Economic and Development in Jainism,*p. 188.

behaviour : it is love without lust. For Jaina monks it means total abstinence, and for laity it means loyalty & commitment in marriage. Any thought, speech or act, which abuses the body, violates this principle. It recognizes not only the dignity of the human body but also the body of nature. For Jains, ecology means living in a relationship of fidelity with nature. Sexual restraint is important in the sense that it will help to minimize the population growth which is also the root cause of ecological depletion.

(e) Non –Possession (*Aparigraha*)

The most important economically and ecologically significant vow for the layperson is the limitation of possession--non-accumulation and non-possessiveness. One should not have more than necessary things. The accumulation of wealth beyond a certain limit is dangerous and this is the root cause of misery of human being in this universe. "There is enough for every body's need but not enough for anybody's greed"[23]. *Aparigraha* means sharing, to live simply, without any pomp and show. "Simple in means, rich in end" [24] is the Jain ecology.

For Jain monks, the *mahavrata* means to have no attachment to anything- wealth, property, animals or grains. But for the laity it means to retain no more than necessary (*Parigraha-viramana - vrata*)[25] One should give his surplus to temple or any other welfare institution. Here, however, we find a contradiction in the sense that inspite of this *mahavrata* the rich people have always formed a major part of the Jaina community. In this context here it is worthwhile to clarify that wealth is not forbidden,but running after wealth and riches is not allowed. This is rather similar to the ascetic Protestantism of the Occident[26].

The practical code of conduct laid down for the Jain householders consists in the observance of the five *vratas* (vows)

---

23 Kumar,Satish "Jain ecology" in Chapple (ed.)*Jainism and Ecology*, p. 189.

24 ibid.p.189

25 Mandawat, S. L, 'Jaina Ethics and Economic prosperity", *Jain Journal* Vol. III No. 1, July, 1968, p. 35.

26 ibid.p. 34.

as discussed and their relevance for the understanding of the ecological question has also been noted.

Apart from these mahavrata, other important principles and teachings of Jainism are as under:

Anckantavada

In the era of global terrorism, ethnicity, violence, racism, casteism, fundamentalism the Jaina philosophy of *anekanta* aims at playing a very crucial role to get rid of the clutches of these monsters. This philosophy of *anekanta* enables us to understand the various dimensions of reality, to reconcile contradictory views, facilitating an attitude of respect for other's viewpoints thereby allowing us to be more understanding and tolerant to other people's views, which will reduce conflicts, tensions and wars. And this very recognition will help us create a non-violent world order .

Anekanta is closely similar to postmodernism doctrine of relative pluralism. It suggests that every field of idea is a field of contending forces and since no representation can capture the subject completely, differences should be recognized. This espouses the idea of tolerance.

Being rooted in the doctrines of *anekantavada*, Jainism does not look upon the universe from the anthropocentric, ethnocentric or egocentric view point. It takes into account the viewpoints of other species i.e. earth, air, water, plant, animal, other communities and nations and other human beings. Thus, it maintains an ecological balance, keeping in view the security of other species, i.e., it protects and preserves them and thereby maintains a balance between man and nature. This is the eco-theology perception in Jainism.

The another major teaching of Jainism is equanimity. It inspires the personal search of every Jain for equanimity (*Samyaktva)* towards both animate beings (*Jiva*) and inanimate substances and objects (*ajiva*). It helps the development of an attitude of give and take and of 'live and let live'. It provides a practical approach to peace, based not on the domination of nation, people and nature, but on calmness of the mind, devoted to the conservation, preservation and protection, for the balance of the universe. This is reflected in passages of *Uttaradhyayana Sutra* as follows :-

> He who verily believes with respect,
> In the truth contained in the nine,
> Which have been named 'fundamentals'
> Since one has equanimity.[27]
>
> (U. S. XXVIII, 15)

Jivadaya means compassion towards all living beings. It means caring for all living beings and also protecting and serving them. It reflects universal friendliness *(Kshama)* and universal fearlessness (*abhaya*). This will be possible only with the help of tolerance. The greatest example of tolerance is the *Paryusanaparva* of the Jains, which leads people to the path of tolerance and thereby maintenance of a friendship between men and men, and even between men and animals. This *parva*, a festival of forgiveness,is generally held between the end of the August and the beginning of September every year, when everyone chants the following verse seeking forgiveness for all misdeeds.

> *Khamemisavva—jive savvajivaKhamantu me/*
> *metti me savva-bhuesuverammajjhamnakenavi.//*

"I pardon all the animals and let all the animals pardon me; I have friendship with all animals and I have no enmity with anybody"[28]

The Jain monastic order and laity follow this with a heart filled with forgiveness and they also pray that it may reign through the world and all living beings may cherish each other as because the misuse of plants and animal beings for our selfish ends leads to extinction of many species,which are responsible for maintaining

---

27 Lalwani,K. C, *Uttaradhyayana Sutra,p.327.*

28 Banerjee, S. R, (ed.),*Prolegomena to Prakritica et. Janica*, (Kolkata: The Asiatic Society, 2005), p. 153.

ecological balance. To maintain a balanced relationship between the human world and the other world it encourages universal love and brotherhood among the people when human beings are ready to shed blood of others for amassing more and more power and wealth making the future of coming generation unsecure and unsafe.

(II) Jain Cosmology

As today's modern world tries to understand traditional values, which enhance the respect of nature, Jainism seeks to improve the shared aim of preserving and respecting all forms of life.

India's one of the most thorough attempts to give a clear picture of cosmology is provided by

Jainism, which combines the place of human being with the continuum of the universe. Umasavati's system of cosmology is accepted by both the major sects (Svetembara and Digambara) of Jainism. It tries to explain the place of the human being in a great moving reality.

According to Jain cosmology, universe has no beginning and no creator. The universe consists of two things –*Jiva* (animate, consciousness) and *ajiva* (inanimate unconsciousness). There are five substances of *ajiva*:[29]

- *Dharma* – the medium of motion
- *Adharma* – the medium of rest
- *Akasha* – space
- *Pudgala* – matter
- *Kala* – time

There are countless souls at different stages of personal evolution like earth, water, air, vegetables, plants, animals, insects, human beings etc. They go through the continuous cycle of death

29 Singhvi,L. M, *The Jain Declaration on Nature*, p.221.

and rebirth till they attain the higher stage of liberation i.e. *moksha* or salvation.

"Mahavira taught that only the one who understood the grave demerit and detriment caused by destruction of plants and trees understood the meaning and merit of reverence for nature. Even metals and stones might have life in them and should not be dealt with recklessly"[30]

As human beings evolve (i.e. having five senses), they have big responsibility in their shared understanding with each other and in their relationship with the rest of the universe. Hence it is this Jain conception of life which views the world as a living, dynamic process in the contemporary context of environmental degradation, requiring protection and care. Jainism also develops a clear and precise code of behavior that seeks to respect different life forms, including material manifestations, and by following it one can ascend to a higher state of spiritual sensitivity for which human beings have an ethical responsibility and cannot escape from it. Thus Jain Culture is a cradle for the creed of environmental preservation, protection and harmony.

Kindness to Animals

In Vedic period people generally made animal sacrifices to satisfy God. The Jain*Tirthankaras* raised their voice against this cruel practice of sacrifice and condemned it as transgressions against the vow of non-violence. It includes avoidance of cruelty to animals and human beings also. It is also forbidden generally to keep animals in captivity, whip, overload them or deprive them of food and drink. The injunction is modified in respect of pet animals to the limit that they may be roped or whipped occasionally but with care, without anger and with due consideration.[31] The stories of *Tirthankaras* underscore the concern for animals and their place within nature, which are also a milestone in the history of protection of animals.

---

30 Ibid., p.222.

31 Singhvi,L. M, *The Jain Declaration on Nature*, p.223.

The other fabled story was of 23rd *Tirthankara* Parsvanatha, who found a snake amid the fire lit by an ascetic, did not remain silent and raised his voice against that form of pain.

During the first half of the second millenium, the great Saiva king Siddharaja of Gurjar, on the advice of Maladhari Acarya Abhayadeva and Acarya Hemacandra, provided protection to animals, beasts and birds. His successor, Kumarapala, is popular for his declaration of non-slaughter. Muhammad Tughlak, being persuaded by Acarya Jinaprabhusuri, at a later period, indulged in many acts of animal protection. Being influenced by the Jain monks Akbar, also legislated on animal protection. The famous *farman* of him is before us which testifies the dynamic character of the principle of non-violence preached by the Jain[32]. Further, consideration for welfare among the Jains is demonstrated by their orientation of vegetarianism with the argument to minimize harm to living beings. Last but not the least, it is worthwhile to mention that various practices and institutions have been established by the Jains for animal protection i.e. *Pinjrapoles* (Special refuges for animals). There are thousands of *pinjrapoles* established and financed by Jains, in the towns and villages of Rajasthan and Gujrat, for serving and protecting the helpless beasts and birds. The efforts of these institutions are focused on protecting domestic herds and animals such as goats, sheep and cattle; at the same time other sick or injured animals may be brought to these refuges for shelter and medical treatment. There are sanctuaries for birds, where food and water are provided to them. Thus, a living being is allowed to complete his life span, in conformity with nature, without any interference in the form of violence. In *Akaranga Sutra* we find the following lines:

All beings are fond of life, like pleasure, hate pain, shun destruction, like life, long to live. To all life is dear.[33] (4)

---

32 PanditSukhalji, *The World Pacifist Meeting and the Role of Jainism*, (Calcutta: Jain reception Committee,(nd)),p.14.

33 Jaina Sutra, Part-I, Akaranga Sutra, trans by Various Oriental Scholars, ed. by F. Muller, Vol.22, MotilalBanarsidass, Delhi, 1994, *The Sacred Books Of the East*, p.19.

The basic thrust here is to provide an environment of preservation and protection of life rather than premature end of life. Therefore, this code of conduct of Jainism, is no doubt, an eco-friendly one.

Vegetarianism

The dietary practice and philosophy of vegetarianism date back to the views of Pythagoras in the 5th century. B.C. Hinduism, Jainism, Zoroastrianism and Buddhism also endorsed this dietary practice and vegetarianism during this period. Historically, support for a vegetarian life style had been stressed in physical, ethical and moral spheres[34] in all societies. The important objective of Jainism is said to be the scientific art of joyful living. Its principles are right faith and right knowledge. Right knowledge leads to salvation from unnatural bondages and helps man enjoying immense and permanent happiness, strength and knowledge[35].

It is relevant here to search why Jains advocate pure and *satvika* vegetarian food. The Jain emphasis on vegetarianism is based purely on a scientific approach to reality. The elements of love and vegetarianism are the integral parts of ecology. Food and *Ahimsa* (Non-violence) have close relationship. Non-violence *(Ahimsa)* necessarily requires taking of vegetarian food. The *satvika* nature promotes alertness, endurance and develops strength with tenacity, calmness or tranquility. Jain acharyas have advocated different kinds of food for different seasons. Even among various kinds of vegetarian food, one has been advised to abstain from garlic and onions for all seasons and leafy vegetables in the rainy seasons. All these depend on the particular climatic conditions and strict adherence may not be possible everywhere. Further, the Acharayas have advised to avoid a high protein diet like *twidal*, *basandal*, as they are *Rajasika* in nature . They are advised not to eat stale food, as in stale food the organism

---

34 Katz,Solomon H,*Encyclopedia of food and culture*, (New York:2003), V.3, p. 488.

35 ibid.p. 2291,Vol. 9.

that develops, destroys the *Satvika* nature of food and makes it *Tamasika*.

There are great chances even for cooked food to develop microorganisms after six hours, if it is not properly preserved. Hence, Jain- Acharyas have advised to eat only freshly prepared food, and drink fresh water which is properly sieved, and to avoid that vegetarian food which is extremely hot, sore and fried. Low intake of fat is also advised.

Further, Jains must not eat fruits of Gular, Angeer, Peepal, and Banagan which are the birth places of mobile beings. It is necessary for a Jain to take his meal during day time because *Himsa* is inevitable when food is prepared or taken in the absence of sunlight. Therefore, Jains have to renounce night eating throughout the year and those who cannot do so, at least do it during the *Chaturmasa* or the four months of the rainy seasons when there is a large growth of insects.

Jain philosophers and sagas ordain that the ideal of brotherhood will remain a mere dream unless the noble man develops the finer feeling of compassion towards all beings.[36] The other arguments given by Jains for the prohibition of flesh eating—The higher the stage of development of the injured being, the heavier the sin of the injury is considered to be committed. Thus from the practical view point the sin of hurting a plant is smaller than that of hurting an animal; the sin of hurting an animal is smaller than that of human being. From this standpoint it can be understood why Jainism forbids flesh eating and insists on the eating of vegetables. Therefore, what is enjoined on Jainas is simply this "Do not destroy life, unless it is absolutely necessary for the maintenance of a higher kind of life.[37]"

Self Restraint and the Avoidance of Waste

The philosophy of self restraint suggests restraint by individuals and setting a physical limit on possession for own

36 SinghNagendra kr. (ed.),*Encyclopaedia of Jainism,* V. 23 p.6046

37 Sangave,VilasAdinath, *Jaina Community – a social survey,* p. 32.

use. These are indicated as the desirable vows by the followers of Jain religion. They are encouraged to observe regular periods of fasting for self-purification and to avoid waste in any form. In fact, using any resource beyond one's needs and misuse of any part of nature is considered as a form of theft. Jains take the cues from the bee that sucks honey in the blossoms of a tree without hurting the blossom and strengthens itself using the earthly resources. In fact, Jainism declares that waste and pollution are the acts of violence. An important example of Jain ecology is the practice of collecting rain water in the family. They cover water tanks in their house roofs to hold sufficient monsoon water. The water tank holds drinking water for the entire year. For Jains, wasting water is a serious offence. Thus, self-restraint and non-waste together will help us to take proper decisions following the criteria of least harm, conservation of resources and the degree to which a mix of projects represents a balance between destruction and preservation of the environment . This is reflective of the concern for the well-being of the world, including the animals and the vegetable kingdom. Thus, in the era of globalization Jainism provides an alternative perspective on issues of prosperity, poverty and ecological balance.

Charity (*Dana*) (Donations, Spiritual Service)

This entails offering with veneration, freshly cooked vegetarian food, drink, shelter and other needs of life to the monks as well as offerings out of compassion to those who are poor and afflicted with misery. Hemacandra considers a great layman (*mahasravaka*) as "one who strews wealth out of devotion in seven fields (*Ksetra*) and out of compassion (*daya*) on the needy"[38]. With this act of *dana* one will be able to destroy his negative *Karma*. In this way a legitimate balance between the three goals of a layperson is maintained, namely, religious pursuits (*dharma*), earning a livelihood (*artha*) and maintenance of the family lineage (*Kama*).

---

38 Jaini,Padmanabh S, *Ecology, Economic and Development in Jainism,*p. 146.

In accordance with the Jain principles of ahimsa and *satya* Jains earn honestly, share one's wealth with others, amass a certain amount of wealth and prosperity to give something for the well-being of society at large. Therefore, the five fundamental teachings and five –fold code of conduct in Jainism would definitely offer this world a viable route plan for humanity and for environmental preservation and protection, peace and harmony in the strife torn universe and also alleviate the greed and pride that lead to disregard the environment.

However, Jainism is not free from criticism. One expression of environmentalism involves tree planting projects. Though Jain lay people might participate in such activities their nuns and monks do not participate, because of the harm caused to the earth in the digging of soil. Digging a well or worshiping the Jinas with cut flowers may both be, on the face of it, slightly faulty, if judged in exclusively doctrinal terms, but ultimately these actions are helpful because they bring about a morally positive disposition in the agent. Yasovijaya makes a significant comment in this respect : "even in activity relating to religion, a little evil caused by violence can be approved.[39]" The type of violence involved in eating, as well as in digging wells or offering worship to the Jinas, is, then, not really violence in true sense of the action.

An expression of environmentalism in India has been to establish forest preserves on property surrounding Jaina temple sites. However, this generally requires blocking access to prevent collection of fodder resulting in further impoverishment of the struggling peasants.

In additionto these questions of organic life and social life, the extensive involvement of the Jains in heavy industries in India raises issues of appropriate economic activity and environmental health. They remained confined to commercial capitalism and failed to create an industrial organization, which seems to be a very important factor in moulding the Jains in the shape of merchant sect, making them refrain from all other economic activities,.

39 Chapple and,(eds.), *Jainism and Ecology*, p.110.

offering lower opportunities to rise.[40] These instances demonstrate the complexities of effectively applying ecological principles on the basis of a religious doctrine.

The ascetic basis of Jainism is declining significantly among large segments of the Jain immigrant community, particularly the youth. They consider it outdated and irrelevant in the modern world. They think that changes need to be made in accordance with the present situation. For example, it was taught by their ancestors not to eat at night. Today, however, with the parents working outside and daily activities extended into late evening, it is not possible to eat early. In addition, health standards are safer than they were hundreds of years ago and hence, it seems acceptable that we eat late at night.

Further, with a certain degree of physical comfort that is afforded by having access to electricity, running water, mechanized transportation, adequate health care, shelter and clothing, it is not possible to carry on without development and industrialization, causing harm to the earth, water, and air. So practising Jain environmental ethic is still the ideal to strive for, even on the part of householders.

In spite of all these blockades, Jainism offers a unique source for the creation of an earth ethic. In the perspective of bio-cosmology, Jainism presents a world-view that stresses the interrelatedness of life forms. Further, its philosophy of *anekant* helps in understanding the nature from different perspectives and thereby increases the quality of tolerance in people. The allied non-violent ethics can easily be extended to embrace the earth ethics. Though it includes a strong emphasis on asceticism that may discourage some adherents from placing too much value on earthly concerns, that Jainism can lead to the enhancement of core human- earth relations is undeniable.

---

40 Mandawat, S. L, Jaina Ethics and Economic prosperity,p.33.

Conclusion

Human beings have accumulated luxury and wealth and squeezed natural resources for selfish purposes. But there is a limit to what nature can endure. Nature has its own way of correcting imperfection via external and internal calamities. External events include earthquakes, floods, storms, fires, hail-storms and landslides. Internal troubles like depression and diseases are sometimes beyond the reach.

Supreme consciousness is evolving constantly. Similarly, in the human mind, *gyan, vigyan*, knowledge and science also grow. But when *gyan-vigyan* is misused for satisfying the egoistic selfish mind, nature demonstrates her power. To understand and control this is beyond human capacity. In one sweep she brings down human arrogance, that makes us think we know it all how things work in the human body and in the universe. Due to the decline in qualities of divinity conferred upon humans by nature, we have become slaves to narrow intellect—that gave it into the manipulative tactics to survive. All spheres, including the religious, social, political, and educational are contorted to satisfy human desires. Lifestyles have become unsuitable. Most have forgotten how to live a life of simplicity, gentleness and brotherhood. Only Karma, action, can cut Karma. Ignite divine qualities within, annihilate *asuric* tendencies as mentioned in Gita, chapter 16, the dignified conduct of Rama and policy of Krishna will assist to crossover.

Therefore, in the chapters of this book, the relation between religion and ecology and their interdependence with each other is well reflected through different religious philosophies, their texts, agamas and granthas.

Chapter 1 discusses about the interdependence and interrelationship between Religion, Society and environment was well acknowledged in India since earliest times. The Vedic seers attached utmost importance to environment and related cosmology, theology and environment in a systematic way through the Vedas which were the guiding force for the society.

The Vedic seers worshiped nature as divine and assigned due values to the objects which formed part of the environment and constituted nature. Mountains, Rivers, Sun, Moon, Stars,Trees, plants, Animals etc. were considered sacred and men in the early ages worshiped them as God. This strong faith formed the basic culture of the society and was transmitted from generation to generation as an inherent trait without any deviation or distortion. Various natural phenomena like seasonal changes, Eclipse, Full moon, New moon were attributed to supernatural forces. Thus, every aspect of natural phenomenon was described as divine action and pre historic human believed this without questioning.

With the advancement of knowledge, especially science and technology man started questioning the validity and veracity of the earlier conclusions and started discarding them as unscientific, redundant, and unacceptable. His voluptuous eyes fell on Nature' s gift to the society and his greed prompted him to devour them in the name of modernization and scientific advancement. This resulted in large scale destruction of Nature causing ecological imbalance.

To check these unsocial, erratic and unethical practices Religion was introduced in a more comprehensible form for the layman bridging environment and religion putting man as the active performer and a binding force in the execution of the act.

The present chapter focuses on the various aspects taking

concrete examples from South India as well as from Sikkim. The data was collected by the author through field visits. Although the term Eco- Theology is a recent coinage introduced by Prof.Lynn white Jr.ofUCLA, the concept is very old and dates back to pre-vedic period. The various details are adumbrated with examples in this chapter. It is also shown that the relationship between Religion, Society,and Environment are intricately intertwined and inseparable.

Chapter 2 highlighted India has a rich ecological and cultural landscape. Both the "devotional model" and the "renouncer model " can contribute for preserving the ecology of India. The latter can help in reducing the over-exploitation of natural resources by limiting one's desire for more and more luxuries, and former can help in restoring natural resources to their original beauty and harmony. A Jain householder is also supposed to avoid injury to *trasa* beings (mobile) and is supposed to minimize injury to *sthavara* beings (immobile) while Buddhism has also emphasized on *Ahimsa* (do no harm), *Karuna* (compassion), and *Metta* (loving kindness). In Hindu religion, many of the gods mentioned in the hymns of Vedas are related to natural phenomena and the ancient Indian philosophy of "Vasudhavkutumbakam "(the whole world is like a family) is very relevant in the present day global environment conservation.

Among other religions, Guru Granth Sahib says that the purpose of human life is to achieve a blissful state in harmony with everything around them including other people, animals and nature. Air is the Guru, Water the Father, and the Earth is the Great Mother.(Guru Granth Sahib).Qur'an, which contains many references to water and other vital natural resources lays down clear guidelines for their conservation and equitable distribution. In the Qur'an, conservation and fair distribution are emphasized. Moreover, like everything in creation, resources are seen foremost as belonging not to humans but to Allah, for whom humans are to hold nature in trust (*amāna*). Another religion present in India is Zoroastrian . Zoroastrians believe that everything including the natural environment has been created pure and should be treated with love and respect. The Avesta and other texts call for the protection of water, earth, fire and air making it, in effect, an ecological religion; some proclaim it as the world's first proponent of ecology.

Thus, a cosmopolitan view gives useful insights in a varied ecological and cultural landscape like India.

Chapter 3 makes an attempt to solve the problem of the exploitation of nature from the perspective of a ***Hindu TāntricPhilosophy***, the ***Trika*** tradition **Kashmir Śaivism**.

Mahatma Gandhi once said, "*There is enough for everybody's need and not for everybody's greed*".

The greed of mankind and the subsequent exploitation of nature led to severe consequences, challenging the survival of the human race. We need an approach to sustainable development, which shall ensure the survival of our civilization without the future generation being compromised. This paper would make an attempt to address this problem, from the perspective of a ***Hindu Tāntric* Philosophy**, the ***Trika*** tradition **Kashmir Śaivism**. The popular idea in religion is to restrain the senses and practise renunciation. For most of the systems, the world is full of sorrows, and therefore withdrawal and introspection is the way out. However, such views often fail to acknowledge the aesthetic needs of a person and the ways of expression. The *Trika* school on the other hand, gives a novel approach towards the world, and acknowledges these subtle material pleasures as meaningful. Thus, in this paper the arguments from their aesthetics, praxis and ontology will be drawn and the focus will be on what thinkers like *Abhinava gupta, Utpala deva, Kshemrāja* and so on, thought of the position of sensual pleasure in Self realization. That is how the understating of the relation between- God, nature and Individual, is an aesthetic realization. Developing on this I would argue that their idea of aesthetic enjoyment holds the key to a novel approach to sustainable development.

Chapter 4 this chapter will focus on the environment and livelihood of the forest dwellers with special reference to their rites and rituals in the Sundarban delta of West Bengal. This will bring forth the unique bond between nature, human and divinity and their interdependence. In order to have better understanding here discussion about the geographical location of this deltas of Sundarban was done, which helps us to understand the occupation and belief of the people residing in that region.

The interaction and interdependence between the natural environment that includes water, soil and forest on the one hand and the religion that includes the entire web of life of human beings, that is, social, political, economic, and cultural milieu is commonly known as eco-theology. It is this aspect of eco theology that suddenly becomes alive in a fragile, dynamic and ecological setting of the region of Sundarban, at a time of great ecological crisis.

Therefore, this chapter will focus on the environment and livelihood of the forest dwellers with special reference to their rites and rituals in the Sundarban delta of West Bengal. This will bring forth the unique bond between nature, human and divinity and their interdependence. Before discussing the livelihood and rites and rituals of forest dwellers of the deltas of Sundarban it is important to know the geographical location of this region which helps us to understand the occupation and belief of the people residing in that region.

Chapter 5 discusses Eco-theology and core of Sikh theology are almost coterminous and synonymous. Since its origin, Sikhism visualizes the entire cosmos and universe as a single unitary entity and its creator a single cosmic power, an invisible impulse and energy that creates, sustains and monitors all its created species. Unlike some Indian and Semitic religions like Hinduism and Islam which worship and eulogize personal deities, Sikhism reposes its faith in the omniscience, omnipresence immanence and transcendence of the one single cosmic power which is synonymous with Nature. It is inherent in the form of an unheard symphony of spheres which in Sikh/ Gurbani parlance has been termed as 'Sabad' or 'Naam'. It is the invocation and worship of this Divine power in all its myriad manifestations with which most of the sacred verses of Sikh Gurus and medieval Indian Saints whose verses are included in Sri Guru Granth Sahib the sacred Sikh text, deal. This entire collection of sacred verses forms one composite melodious orchestra set to music in praise of the ecologically composite Nature and its creative force to cite Guru Nanak's first invocatory verse, the Mool Mantra, Arti in Raag Dhanasari, two Bara Mahan verses in Raga Majh and Raga Tukhari and various other verses listed under various other Raagas such as Bihagra, Basant, Malhar, Mali Gauda, Prabhati to name a few, with an abundant of imagery from the animal kingdom, world of vegetation and natural phenomena. Digging of wells, water tanks, planting of mangroves, construction of Golden Temple in the centre of a pool of water and other major Sikh shrines at Goindwal, TaranTaran and Muktsar along with some rituals and folk songs of Sikhs/ Punjab and Sikh agricultural practices show a close proximity to nature.

Chapter 6 discusses how the *Guru Granth Sahib* makes a vivid mention of Mother Nature in multifarious forms. The two words '*Waho-Waho*' refer to the appreciation of the written text and the moment when we open our eyes that unveil the mystics of nature. This is the moment of self realization. The Sikh Scriptural portrayal of Nature urges one to be a part therein. It is not for any material gain. Through His experiences, being one with Nature, as a way to infinity *Sri Guru Nanak Devji,* the first *Guru* referred to it as *Qudrat,*that comes from the Arabic word *qudra.* In *Raga, Asa De Vaar,* the emphasis in the first *Raga* out of the 31 *Ragas,* is on Nature. Nature like God Almighty is infinite and beyond comprehension. The humans create their surroundings as a reflection of their inner state. Spirit of humility and prayers are two ways in which human beings can become part of Nature and respect others. The History of the *Gurus* unfolds stories where the love for animals, birds, trees, vegetation, rivers, mountains, sky, etc. can be seen. The belief is that ecological balance is attained when all have equal rights of Life and sustenance. The article will look into the intervention of spirit referred to in Text as the Ultimate Truth. It is similar to the aesthetic experience that each artist undergoes. The experience is comparable to that of a *Yogi* or the one in penance irrespective of religious practice. *Guru Granth Sahib* and the teachings are for the betterment of human being relating to Universal brotherhood and kindness. By being close to the environment and Nature, we all become creative and abundant like nature.

Chapter 7 discusses after attaining the *Bodhi,Shakyaputra* Gautama presented his expertise in Magadha *janapada* adjacent to Bodhi-tree. Those are now available in three *Piṭaka* literatures .Whereas, his teachings in Kashmir in four *Sarvāstivad, Agama* texts are available in Chinese renderings. Resultantly, Kashmirian Buddhism was generated with a distinct outlook than what Shakyaputra Gautama had delivered. Most of the teachings of Shakyaputra Gautama delineated in Magadha emphasize that the ephemeral nature of animate is dependent to ecology,whereas, *Sarvāstivada* means that everything is existent. Apparently, Kashmirian Buddhist interpretations did bring forth a separate outlook with relativity, elucidated in their *Āgamas*. The paper attempts to elucidate outlooks on *Sarvāstivada* Buddhist understanding.

Chapter 8 highlighted that humankind has been blessed with a host of humanistic religious teachers and being a Buddhist, the relevant teachings of the Buddha come to my mind and my view is that such teachings serve as the most assured medium of intervention. The humanistic concern of the Buddha can very clearly be seen from a number of his early discourses. Buddhism plays a very important role, in connection with the environmental problems and considers environmental crisis as a part and parcel of man's predicament, his *dukkha*. Buddhism induces people to protect and conserve the environment making it a part of their virtuous living. The interdependent nature of man and environment is very well explained in Buddhism. Buddha points out both the psychological and material causes that propel man to unethical living, forcing to resort to unscrupulous means to exploit nature and natural resources. Buddhism addresses many issues that have immediate impact on day to day life of the people. The protection as well as the conservation of the environment is one major aspect among them. Trees and groves have been closely linked with the life of monks, especially with the Buddha. There are many precepts and rules meant to be observed by the *bhikkhus* for the purpose of protecting and conserving the environment. With his deep personal experience, whenever the Buddha found the occasion, did his best to inculcate the listeners with an environmentally friendly attitude. How political leadership has a great responsibility by setting an example in the protection and conservation of nature and environment is a strong positive reminder in Buddhism. To strengthen this ethical foundation the Buddha warns the followers about the dreadful pitfalls that are found in the way of ostentatious living.

Chapter 9 explained that Jain teachings emphasize that life suffuses all aspects of a multi-story universe. From the infernal realms to the heavens and beyond, life takes many expressions. Particles of karma shroud each living unit (*jīva*), obscuring its innate energy, consciousness, and bliss. For more than 2500 years, Jains have been practising to shake off the karmic material through the purification known as *tapas*, by observing vows that seek to minimize harm to all other forms of life as best possible. The lessons learned about how to avoid harm to other beings in order to purify oneself have resulted to an overall lifestyle that enhances personal and societal well-being. This chapter will explore how the Jain system of protection of life can be applied within the important realm of environmental ethics.

[1] Adapted from the website of the Forum on Religion and Ecology: https://fore.yale.edu/World-Religions/Jainism/Overview-Essay

Chapter 10 highlighted that the Karma theory is a unique identity of Jainism in propounding the message of self-restraint in a straight way. Theist schools of Philosophies advocate the life of human beings is for karma, in contrast with those of heavenly beings and hellish beings, as they have the life of enjoyment and suffering respectively. And those, the consequences of karma, are accumulated only in a mundane life. So self-restraint, in one sense, is the means of violence free life, which holds the practical mission of the ideology of '*live and let live*'. Jainism staunchly believes in an existential mode of life in which all living beings hold equal importance. This is one of the prime sources of eco theology. The ethical doctrines preached in both the schools of Jainism (Śvetāmbara and Digambara) are recorded in the canonical treatises. The seed of philosophy is preserved in the canons in a dormant state. Be it the Śvetāmbara canons starting from the *Ācārāṅga, Sthānāṅga, Bhagavatīsūtra, Uttarādhyayana* and *Daśavaikālika* and so on or the Digambara philosophical treatises of Kundakunda, Vaṭṭakera and the like, the sole teaching is focally framed on self-restraint. This very important act of life leads to the path of emancipation through the purification of one's physical, mental, emotional and spiritual beings. Co-existential ethos is the pivotal point that Jainism cherishes for its candid approach towards ethical doctrines. It not only advocates preventing violence from physical level, but from the vocal and the mental states also. The very first canon of the Śvetāmbara sect, the *Ācārāṅgasūtra* starts with the self-introspection and prevention of weapons. It teaches the violence-free life in a subtle way. Jainism preaches "*parasparopagrahaḥjīvānām*" inter-dependency to each other, from one-sensed being to the five-sensed creatures. It pleads for the universal kinship, beyond the knot of human relation. It warns the killer that there is no difference between him and the victim in a real sense. In the event of eco theological studies, Jainism can show the path of tranquility, peace and bliss in human life.

Chapter 11 discusses about the mutual existence and sustenance of nature and human beings. Nature and human beings are close to each other for mutual existence and sustenance. The mutual interdependence, relationship between nature, humans, plants and animals has always been discussed in the history of human civilization at different periods, in different religions of the world. Jainism is one among other ancient religions of the world, highlighting this issue. Jain thinkers, at length, discussed how one could protect the environment and save oneself, nation, society and all creatures from natural disaster, through non-violence and non-possession. This Chapter attempts to illuminate how Jainism has addressed questions of ecology and environment and created a consciousness regarding the interconnectedness and interdependence of all natural systems. Through the Jain Declaration on nature which is broadly divided into three main parts viz ;

I. The Jain teaching

II. The Jain cosmology and

III. The Jain Code of conduct.

All these will reflect the essence of eco-theology in Jainism.

BIBLIOGRAPHY

1. Abhidhanacintamaniby Hemchndra (ed.) Bohtlinck and Rice, St. Petesberg, 1847; Bhavanagar, V. E. 2441, Pt. I, 1914; pt. II, 1919.

2. Acaranga Sutra [P]. Edited by Hermann Jacobi. Longon: The Pali Text Society, 1882.

3. Acaranga Sutra, ed., as the Ayaramga Sutra of the Svetambara Jains by H. Jacobi. London (Pali Text Society) 1882.

4. Adipurana of Jinasena. Pts. 1-2, Sanskrit text with Hindi tr. Pannalal Jain. Varanasi (BJP) 1963-1965.

5. *Bhagawati Sutra* [P] with Tika [S] of Abhayadeva, Sanskrit translation by Ramacandragani, and Gujarati translation by Meghrajgani. Edited by RsiNanakcand. Bonaras: Ray DhanpatisirphBahadurAgamSarpgrah, 1882.

6. *Dasavaikalika Sutra* [P]. Edited by Ernst Leumann, with English translation by Walther Schubring. Ahmedabad: AnandjiKalianji, 1932.

7. *Kalpa-Sutra And Nava Tattva*, tr. by Rev. J. Stevenson, D. D. London. Printed for The Oriental Translation Fund of Great Britain And Ireland.

8. *Tattvartha-sutra* of Umasvati, Sanskrit text with tr. by L. Jaini, Arah, 1920.

9. *Tiloyapannati*(Ed.) A. Upadhye and H. L. Jain, Sholapur, 1943.

10. Babb, Lawrence A, *The Divine Hierarchy : Popular*

Hinduism in Central India. New York : Columbia University Press, 1975.

11. Banerjee, S.R., Prolegomena to Prakritica et Jainica; Kolkata: The Asiatic Society, 2005.
12. Banerjee, SatyaRanjan and Ganesh Lalwani (ed.),Weber's Sacred Literature of the Jains, Jain Bhawan, Calcutta, 1999.
13. Barnes, Michael(ed.) Reflection and Environmental Consciousness, Lanham, Maryland : University Press of America, 1994.
14. Chan Chreek, K L and Jain, Makesh K. (eds.), Jaina Philosophy, New Delhi:Shree Publishers and Distributors, Vol. I and II, 2004.
15. Chapple, Christopher Key (ed), Jainism and Ecology, Cambridge:Harvard Divinity School,2002. Dandas, Paul, Food and Freedom,TheJaina Sectarian Debate on the Nature of the Kevalin. Religion 15, 1985.
16. Gier, Nicholas F, *The Virtue of Non-Violence from Gautama to Gandhi*, NewYork:State University of New York Press, 2004.
17. Jain, D. C. "Vegetarianism and its Role in Environmental Preservation.",in *Medieval Jainism: Culture and Environment*, (eds.) PremSuman Jain and Raj Mal Lodha. 103-108. New Delhi : Ashish Publishing House. 1990.
18. Rampkuria, S.C.,*Jainism as a faith and Religion*, Calcutta: 28th Jan 1946.
19. Sangave, Vilas A.S., *Aspects of Jain Religion*, New Delhi: BharatiyaJnanpith 2nd edn. 1999.
20. Sethia, Tara [ed],*Ahimsa, Anekanta and Jainism*, Vol. XXI, Delhi : MotilalBanarsidass Publication Pvt. Ltd., [First Edn.], 2004.
21. Singhvi,L.M,"Environmental Wisdom in Ancient India." http://www.ecomall.com/greenshopping/eastgreen.htm.
22. Zimmer, Heinrich, Philosophies of India, Joseph Campbell(ed.) Princeton: Princeton University Press, Bollingen Series, 1951.

Index

Chapter 1

J

K

L

M

N

O

P

R

S

T

U

V

Chapter 2

Chapter 3

Chapter 4

Chapter 5

Chapter 6

Chapter 7

Chapter 8

Chapter 9

Chapter 10

Chapter 11